Focke-Wulf Fw 190 "Long Nose"
An Illustrated History of the Fw 190D Series

Also by the Author
Focke-Wulf Ta 152: The Story of the Luftwaffe's Late-War, High-Altitude Fighter

Focke-Wulf Fw 190 "Long Nose"
An Illustrated History of the Fw 190D Series

Dietmar Hermann
Translated from the German by David Johnston

Schiffer Military History
Atglen, PA

Dust jacket and color profile artwork by S.W. Ferguson, Colorado Springs, CO.

LAMENT FOR THE LANGNASEN
The cover art displays the DORA 9, "White 2", of *Lt*. Karl Ossenkop in the final seconds of his combat career. Originally with III./JG 54, who introduced the DORA 9 to the front in the September of 1944, Ossenkop's *Gruppe* had recently moved their operations in the spring of 1945 to the vestige elements of JG 26. On 17 April, the *Leutnant's staffel* flew an armed reconnaissance on the foggy deck of the Dutch countryside where they encountered a flight of RAF Spitfires. That brief skirmish drove them higher into the broken cloud cover where they were ambushed by the RAF Tempests of No.80 Squadron. Ossenkop's "tired grey" veteran DORA was hit by several 20mm rounds that forced him to bail out while his wingmen fell victim to both the Tempests and the Luftwaffe anti-aircraft batteries below. As of that fateful morning, three more of his wingmen had been killed. In a matter of only a few days, all DORA operations ceased.

Dedication
This book is dedicated to my youngest son Luke Lennart.

Book design by Robert Biondi.

Copyright © 2003 by Dietmar Hermann.
Library of Congress Catalog Number: 2003106080.

All rights reserved. No part of this work may be reproduced or used in any forms or by any means – graphic, electronic or mechanical, including photocopying or information storage and retrieval systems – without written permission from the publisher.

The scanning, uploading and distribution of this book or any part thereof via the Internet or via any other means without the permission of the publisher is illegal and punishable by law. Please purchase only authorized editions and do not participate in or encourage the electronic piracy of copyrighted materials.

"Schiffer," "Schiffer Publishing Ltd. & Design," and the "Design of pen and ink well" are registered trademarks of Schiffer Publishing, Ltd.

Printed in China.
ISBN: 0-7643-1876-4

We are always looking for people to write books on new and related subjects. If you have an idea for a book, please contact us at the address below.

Published by Schiffer Publishing Ltd. 4880 Lower Valley Road Atglen, PA 19310 Phone: (610) 593-1777 FAX: (610) 593-2002 E-mail: Info@schifferbooks.com. Visit our web site at: www.schifferbooks.com Please write for a free catalog. This book may be purchased from the publisher. Please include $3.95 postage. Try your bookstore first.	In Europe, Schiffer books are distributed by: Bushwood Books 6 Marksbury Ave. Kew Gardens Surrey TW9 4JF England Phone: 44 (0)20 8392-8585 FAX: 44 (0)20 8392-9876 E-mail: Bushwd@aol.com. Free postage in the UK. Europe: air mail at cost. Try your bookstore first.

Contents

Foreword 7

Chapter 1   **The Beginning: Radial-Engined Variants of the Fw 190** 8

Chapter 2   **Development of the DB 603** 12
         2.1 The Engine Test-Beds Fw 190 V13, Fw 190 V15 and Fw 190 V16 17
         2.2 The Fw 190 C-1 and C-2 28
         2.3 The Planned Prototypes for the Fw 190 C Series 33

Chapter 3   **Development of the Junkers Jumo 213** 36
         3.1 The Jumo 213 Engine in the Fw 190 37
         3.2 The Fw 190 V17 Finally Takes to the Air 38
         3.3 Preparations for Production – The Prototypes 43
         3.4 The Production Fw 190 D-1/D-2 with Jumo 213 Standard Power Plant 46
         3.5 Installation Experiments with the V19 52

Chapter 4   **The Fw 190 D becomes the Ta 153** 63
         4.1 The Renaming 64
         4.2 Performance Comparison with the Me 209 64

Chapter 5   **The Fw 190 D-9 finally enters Production** 66
         5.1 Focke-Wulf Technical Description No. 268: The Fw 190 D-9 67
         5.2 The First Prototypes 81
         5.3 The Fw 190 V17/U1, Fw 190 V53 and Fw 190 V54 in Detail 89
         5.4 Production Begins 91
         5.5 Testing the D-9 96
         5.6 Fw 190 D-9 Testing Report by the *E-Stelle Rechlin* 99
         5.7 The Jumo 213 A Engine in the Fw 190 D-9 102
         5.8 Fw 190 D-9/R14 Torpedo-Carrying Aircraft 108

Chapter 6	**Operational History of the Fw 190 D-9** 110
	6.1 Conversion of III./JG 54 110
	6.2 A Fighter Pilot's Opinion of the Fw 190 D-9 118
	6.3 The D-9 Compared to Fighter Aircraft of the Allies 121
	6.4 The Fw 190 D-9 with R4M Air-to-Air Rockets 125
	6.5 The Fw 190 D-9 with *Panzerblitz* and Underwing Bomb Racks 126

Chapter 7	**The Fw 190 D-10 is Stillborn** 127

Chapter 8	**The Fw 190 D-11 – The Last Minute Fighter** 128
	8.1 The Prototypes 131
	8.2 Capsule Histories of the Other Fw 190 D-11 Prototypes 137
	8.3 Report on Testing 140
	8.4 Further Development and Fw 190 D-11 Performance Enhancement 141
	8.5 List of Fw 190 D-11 Prototypes 142

Chapter 9	**The Fw 190 D-12/D-13 – The Fastest Doras come too Late** 143
	9.1 New Requirements 143
	9.2 Prototypes for the new Variants 149
	9.3 The New Prototypes 150
	9.4 Problems with Jumo 213 F 153
	9.5 Production 155
	9.6 Comparison Flight between the Fw 190 D-13 and the Hawker Tempest .. 157
	9.7 The Focke-Wulf Fw 190 D-12/R14 170

Chapter 10	**Rebirth of an Old Idea: The Fw 190 and Daimler-Benz Engines** 174
	10.1 The Fw 190 D-14 and D-15 175
	10.2 The Fw 190 V76 and V77 Prototypes 180
	10.3 The Two Fw 190 D-14 Prototypes 182
	10.4 Results of Testing 183
	10.5 The Big Mistake 183

Chapter 11	**The End** 188

	Bibliography 197
	Color Aircraft Profiles 202

Foreword

In 1940 Focke-Wulf was already thinking about future development of the Fw 190, even as the first pre-production aircraft were leaving the factory in Bremen. One of the most promising ideas was replacing the BMW 801 radial engine with a liquid-cooled in-line engine from Junkers or Daimler Benz, however the RLM delayed development and production approval for a version of the Fw 190 powered by the new Daimler Benz DB 603 or Junkers Jumo 213. The proposed Fw 190 C and D series progressed no farther than a handful of prototypes. From the Fw 190 C and D – which had nothing to do with the later Fw 190 D-9 – development progressed to an entirely new machine, the Focke-Wulf Ta 153.

The German State Aviation Ministry (RLM) wanted to select one standard fighter, however, and it therefore pitted the development of the Focke-Wulf Ta 153 against the Messerschmitt Me 209. The rapidly deteriorating military situation led to the abandonment of the Ta 153 and to other drastic changes. Simplification and standardization for mass production became the byword. This was the actual starting point in the development of the Ta 152, which was to completely replace the Fw 190.

As a result of the RLM's inability to make a decision, there was no significant improvement in the Fw 190 A powered by the BMW 801 radial engine for three years. The improved 2,000-h.p. BMW 801 E never entered production. At the beginning of 1944, however, pressure from the war forced the RLM to act. It was decided that existing Fw 190 airframes would be fitted with the Jumo 213 standard power plant as an interim solution pending introduction of the Ta 152. The new series, the Fw 190 D-9, was the result of a fairly simple modification of the existing production variant, the Fw 190 A-8. The aircraft's lengthened forward fuselage resulted in the apt nickname "Long Nose". Further delays in construction of the Ta 152 resulted in additional versions up to the D-15.

This book describes the development of the Fw 190 with in-line engines. In terms of production, the Fw 190 D-9 represented the apex. 1,500 examples of the Fw 190 D-9 were completed by the end of the war, making it one of the major production versions of the Fw 190.

CHAPTER ONE

The Beginning: Radial-Engined Variants of the Fw 190

Development of the Fw 190 began in 1938. The first prototype of the new fighter, which was assigned the RLM designation Fw 190, was completed in the summer of 1939. The Fw 190 V1, powered by a BMW 139 radial engine, took to the air for the first time on 1 June 1939. Development of the BMW 139 was subsequently abandoned, however, and the Fw 190 had to be modified to accept the new BMW 801. Focke-Wulf took this opportunity to redesign the Fw 190, and the Fw 190 V5 was the first true production prototype. The RLM placed an order for a pre-production series. Designated the Fw 190 A-0, these aircraft were used to ready the type for front-line service. The first production aircraft were issued to a Fw 190 test detachment in Rechlin. A number of shortcomings were found, and their elimination delayed the Fw 190's entry into service.

The Fw 190 V1 was the forerunner of all later Fw 190 variants.

The Focke-Wulf Fw 190 was the first *Luftwaffe* fighter to be powered by the new BMW 801, a 14-cylinder air-cooled radial engine. The first production series, the Fw 190 A, began reaching *Luftwaffe* units in June 1941. Quantity production began, and by January 1942 Focke-Wulf had completed 102 examples of the Fw 190 A-1. The new aircraft's development potential was great, and production of an improved version, the Fw 190 A-2, began in August 1942. This was followed by the A-3, which was equipped with a more powerful BMW 801 D engine.

The first units to receive the Fw 190 A were the fighter wings JG 26 *Schlageter* and JG 2 *Richthofen*, both based on the Channel Coast. Following the attack on the Soviet Union, these units were for a time the only fighter wings based in the west. These two *Jagdgeschwader* were issued the most modern fighter aircraft available in an effort to counter the growing materiel superiority of the Allies. Immediately upon entering service the Fw 190 proved superior to the Spitfire Vb, then the Royal Air

Left: The Fw 190 V5 was the actual prototype for the initial production version of the Fw 190 powered by the new BMW 801 radial engine.

Below: This Fw 190 A-1, *Werknummer* 067, manufacturer's code TI+DQ, is prepared for another flight.

The first Fw 190 A-0s in front of the hangar doors in Bremen.

Force's standard fighter. At last the *Luftwaffe* had the superior fighter it had been seeking. Such a machine had been lacking one year earlier in the heavy fighting over England. Technologically, Germany had gained a lead in fighter design. Of course this advantage would only last for a time, as the Allies would obviously devote much effort to improving their fighters in order to overtake the Fw 190 or exploit its weaknesses. And the fighter did have one weakness, its power plant.

The BMW 801 D was an outstanding engine at altitudes up to 6000 meters, but above 6000 meters its performance dropped off sharply. BMW had already begun work on improved engines, however this would take time, time which the fighter pilots at the front did not have. The quality of the airframes and engines they were given was of vital importance to the pilots, both Allied and German. Chief designer Professor Kurt Tank was well aware of the Fw 190's shortcomings at high altitude, and he therefore directed Focke-Wulf's development department to search for ways to improve the type's performance by using existing engines with better high-altitude performance than the BMW 801 D.

The Focke-Wulf designers very soon found a suitable power plant, the new DB 603 A liquid-cooled in-line engine by Daimler Benz. Later they also turned to the Jumo 213, another liquid-cooled power plant. But even with official approval, could these engines be adapted to power a new version of the Fw 190? And could the changed engine geometry be married to the airframe of the Fw 190?

Until these questions could be answered, the BMW 801 remained central to further developments in the Fw 190 series. In the interim Focke-Wulf initiated efforts to improve the high-altitude performance of the BMW 801 and adapt the Fw 190 for the high-altitude fighter role. In addition to various high-altitude fighter designs powered by the BMW 801, Focke-Wulf projected a number of variants powered by the DB 603. The RLM gave its approval for prototypes to be built for the purpose of

Fw 190 A-1, Red 17. The first production aircraft were issued to the fighter units JG 2 *Richthofen* and JG 26 *Schlageter*, both of which were based in the west.

determining the suitability of the DB 603 and Jumo 213. With this, Focke-Wulf initiated the interesting technical developments which will be examined in detail here. These developments could have led to a new series much sooner, however the decision to introduce a new and improved variant of the Fw 190 rested with the *Reichsluftfahrtministerium* (State Aviation Ministry), not the manufacturer.

In addition, Focke-Wulf still faced stiff from its main rival Messerschmitt. At that time Messerschmitt was also working on new fighter projects, such as the Me 309 and later the Me 209. At that time it was accepted practice that only one of the two companies should win the technical race. This book examines the development path of the long-nosed variants of the Fw 190. The experience which Focke-Wulf gained in designing and building these prototypes led two years later to the development and construction of the successful Focke-Wulf Fw 190 D-9, considered to be the best German piston-engined fighter of its day.

CHAPTER TWO

Development of the DB 603

The engine manufacturer Daimler Benz first proposed development of the DB 603 to the RLM in September 1936. Initial development work on the DB 603 had to be halted six months later, in favor of other, higher priority projects. Not until the end of 1939 was there a renewal in official interest in the DB 603. This did not occur by chance, for the then director of Daimler Benz, Nallinger, sent a report to *General* Udet and to *Generalstabsingenieur* Lucht on the state of development of the DB 603, obviously eyeing the potential of license production abroad. The letter was dated 2 December 1939.

A short time later, in February 1940, Daimler Benz and the RLM concluded an agreement for batches of 40 and 80 so-called "Zero Series"

The DB 603 A was intended for installation in the Fw 190 and Me 309. (Daimler-Chrysler Archive)

engines, to be delivered from October 1940 to September 1941. The precise delivery sequence was laid down on 14 June 1940:

36 DB 603 A	(No. 101-136)	with standard supercharger
4 DB 603 W/X	(No. 137-140)	for DB 613 V1 and V2
60 DB 603 A-0	(No. 141-200)	with standard supercharger
20 DB 603 W/X	(No. 201-220)	for ten DB 613
10 DB 603 D	(No. 221-230)	with limited supercharger (for 7000 m)

Focke-Wulf was interested in installing the DB 603 in the Fw 190 and began initial calculations. An internal Daimler Benz memo dated 6 February 1940 states:

"The Focke-Wulf company has advised that it has looked into the installation of the DB 603 engine in its Fw 190 machine and has come up with the following results compared to the currently anticipated engine (BMW 801):

Installation very good
Increase in speed of 50 km/h
Reduction in gross weight

Forward view of the DB 603. (Daimler-Chrysler)

Me 309 in flight. The Me 309 was to have replaced the Bf 109 as the *Luftwaffe*'s standard fighter. (DASA via Ebert)

Me 410 A-3. Beginning in 1943, the DB 603 was installed in the Messerschmitt Me 410, which was built in large numbers.

Installation of the DB 603 in the twin-engined aircraft[1] currently in development can be undertaken just as easily, with similar advantages. Herr Dir. Tank and Herr Kaether are flying to Berlin to convince the RLM that these aircraft should be converted to the DB 603."

Focke-Wulf produced more detailed estimates. Estimated maximum speed at 6000 m was 745 km/h with the DB 603 compared to 700 km/h with the BMW 801. The estimated weight of the DB 603-powered Fw 190 was 40 kg less than that of the BMW 801 version, even when the weight of armor for the annular radiator and oil cooler was included. The Focke-Wulf calculations did not suggest any problems with the center of gravity.

Things were not as simple as they seemed, however. Approval for the installation of the DB 603 in the Fw 190 was no immediately forthcoming. Nevertheless, development work on the engine for the Fw 190 continued. Focke-Wulf responded to Daimler Benz on this topic on 12 February 1940: "In the RLM they told us that, according to existing information, the performance of the Fw 190 with the BMW 801 will suffice for the immediate future, but that we should be prepared at any time to improve the machine's performance with your engine."

Several conferences were subsequently held to discuss the installation of the DB 603 in the airframes of the Fw 190 and the Me 309, for example at Daimler Benz on 17 July 1942 concerning the installation of weapons in the DB 603 and at the RLM on 4 August 1942 concerning the installation of the engine in the Me 309 and Fw 190. It was decided that both fighter aircraft would be built with the DB 603. Whereas a BMW 801-powered version of the Fw 190 was already in production and its airframe "only" had to be adapted to accept the new power plant and, the Me 309 was a completely new development.

For engine trials, a pre-production DB 603 (No. 136) was installed in a Fw 190 pre-production machine, *Werknummer* 0 036. The design, or more accurately the redesign of the type, was thus based on the Fw 190 A-0. The aircraft, which was assigned the internal Focke-Wulf prototype designation Fw 190 V13, made its successful first flight at Bremen in March 1942. What was the competition doing at this time? Not until four months later, on 18 July 1942, did the Me 309 V1 (GE+CU) take to the air at Augsburg with test pilot Karl Bauer at the controls.

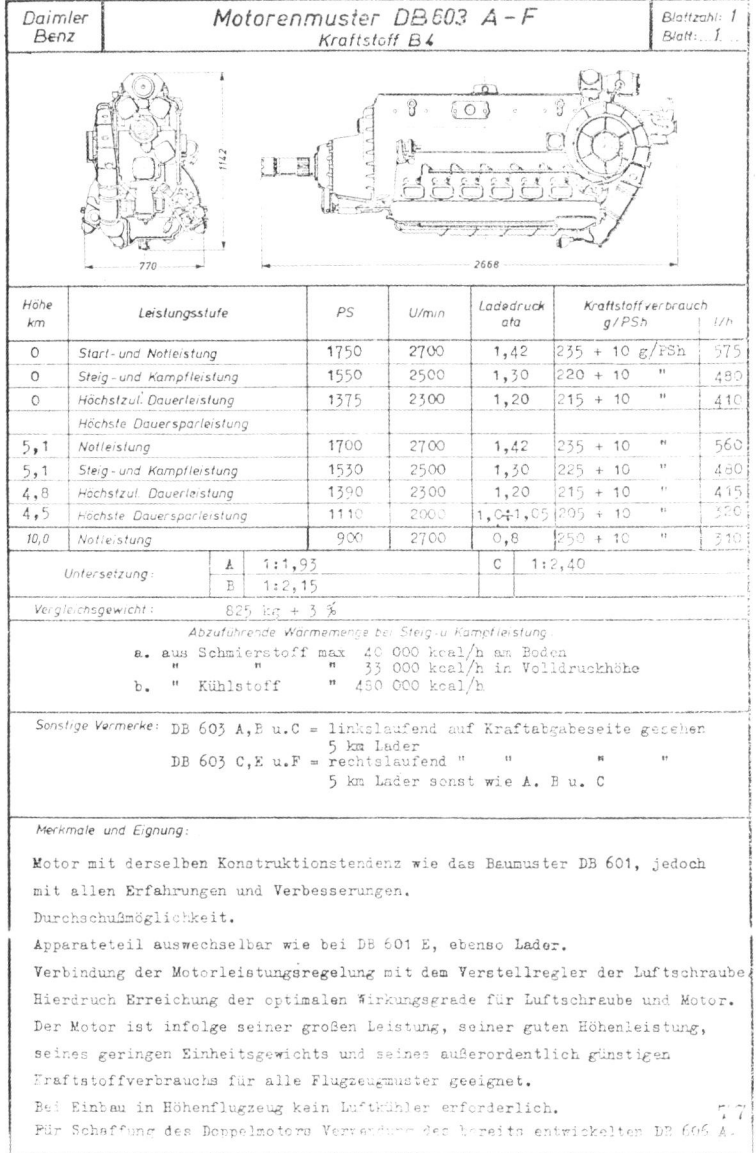

Specification sheet for the 1,750-h.p. Daimler Benz DB 603 A engine. (Daimler-Chrysler)

Preparations for the experimental installation of the DB 603 A in the airframe of the Fw 190.

The DB 603 A, with its enormous capacity of 44.5 liters, was already producing 1,750 h.p. at that time. This performance was achieved at 2,700 rpm, which initially could only be maintained for one minute. Maximum continuous power at low level was 1,375 h.p. at 2,300 rpm. The engine's maximum boost altitude was 5700 m. The single-stage engine was, however, suitable both for water-methanol and GM-1 injection (for further information see the engine specification sheets for the DB 603 A-E and DB 603 B). Daimler Benz had already initiated work on versions of the DB 603 with improved high-altitude performance, such as the DB 603 E and DB 603 G. These engines entered production in 1943 and 1944, respectively, and proved themselves in service in the Me 410 B and He 219 A.

2.1 The Engine Test-Beds Fw 190 V13, Fw 190 V15 and Fw 190 V16

The first Fw 190 powered by a Daimler Benz liquid-cooled engine flew in March 1942. The aircraft, which Focke-Wulf designated the Fw 190 V13, was fitted with one of the first DB 603 A-0 pre-production engines. The prototype, *Werknummer* 0036, entered testing without serious difficulties. Hans Sander, Focke-Wulf's chief test pilot, flew SK+JS extensively during the initial phase of testing. Like the Fw 190 V15 and V16 which followed, the V13 was equipped with a ventral oil cooler and was unarmed.

In an effort to preserve aerodynamic cleanliness, the V13 was initially fitted with a so-called "Stovepipe Intake Shaft". In adopting this, Focke-Wulf attempted to imitate the BMW 801 arrangement. Instead of an external scoop, the supercharger air intake consisted of a pipe located between the twin oil coolers. This arrangement did not prove itself in testing, however, as it reduced the engine's high-altitude performance.

Forward view of the first Fw 190 equipped with the Daimler Benz DB 603 in-line engine. Focke-Wulf succeeded in fitting the engine into the airframe perfectly without a major redesign. (Company Photograph)

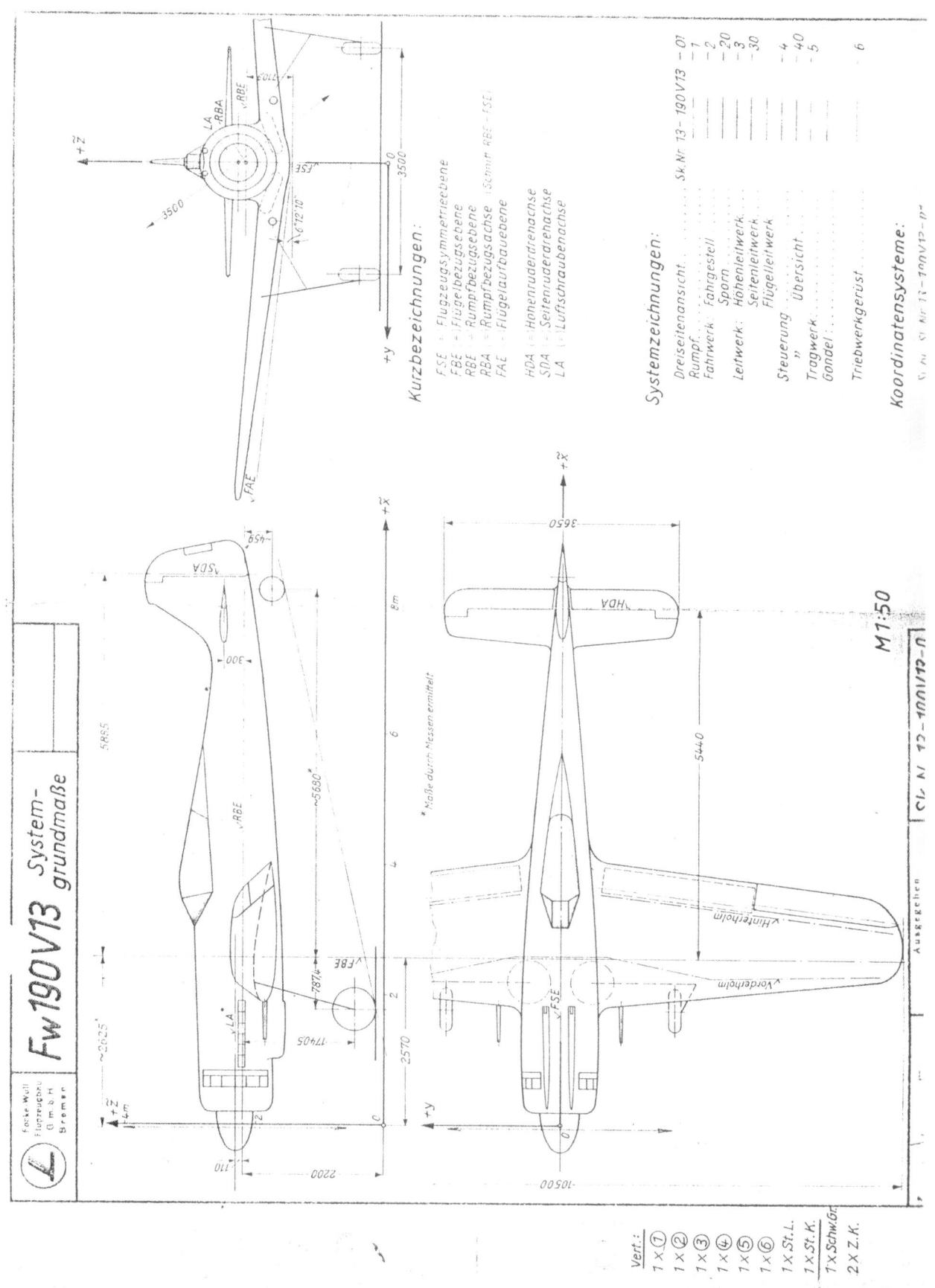

	Stovepipe	External Scoop
Loss of supercharger effectiveness	5305 m	5890 m
Maximum boost altitude in level flight	5705 m	6950 m

Both measurements were made at combat power (2,500 rpm) and 1.3 atm of boost.

Later, when the V15 and V16 began flight trials, it was shown that the achievable maximum boost altitude with the stovepipe design was 1500 meters less than with a conventional external supercharger air intake. As well, use of the external scoop did not result in any reduction in maximum speed. Focke-Wulf therefore decided to adopt a conventional supercharger air intake similar to that already in use on the Bf 109. The V13's takeoff weight was 3640 kg, which was reduced to 3380 kg for landing. On 9 April 1942 the Fw 190 V13 achieved a speed of 557 km/h at a height of 500 meters and on 18 April reached 650 km/h at an altitude of 5950 meters. The Fw 190 V13 made its 35th and last flight on 30 July 1942. On that day pilot Hopfer took the aircraft up for an initial familiarization flight, which ended with the V13 crash-landing at the Hamburg-Wenzendorf test center. Damage was such that the aircraft was not rebuilt.

The second engine test-bed was the Fw 190 V15, *Werknummer* 0037, manufacturer's code CF+OV. Hans Sander took the aircraft into the air for the first time on 9 May 1942. The V15 was fitted with an external supercharger air intake, which resulted in a significant improvement in maximum boost altitude. The spacing between the external scoop initially used with the DB 603 A-0 (211) and the airframe was 100 mm. When the new DB 603 A-1 (*Werknummer* 17 641) was installed, spacing from the engine cowling was reduced to 60 mm. On 19 May 1942 the Fw 190 V15 went to Rechlin for the first time.

Opposite: Focke-Wulf drawing of the Fw 190 V13.

Side view of the Fw 190 V13, SK+JS, in Bremen. Although the engine was liquid-cooled, the use of an annular radiator gave the aircraft the appearance of having a radial engine.

The Fw 190 V13 in the hangar with engine access panels open. The bend in front of the supercharger for the engine intake shaft, the so-called "Stovepipe" is clearly visible. The presence of the stovepipe made necessary a small, but clearly visible bulge in the right access panel.

Opposite
Top: Another interesting detail view of the DB 603 A engine in the airframe of the Fw 190 V13. Note the two blast tubes in the radiator fairing, for the possible installation of machine-guns. The ventral oil cooler panel is open here.

Bottom: Fw 190 V13 was also fitted with a mock-up of an external stores carrier (ETC).

While still powered by the DB 603 A-0, in June 1942 the V15 achieved maximum speeds of 696 km/h at 6950 meters and 575 at a height of 400 meters at maximum combat power. In both cases the aircraft was flown with the cooling gills closed. This performance was not matched until late 1944, by the Focke-Wulf Ta 152 C, which was powered by a DB 603 E engine. The later Focke-Wulf Ta 152 CV 6 experimental aircraft, powered by a DB 603 E engine with MW 50 boost (emergency power = 2,700 rpm), achieved similar speeds but was significantly heavier (4370 kg). During flight testing the V15 had a gross weight of 3607 kg. As well, all seams were filled and the aircraft was polished. Focke-Wulf expected a further increase in speed through the adoption of a more streamlined engine cowling.

Like the V13, the V15's radio equipment consisted of a FuG VIIa and a FuG 25. Focke-Wulf was still test-flying the V15 from Langenhagen in May 1943. There it was fitted with a wooden four-bladed propeller for the first time. Until the last known flight report the V15 was flown unarmed, although it did have bulged fairings over the cannon ammunition feeds. The aircraft was flown with 15 kg of ballast in the jacking tube and 12 kg in the vertical fin.

As well, the V15 was experimentally fitted with the exhaust piping for the Hirth exhaust-driven turbosupercharger which was later installed

The Fw 190 V15, *Werknummer* 0 037, was the second Fw 190 equipped with the DB 603 in-line engine. It bore the manufacturer's code CF+OV. Unlike the V13, it was fitted with an external supercharger air intake.

in the prototype of the *Höhenjäger 2* (High-Altitude Fighter 2), the so-called *Kängeruh* (Kangaroo). The V15 was retained as an experimental aircraft until the end of the war and was captured in good condition at Göttingen on 18 April 1945. It was later scrapped.

The final DB 603 A test-bed produced by Focke-Wulf was designated the Fw 190 V16. This aircraft, *Werknummer* 0038, CF+OW, flew for the first time on 2 August 1942. On 2 August 1942 the V16 was transferred to the Daimler Benz research facility at Stuttgart-Echterdingen. There, under the direction of *Flugkapitän* Ellenrieder, the aircraft was test-flown extensively. The resulting performance figures were found to be almost identical to those achieved by Focke-Wulf, the difference being only plus-minus 1%. In the hands of Daimler Benz the V16 achieved a maximum speed of 724 km/h at an altitude of 7000 m at emergency power (2,700 rpm). The engine used was the DB 603 A with standard supercharger. Daimler Benz made various modifications to the engine and installed the DB 603 G supercharger. With this combination of DB 603 A engine and

Unlike the Fw 190 V13, the V15 and V16 were equipped with an external supercharger air intake, which is clearly visible in this photograph.

DB 603 G supercharger, the V16 achieved a maximum speed of 722 km/h at 9000 meters. Low-level rate of climb at combat power was 17.5 m/s and this remained virtually constant to an altitude of 4500 meters. In contrast to the Jumo-powered Fw 190 D-9 which came later, the DB 603-powered Fw 190 retained its low-level climb rate better. Daimler Benz noted that the aircraft's rate of climb could be further improved through the use of a broad-blade propeller. The estimated improvement was 1 to 1.5 m/s.

In the summer of 1944 the DB 603 E V83 engine was installed in the V16. So equipped, it achieved a low-level rate of climb of 22 m/s using MW 50 boost. The aircraft was fitted with mock-up weapons and ballast.

Photographs depicting more than one DB 603-powered Fw 190 are rare. Seen here are the V15, with engine access panels open, and, in the background, the V13, SK+JS.

Two DB 603-powered Fw 190s are also visible in this photograph. The projecting ventral oil cooler is clearly visible.

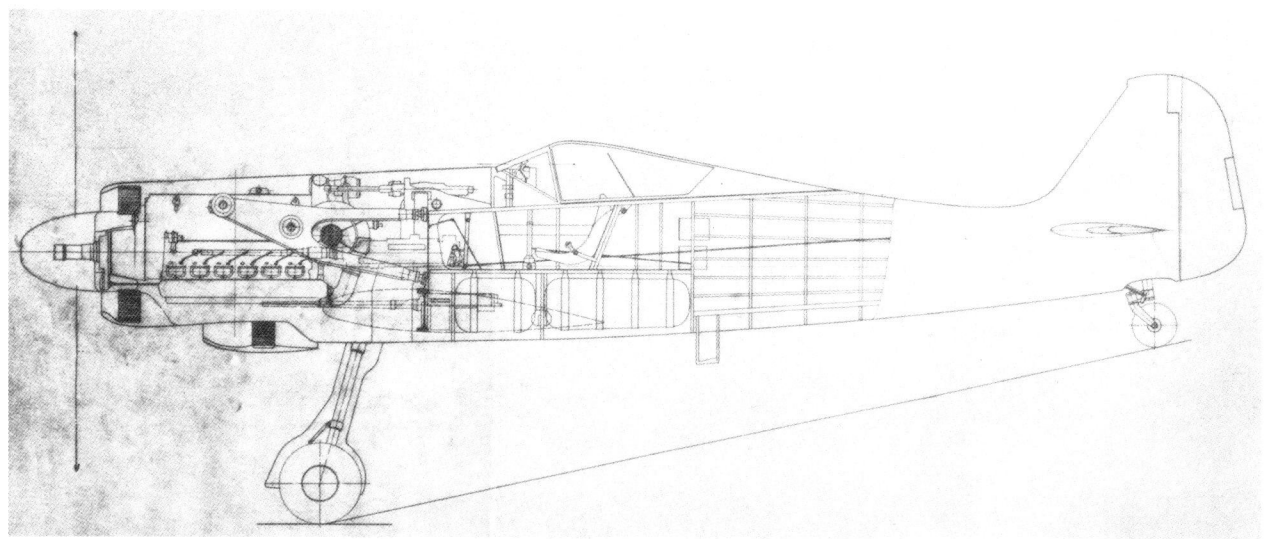

Side-view of the Fw 190 with DB 603 and ventral oil cooler, representative of the Fw 190 V13, V15 and V16.

Allied impression of the new Fw 190 powered by the DB 603 in service at the front. It is amazing how well the Allies were informed about German aircraft developments.

The V16 easily reached altitudes of 12000 meters. With the new engine the V16's gross weight rose to 3765 kg.

On 14 August 1944 the V16 sustained 65% damage in a heavy bombing raid on Echterdingen. It appears to have been rebuilt, however, for a Daimler Benz document dated December 1944 contains a note that the Fw 190 V16 was present and supposedly undergoing conversion.

Summary of Testing

With the first three test-beds Focke-Wulf obtained valuable information on the installation of in-line engines in the standard Fw 190 A airframe. These engines were successfully installed in the airframe and conversion costs were minimal. The performance of the three test-beds, especially at high altitude, was convincing. Nevertheless, this does not appear to have made any lasting impression on the officials in the RLM, for instead of accelerating development of this promising engine-airframe combination, the Fw 190 C series was shelved at the beginning of 1943. With its performance and armament, the Fw 190 C would have been a useful addition to the *Reichsverteidigung* (Defense of the Reich). Instead, however, the RLM halted development of the Fw 190 with conventional DB 603 engines for more than two years.

Forward view of the Fw 190 V15. Clearly visible are the two muzzle openings in the radiator fairing for the fuselage-mounted weapons.

Three highly-interesting views of the Fw 190 V16. All three were probably taken during testing by Daimler Benz at Echterdingen.

Opposite
The airspeed data sheet for the Fw 190 V16 documents the outstanding performance of the Fw 190 with the DB 603 A. Performance was enhanced further with use of the G-type supercharger. Thus equipped, the V16 achieved speeds of 570 km/h at low level and 722 km/h at a height of 8500 meters. These speeds were achieved in 1943. (Daimler Benz Document)

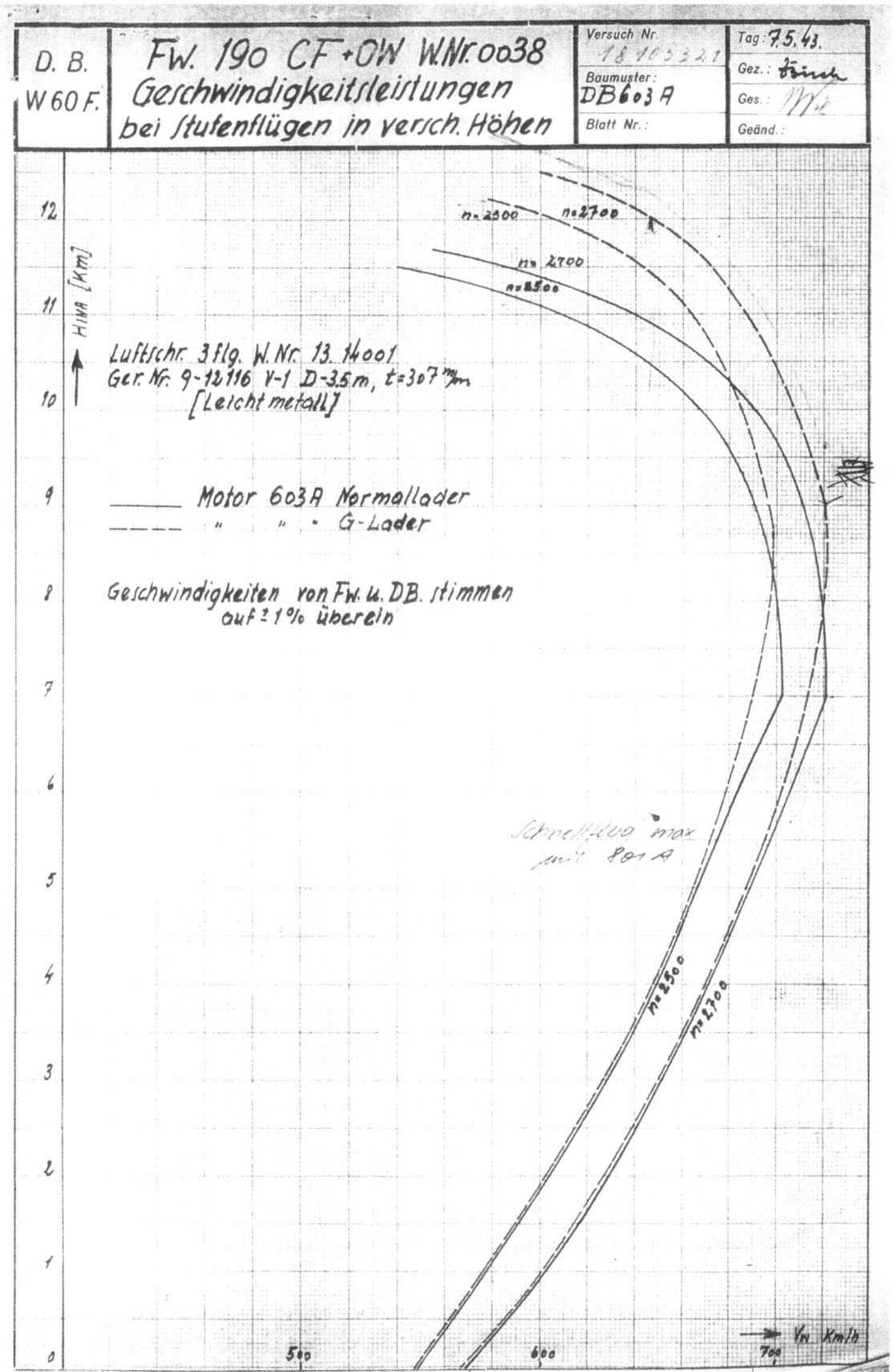

2.2 The Fw 190 C-1 and C-2

Focke-Wulf initially planned two production versions of the Fw 190 powered by the DB 603 in-line engine, designated the Fw 190 C-1 and C-2. While the Fw 190 C-1 was a conventional fighter without a pressurized cockpit, the Fw 190 C-2 was equipped with pressurization and was intended for the high-altitude fighter role. Both versions were to carry a standard armament of two MG 131 machine-guns in the fuselage, two MG 151 cannon in the wing roots and one engine-mounted cannon (MG 151, MK 103 or MK 108). Two additional MG 151 cannon could be installed in the outer wings. The Fw 190 C-1 was designed to carry a rack beneath the fuselage for either 500 kg of bombs or a jettisonable 300-liter fuel tank. Radio equipment consisted of a FuG 16 ZY and FuG 25a for the Fw 190 C-1 and a FuG 16 Z and FuG 25a for the Fw 190 C-2.

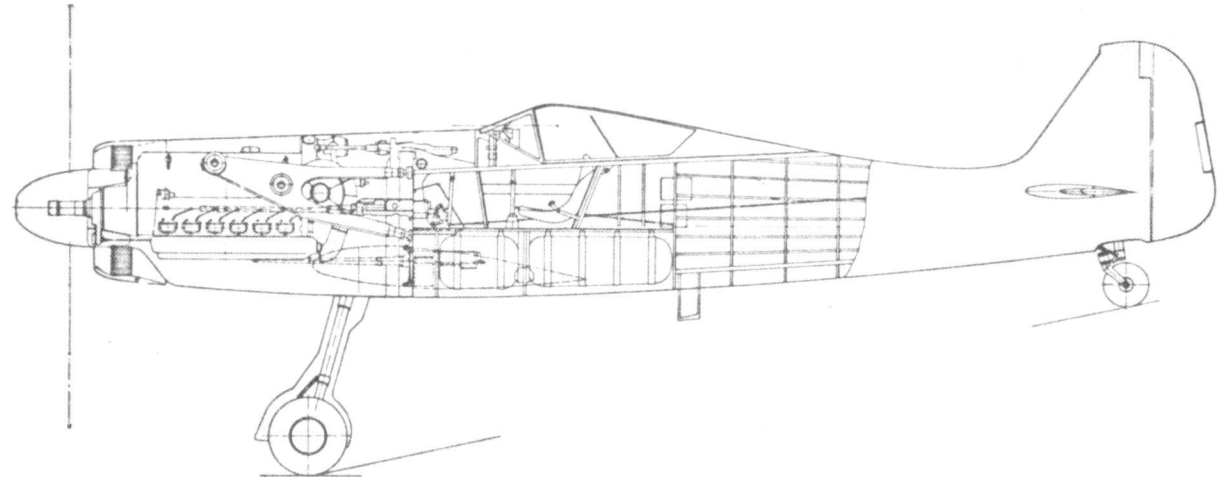

Side-view drawing of the Focke-Wulf Fw 190 C.

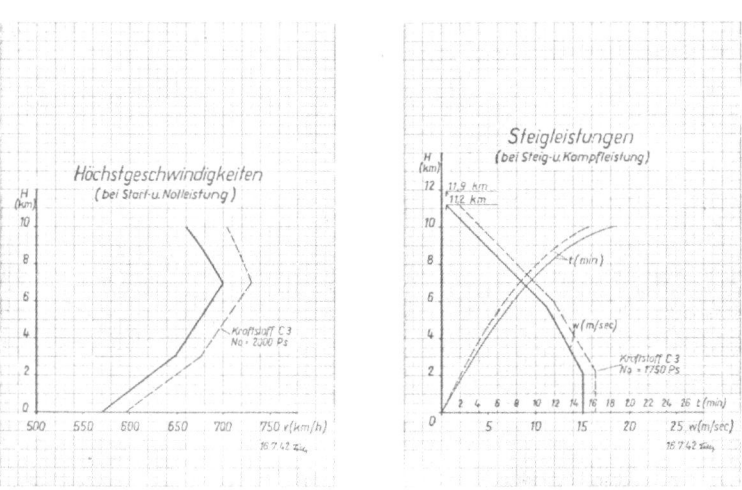

Performance figures for the Fw 190 C. Maximum speed was 700 km/h, which increased to 730 km/h using C3 fuel.

Focke-Wulf had even devised a production schedule for the series. According to Delivery Plan LC 21 of December 1942, production of the Fw 190 C was to have begun in March 1943 and continued until March 1944. Total production was to have been just 727 aircraft. Focke-Wulf also assigned production designations:

Fw 190 C-1　version 190. 0 310
Fw 190 C-2　version 190. 0 320

In spite of these intensive preparations for manufacturing the Fw 190 C, the type did not enter quantity production. The competing design from Messerschmitt, the Me 309, suffered a similar fate. Messerschmitt had run into serious problems with the Me 309's tricycle undercarriage, retractable ventral radiator and Me P6 braking propeller. In contrast, there had been virtually no complaints about the DB 603 A-powered Fw 190. Official documents reveal that even the RLM viewed the building of the Fw 190 with an in-line engine as low risk. It was felt that technical problems were unlikely to arise as the modifications to the Fw 190's airframe were minimal. The planned Fw 190 C series with the DB 603 was still entered in company documents in December 1942, but in January 1943 it was struck from the list.

The cockpit of the Fw 190 V15. Note the centrally-mounted instruments for monitoring coolant and oil temperatures. The corresponding switches are on the right.

The annular radiators of later series prototypes were much more efficient aerodynamically, further improving the maximum speed of the Fw 190.

All of this was the result of a decision made by the RLM on 26 January 1943 to produce the Fw 190 C with the Jumo 213 engine instead of the DB 603. A possible explanation for this fatal delay may possibly be found in the engine question. The heavy fighter, or *Zerstörer* role was still seen as vitally important by the *Luftwaffe*. The Messerschmitt Me 410 A, which had been derived from the Me 210, was about to enter production in January 1943 and was to fill the *Zerstörer* role. Unlike the Me 210, the Me 410 A was powered by the DB 603, and the RLM decided to allocate the bulk of DB 603 production to that aircraft. The serious shortage of capable *Zerstörer* apparently did not allow for the production of two front-line aircraft equipped with the DB 603.

A little more than a year later, in April 1944, the improved Me 410 B began leaving the production line. It was powered by the improved DB 603 G, which produced 1,900 h.p. and also had an improved maximum boost altitude of 8300 meters. This improved engine would have significantly enhanced the performance of the Fw 190 C, but in April 1944 the type was not in production. A total of 1,160 examples of the Messerschmitt Me 410 were built in 1943 and 1944, requiring 2,320 DB 603 engines.

The Me 410 was also employed as a heavy fighter to counter the growing Allied bombing campaign against Germany. Against the smaller, lighter and more maneuverable P-47 Thunderbolt and P-51 Mustang escort fighters the Me 410 had virtually no chance. Losses in machines and

Development of the DB 603

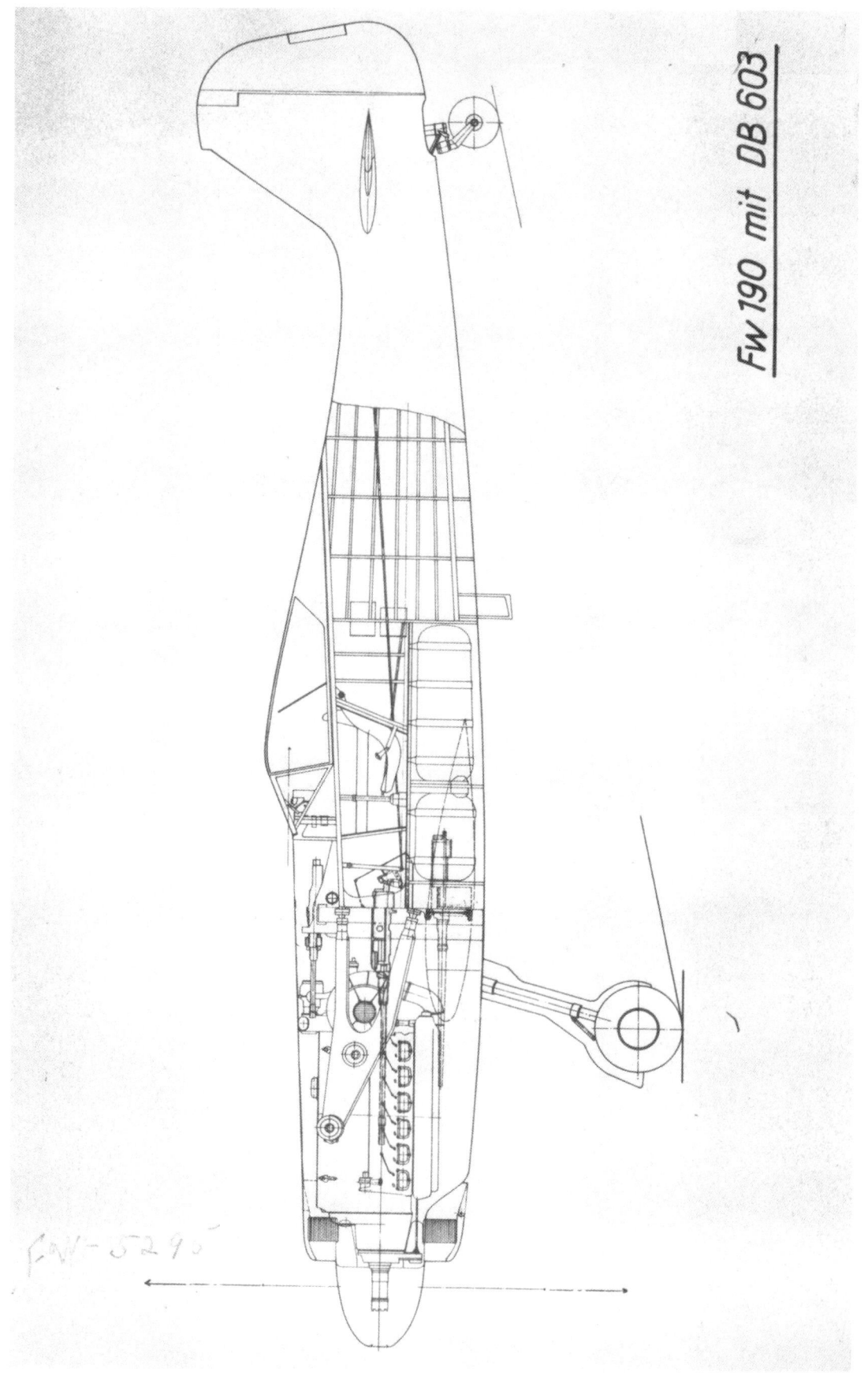

Fw 190 mit DB 603

The Me 309 was the direct counterpart of the DB 603-powered Fw 190. The design of the Me 309 included many innovative features which caused numerous problems. (DASA Munich)

experienced pilots were heavy. By this time at the latest, it was obvious that the RLM's decision not to produce a version of the Fw 190 powered by the DB 603 had been a mistake. The Fw 190 C would have given the *Luftwaffe* a much more effective weapon during the critical phase of the air war over Germany. In the spring of 1944 the pilots of the *Reichsverteidigung* were still flying the Fw 190 A, which was inferior to the Allied escort fighters. The result was heavy losses in machines and experienced pilots.

Not until the Me 410 *Zerstörer* was struck from the *Luftwaffe*'s procurement plans was Focke-Wulf successful in getting a fighter powered by a Daimler Benz in-line engine into production in the form of the new Ta 152 C equipped with the powerful DB 603 EM or LA engine. Production was cut short by the end of the war before it could get fully under way.

This photograph of the Fw 190 V16 shows very well the characteristics of the air intakes for the annular radiator and the ventral oil cooler. Like the annular radiator, the ventral oil cooler was equipped with adjustable cooling flaps.

2.3 The Planned Prototypes for the Fw 190 C Series

A total of six prototypes were planned for the Fw 190 C series, all of which were to be conversions of Fw 190 A-0 airframes. The ventral oil cooler of the V13, V15 and V16 engine test-beds was to be deleted in favor of an annular cooler in the aircraft nose.

Aircraft Program No. 222/2 of 1 Nov. 1942 – Prototypes					
Fw 190	1 DB 603	V15	in testing	0 037	General handling and performance trials aircraft, testing of exhaust piping for turbosupercharger.
Fw 190	1 Jumo 213 A-0	V17	in testing	0 039	General handling and engine performance trials aircraft.
Fw 190	1 DB 603 A-1	V18	under construction	0 040	Conversion to DB 603 A-1 (high-altitude fighter with turbosupercharger)
Fw 190	1 DB 603 A-1	V19	under construction	0 041	Dural construction
Fw 190	1 DB 603 A-1	V20	under construction	0 042	Dural construction
Fw 190	1 DB 603 A-1	V21	under construction	0 043	Dural construction
Fw 190	1 Jumo 213 A	V22	under construction	0 044	Zinc-aluminum alloy
Fw 190	1 Jumo 213 A	V23	under construction	0 045	Zinc-aluminum alloy
Fw 190	1 DB 603 A-1	V25	under construction	0 050	Zinc-aluminum alloy, mid-November
Fw 190	1 DB 603 A-1	V26	under construction	0 051	Zinc-aluminum alloy, end-November
Fw 190	1 DB 603 A-1	V27	under construction	0 052	Zinc-aluminum alloy, early December
Fw 190	no engine	V28	under construction	0053	Non-flying Dural airframe for static tests
Fw 190	1 DB 603 A-1	V29	under construction	0054	High-altitude fighter with turbosupercharger
Fw 190	1 DB 603 A-1	V30	under construction	0055	High-altitude fighter with turbosupercharger
Fw 190	1 DB 603 A-1	V31	under construction	0056	High-altitude fighter with turbosupercharger
Fw 190	1 DB 603 A-1	V32	under construction	0057	High-altitude fighter with turbosupercharger
Fw 190	1 DB 603 A-1	V33	under construction	0058	High-altitude fighter with turbosupercharger
Fw 190	1 BMW 801 D		under construction	669	Test-bed for increased wing loads, Jaborei A-4/U8
Fw 190	1 BMW 801 D		under construction	670	Test-bed for increased wing loads, Jaborei A-4/U8
Fw 190	1 BMW 801 D		under construction	270	Test-bed for increased wing loads, Jaborei A-3/U1

This Focke-Wulf prototype summary from late 1942 makes it clear that the company had great hopes for the DB 603-powered Fw 190 at that time.

The first two Fw 190 C prototypes, the Fw 190 V19 and V20, were to have been unarmed and not equipped with a pressurized cockpit. A pressurized cockpit and an armament of two MG 131s over the engine, two MG 151s in the wing roots and one engine-mounted MG 151 cannon were planned for all the other prototypes. For center of gravity reasons, all prototypes were to have been built with a forward-swept wing with an area of 18.3 square meters. The V19, V20 and V21 prototypes were to be constructed using the conventional Dural stressed-skin method, however the V25, V26 and V27 were to have been built using zinc-aluminum alloy.

The cancellation of the Fw 190 C series had direct effects on the planned prototypes. None was ever completed as a Fw 190 C prototype. The Fw 190 V19 to V21 and V25 prototypes were later used in the Fw

190 D/Ta 152 A test program, although they were then equipped with the new Jumo 213 C standard engine.

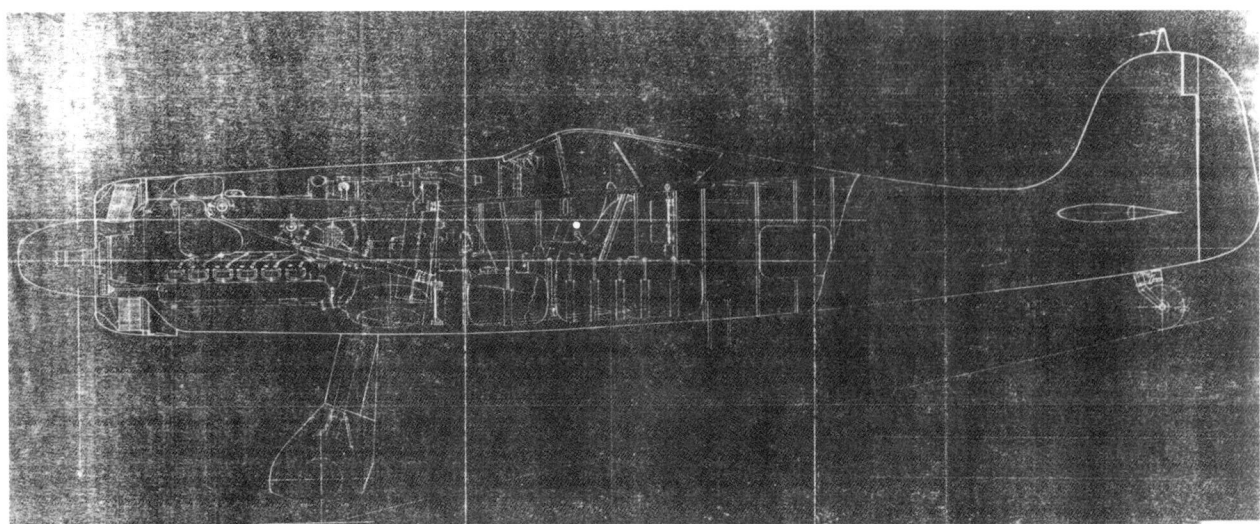

Blueprint of the Fw 190 V19, still powered by the DB 603.

Summary of the Planned Prototypes for the Fw 190 C Series with DB 603 Engine

Prototype:

Fw 190 V19	Werknummer 0 041	no pressurized cockpit	no armament	Feb. 1943
Fw 190 V20	Werknummer 0 042	no pressurized cockpit	no armament	Feb. 1943

Test:

Fw 190 V21	Werknummer 0 043	pressurized cockpit	2 MG 131 + 2 MG 151 + MG 151	March 1943
Fw 190 V25	Werknummer 0 050	pressurized cockpit	2 MG 131 + 2 MG 151 + MG 151	March 1943
Fw 190 V26	Werknummer 0 051	pressurized cockpit	2 MG 131 + 2 MG 151 + MG 151	March 1943
Fw 190 V27	Werknummer 0 052	pressurized cockpit	2 MG 131 + 2 MG 151 + MG 151	March 1943

Source: FW document dated 18 Nov. 1942

Note: Curiously, after the Focke-Wulf statement of 7 August 1942 the Fw 190 prototypes with exhaust-driven turbosupercharger were assigned the highest priority level. Next came the twin-engined Fw 187 being converted to the DB 605 and then the remaining Fw 190 prototypes. The ready-to-fly dates for the turbosupercharger-equipped aircraft were in the period Nov. to Dec. 1942. This ruling by the RLM explains the late ready-to-fly dates in the table above.

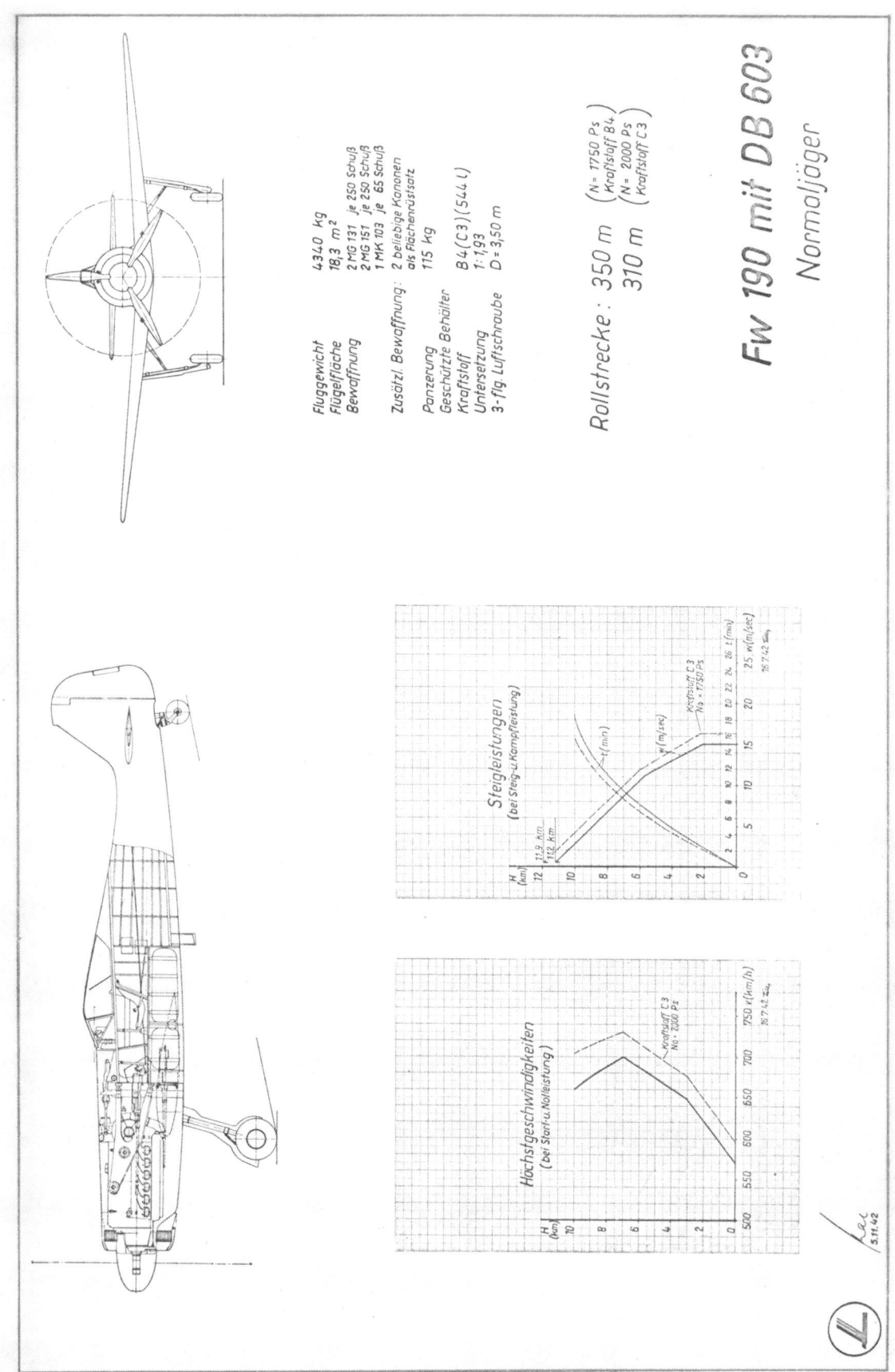

CHAPTER THREE

Development of the Junkers Jumo 213

The later developments in the Fw 190 series were closely associated with the development of the Junkers Jumo 213 engine. Junkers developed the new Jumo 213 from the twelve-cylinder in-line Jumo 211, retaining its 34.79-liter displacement but increasing engine revolutions.

The development history of the Jumo 213 is another example of the sometimes shortsighted decisions made by the RLM at that time. In October 1940 the Jumo 213 was dropped from the production program and its subsequent development was severely restricted. This decision

The new Jumo 213 was installed in the airframe of the Fw 190 V17. Here it has already been attached to the new engine bearers.

was supposed to force the development of the Jumo 222, which was to power the new Bomber B (Ju 288).

Not until early 1942 did the RLM decided to produce the Jumo 213 as a replacement for the Jumo 211. The Jumo 213 had never been planned purely as a bomber engine, however. Installation experiments requested by the RLM for the Bf 109, Me 309 and Fw 190 in mid-1941 showed that, from the beginning, the Jumo 213 was also thought of as a fighter engine. The first installation mock-ups of the Jumo 213 were delivered to Messerschmitt for the Me 309 and Focke-Wulf for the Fw 190 in July 1942. That same month the first consideration was given to using the engine in the Ju 88/Ju 188 series of aircraft.

3.1 The Jumo 213 Engine in the Fw 190

The first concrete plans by Focke-Wulf to create a version of the Fw 190 powered by the new Jumo 213 engine were initiated in November 1941. With planning for the DB 603-powered Fw 190 already at an advanced stage, the RLM request required a reassignment of resources in the Focke-Wulf design department. From then on, development work on the two variants of the Fw 190 with the DB 603 and Jumo 213 was to proceed in parallel. Five experimental aircraft were to be built with the Jumo 213 engine.

The first two prototypes, the V17 and V18, were intended to be nothing more than engine test-beds for the Jumo 213 and were essentially modified Fw 190 A airframes. No armament was foreseen. The true prototypes for the new series were to have been the Fw 190 V19 to V23 (*Werknummer* 0 041 to 0 045). The internal Focke-Wulf project designations were Fw 190 Wb-1 and Fw 190 Ra-1. The Fw 190 Ra-1 differed markedly from the A-series in a number of respects. The most significant were the new forward-swept wing, which was located farther forward than before, and the change to an hydraulically-actuated undercarriage.

Installation of the new Jumo 213 in the Fw 190 V17.

The Jumo 213 gave the nose of the Fw 190 an entirely different appearance.

Opposite
Design drawing of the new forward-swept wing intended for the Fw 190 C and the later Fw 190 D.

While the first Fw 190s powered by the DB 603 had begun long-term testing in the first half of 1942, the first prototypes of the Fw 190 with the new Jumo 213 engine were not yet ready to fly. The reason for this was the engine, not the airframe. Junkers was not able to deliver the first engine to Focke-Wulf for installation until the end of July 1942.

3.2 The Fw 190 V17 Finally Takes to the Air

The installation of the Jumo 213 A in the Fw 190 airframe was seriously delayed as a result of delays in the arrival of the engine. Consequently the Fw 190 V17 did not make its first ground runs with the new engine until 13 September 1942. On 26 September at Bremen, Focke-Wulf's well-known and experienced chief test pilot Hans Sander took the V17 (*Werknummer* 0 039, CF+OX) into the air for the first time. Aerodynamically the V17 made a good impression.

Like the DB 603 A-powered prototypes, the V17 was fitted with an annular radiator, however unlike those machines the V17 was built from the outset with the nose-mounted oil cooler. Kurt Tank's design team adopted this arrangement to minimize subsequent modifications. Minimizing the number of modifications would significantly ease the process of introducing the new type into the Fw 190 A production line. In this way many of the existing jigs could be used for the new variant and the drop in production during the changeover would be minimized.

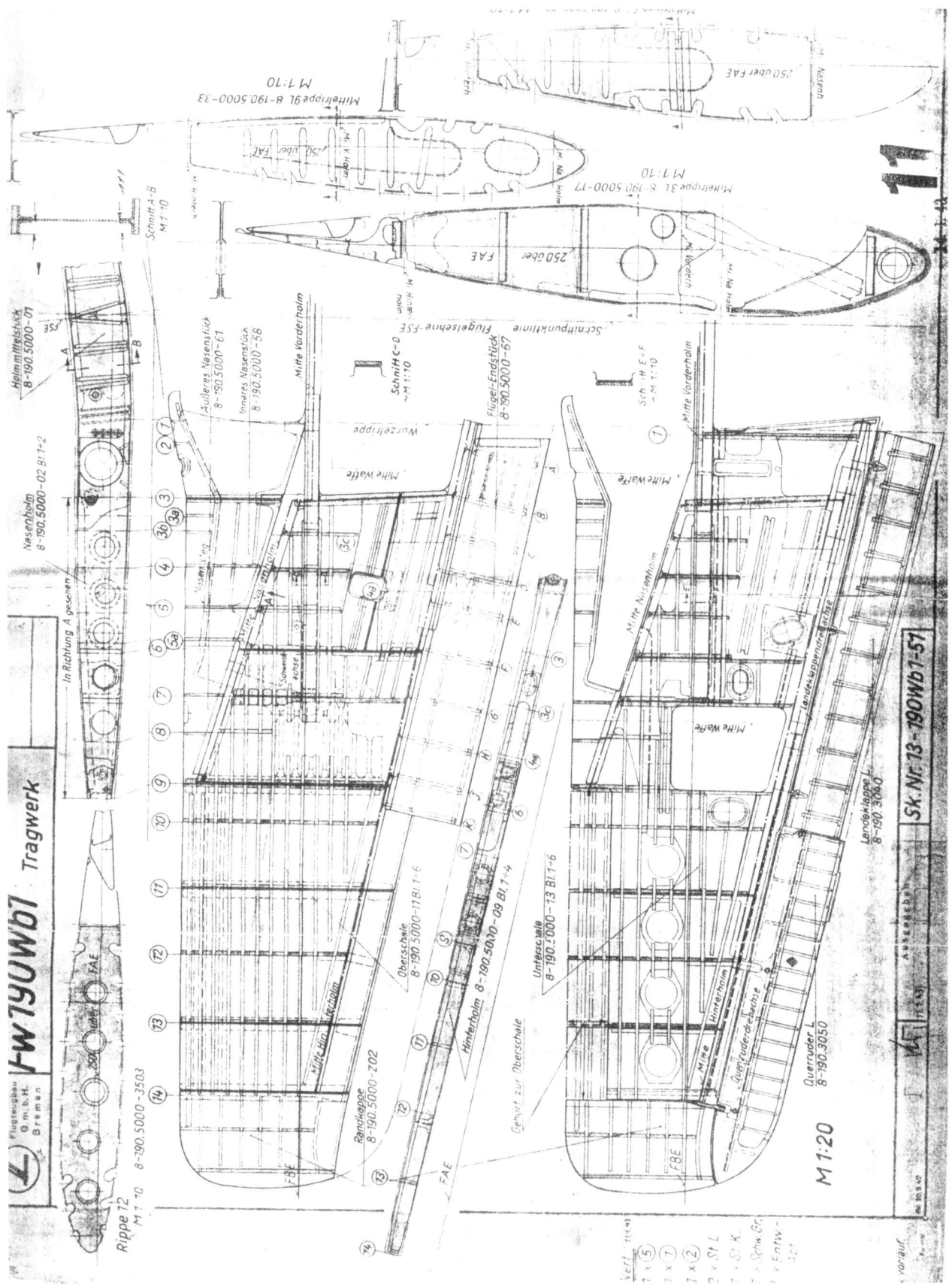

The Fw 190 V17 did not have the relocated and redesigned wing which had been planned, and ballast was initially required to compensate for the additional engine weight. The ballast was distributed as follows: 130 kg of lead plates in the radio compartment, 12 kg in the vertical fin and 15 kg in the jacking tube. Not until later was an elegant solution found for the lengthened engine compartment: instead of installing ballast, the rear fuselage was lengthened through the insertion of a 500-mm section. This eliminated the center of gravity problem and also increased directional stability. This fuselage insert would later play an important role. The Fw 190 V17 was unarmed and takeoff weight with full fuel was 3900 kg.

During flight testing the airframe gave little cause for complaint, however there were unforeseen technical problems with the Jumo 213. From the very beginning, the V17 demonstrated serious resonance phenomenon between the engine and airframe. Heavy vibration made the aircraft almost impossible to fly. Unless it was eliminated, the machine would be useless as a fighter, as the vibration would make it impossible to aim using the reflector gunsight. An intensive search for the cause was initiated and valuable time was lost as a result. Numerous engine problems seriously hampered the testing of the V17. The aircraft did not make its ninth test flight until 11 January 1943. During testing in March 1943 the V17 demonstrated an initial climb rate of 18 m/s. It was able to maintain this to 1800 meters, after which the rate of climb fell off. At 4500 meters

Opposite
Unlike the first Fw 190s with the Daimler Benz DB 603 A engine (photo above), there was no requirement to install the oil cooler beneath the fuselage. The radiator and oil cooler were housed in an annular arrangement in the fuselage nose. (Focke-Wulf)

Above: Close-up of the new Jumo 213 engine cowling with external supercharger air intake. (Focke-Wulf)

Test pilot Bernhard Märschel.

the rate of climb was 15 m./s. At that time operation of the Jumo 213 A was restricted in the 2,650 to 2,950 rpm range. Modifications to the engine mounts did nothing to solve the problem. The engine also ran rough at 3,000 rpm. Very often the exhaust stubs even separated at the flange. As well as the standard VS 9 propeller, a VS 10 unit was used experimentally for a time in an attempt to reduce vibration. All of this showed that six months after the prototype's first flight the initial problems with the Jumo 213 had not yet been ironed out. Another problem encountered at that time was getting the two cooling gill sections to retract simultaneously, which made it difficult to accurately measure the aircraft's maximum speed. One month later, on 30 April 1943, the Fw 190 V17 was test-flown in Rechlin.

The cause for the serious engine vibration was later found to be crankshaft resonance in the continuous speed range. While Junkers sought to eliminate the problem by installing a spoke wheel between the crankshaft and the propeller, to shift the resonance into an rpm range which was not disruptive, the *E-Stelle Rechlin* sought another way. Theoretical calculations showed that changing the firing sequence should eliminate the resonance. Experiments were so successful that Junkers abandoned its experiments and adopted the "Rechlin Firing Sequence". All Jumo 213 engines were recalled and modified. The downside of this action was an 8% loss in performance, for the exhaust and intake lines were optimized for the original firing sequence. These modifications began in the summer of 1943.

Right and opposite top: Two views of Fw 190 V17 taken during testing in Langenhagen.

The Fw 190 V17 underwent a number of changes during the course of testing until spring 1944. The final flight by the "old" Fw 190 V17, *Werknummer* 0039, manufacturer's code CF+OX, was made by Focke-Wulf test pilot Bernhard Märschel on 13 April 1944, when he flew the aircraft from the Focke-Wulf testing center in Langenhagen to the prototype works in Adelheide. There, in just one month, the Fw 190 V17 was converted into the Fw 190 V17/U1, the first prototype of the new D-9 series.

3.3 Preparations for Production – The Prototypes

As a result of the technical difficulties encountered with the Jumo 213, the DB 603 engine appeared to have pulled ahead in the race to power the new Fw 190. Of the five originally-planned prototypes (Fw 190 V19 to V23), only the V22 and V23 were left for trials with the Jumo 213, the V19 to V21 having been allocated for DB 603 variants. Time continued to pass, however. In December 1942 the six prototypes under construction (Fw 190 V19, V20, V21, V25, V26 and V27) were still viewed as test-beds for the Fw 190 C to be powered by the DB 603. But then, on 26

Side view of the Fw 190 V17. the V17 was the first prototype to be powered by the Jumo 213. Note the weights installed in the jacking tube in the rear fuselage.

The engine installation in the Fw 190 V19 was changed from that of the V17. The propeller spinner, radiator intake with cooling gills and radiator fairing were unchanged.

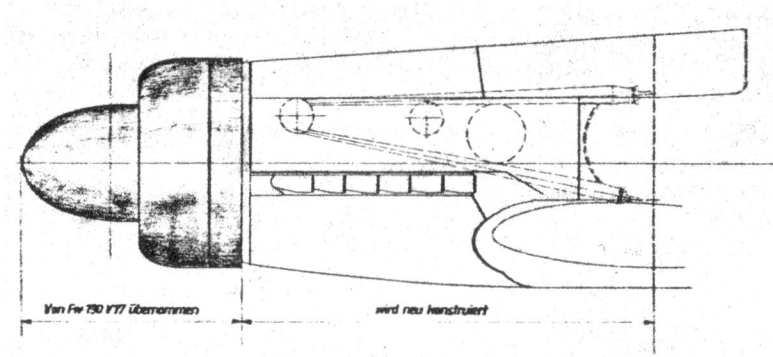

January 1943, the RLM made the "final decision" that the Fw 190 C would be placed in production, but with the Junkers Jumo 213 engine instead of the DB 603. This contradicts the oft-repeated claim that the Fw 190 C was only planned with the DB 603 and that the later Fw 190 D was supposed to receive the Jumo 213.

Work was initially halted on the Fw 190 C prototypes in the Focke-Wulf prototype works in Adelheide, and the aircraft would have to be modified to accept the Jumo 213 engine in keeping with the RLM's decision. As the graphic below shows, considerable modification was required for the prototypes to accept the Jumo 213 engine as installed in the V17. Only the forward part of the power plant was usable.

Everything else, from the firewall to the motor mounts and the radiator assembly, had to be redesigned. Orders were given for the necessary modifications to the six prototypes to be completed as soon as possible, however the target date for the completion of design work was mid-April

In the foreground the Jumo 213 standard power plant, ready for installation. The aircraft in the background may be the Fw 190 V20.

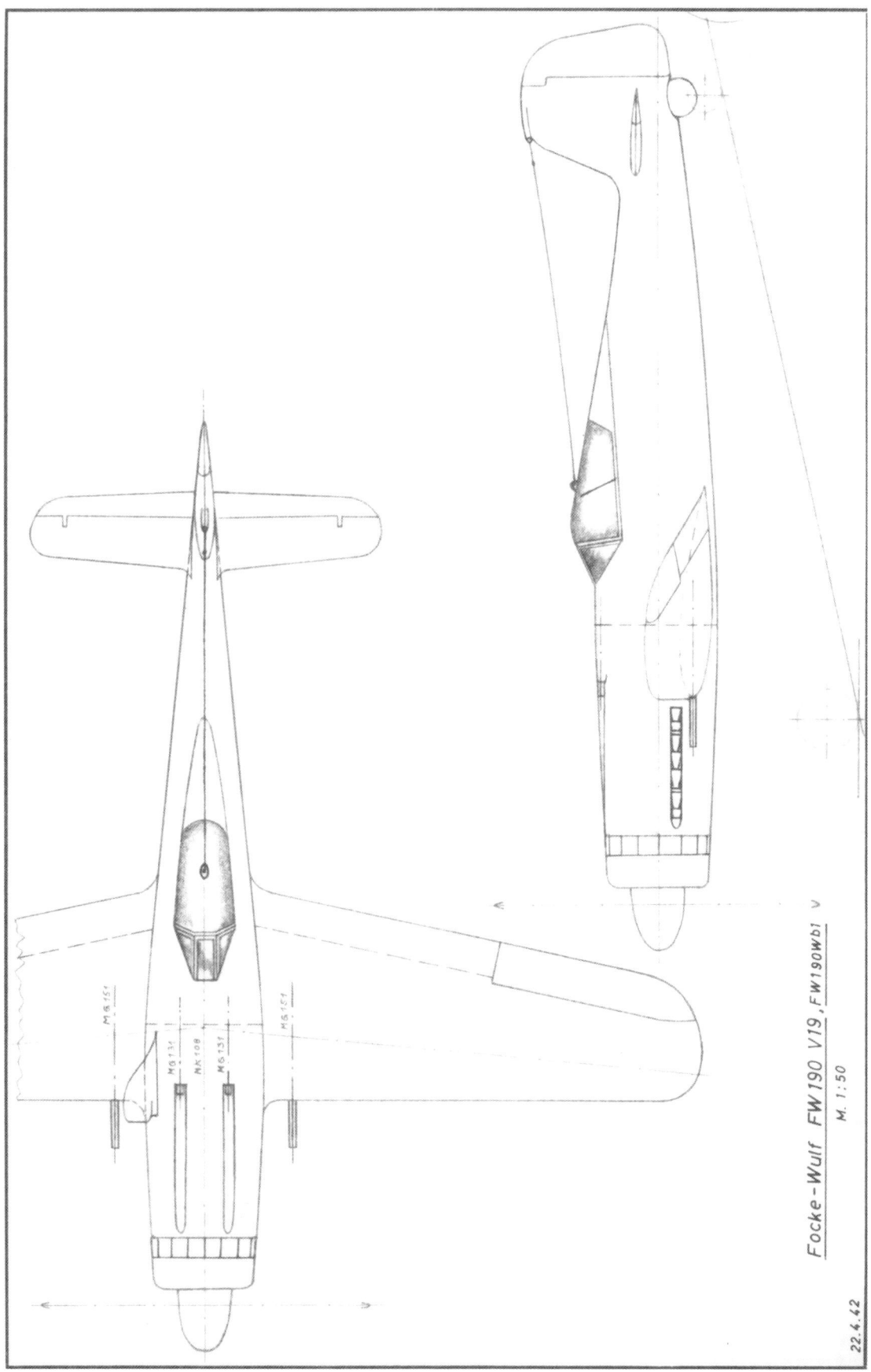

1943. Until then all work on the prototypes would have to be halted. Much time was lost, but this halt also represented a tragic delay in the development of the in-line-engined Fw 190 which would never be made good.

In the course of the other Focke-Wulf effort to develop a high-altitude fighter – development and testing of the so-called "V19 Version" – only two prototypes were built with a pressurized cockpit, the Fw 190 V26 and V27. Focke-Wulf already had enough experimental aircraft equipped with pressurized cockpits to conduct long-term trials: four Fw 190 B-0s, one Fw 190 B-1 and five aircraft equipped with turbosuperchargers.

With the change to a Jumo-powered version of the Fw 190 C, the V17 again came to have special significance, for at that time it was the only Fw 190 prototype with the Jumo 213 engine. Time was working against Focke-Wulf. On 3 June 1943 the RLM cancelled the Fw 190 V22 and V23 prototypes for the Fw 190 D and the Fw 190 V26 and V27 intended for high-altitude trials. All that remained for series testing of the Fw 190 C were the Fw 190 V17 and five other prototypes, of which the V28 was earmarked exclusively for static testing. A Focke-Wulf document dated 4 December 1942 and revised on 29 May 1943 lists the following prototypes for the Fw 190 C:

Fw 190 C Prototypes with the Jumo 213 Engine		
Fw 190 V19	*Werknummer* 0 041	Annular radiator, lengthened rear fuselage, motor relocated forward, no pressurized cockpit
Fw 190 V20	*Werknummer* 0 042	Similar to the V19
Fw 190 V21	*Werknummer* 0 043	Similar to the V19
Fw 190 V25	*Werknummer* 0 050	Similar to the V19
Fw 190 V28	*Werknummer* 0 053	Static test aircraft, similar to the V19

3.4 The Production Fw 190 D-1/D-2 with Jumo 213 Standard Power Plant

In spring 1943 the RLM instructed Focke-Wulf to install the Jumo 213 standard engine in the Fw 190 series. The Fw 190 C series thus became the Fw 190 D. Focke-Wulf initially planned two variants equipped with the Jumo 213 designated the Fw 190 D-1 and D-2. The Fw 190 D-1 was a conventional fighter, while the D-2 was a high-altitude version equipped with a pressurized cockpit. Both versions were to carry a standard armament of two MG 131 machine-guns in the fuselage, two MG 151 cannon in the wing roots and two MG 151s in the outer wings. A 500-kg bomb or a 300-liter fuel tank could be carried beneath the fuselage. Radio equipment was to consist of a FuG 16 and FuG 25a. The D-1 was designated variant 190.0410 and the D-2 190.0420.

Installation of the Jumo 213 standard power plant meant that work on the prototypes had to be halted again in June 1943, as the Fw 190 V20,

Fw 190 V20 with Jumo 213 standard power plant and flame damper system as planned for the production version of the Ta 152 A.

V21 and V25 now had to be modified to accept the new engine. The exception was the Fw 190 V19, which was on the verge of completion and thus the only Fw 190 built to the original Fw 190 C standard. After all the delays and reverses, the Fw 190 V19, *Werknummer* 0 041, did not begin flight testing until 7 July 1943. In addition to the forward-swept wing it had the extended rear fuselage which was later to be a feature of all long-nosed Fw 190s. Although the machine was tested for some time, no photographs of V19 have been found. During initial testing the Fw 190 V19 was damaged in a belly landing after the locking bolts for the starboard main landing gear failed. The damage was repaired and the machine resumed testing. Then, on 16 February 1944, the V19 was involved in a forced landing that resulted in 70% damage. This time it was not repaired.

The fact that the RLM was not exactly pushing the Fw 190 D series either, is shown by the first flight of the second prototype, the Fw 190 V20, *Werknummer* 0 042, manufacturer's code TI+IG. Not until 23 November 1943, almost six months after the V19, did chief test pilot Hans Sander make the first flight in the V20. When it did fly, the V20 was a prototype for the new Ta 152 A, not the Fw 190 D. By that stage of the war the shortage of materials was making itself felt. The magic formula was simplification and standardization. On 17 August 1943 the simplification and standardization of the Fw 190 D led the RLM to rename the series, in the process incorporating the name of the designer Kurt Tank (Ta) in the designation. Significant changes were to flow into the

Initially intended as a prototype of the Fw 190 C, the Fw 190 V20 was eventually completed as a prototype of the Ta 152 A. Here the flame dampers are seen during removal.

Side view of the Fw 190 V20. It was the first Fw 190 to be equipped with the Jumo 213 standard power plant.

new series, now designated Ta 152 A-1 and Ta 152 A-2. The most significant design changes were the planned flame-damping system for the Jumo 213 C standard power plant, the hydraulic system for the undercarriage and landing flaps, the tail surfaces originally planned for the C-series (the so-called "C Tail"), and a wing of greater area (19.5 m²). One day after its maiden flight the V20 was flown by test pilot Bernhard Märschel from Langenhagen to Barth on the Baltic Sea. There the machine was demonstrated to the senior operations staff of the RLM.

The Fw 190 V20 was the first prototype to have a flame-damping system. Focke-Wulf suspected that the system would result in a considerable speed loss and this was confirmed in flight testing. With the flame dampers the Fw 190 V20 achieved a maximum speed of just 675 km/h at a height of 7600 meters. During testing, therefore, the flame dampers were removed. Without them the aircraft achieved a maximum

The Fw 190 V21, *Werknummer* 0043, TI+IH, flew for the first time on 13 March 1944.

speed of 692 km/h at a height of 7000 meters, which was about 35 km/h less than expected.

The third prototype was the Fw 190 V21, *Werknummer* 0 043, manufacturer's code TI+IH. The V21 flew for the first time on 13 March 1944 with Focke-Wulf test pilot Bernhard Märschel at the controls. Like the V20, the V21 was equipped with the Jumo 213 standard power plant and the characteristic flame-damping system. During initial testing the V21 exhibited excessively low coolant temperatures at low outside air temperatures. This problem was quickly solved by modifying the cooling gill actuating rods, which resulted in a significant improvement in engine operating conditions in winter. The V21 encountered problems with rough engine running, and, like the V20, it was fitted with a new propeller which improved the situation. The flame-damping system of the Fw 190 V21 was somewhat different from that of the V20, with an 85% straight-cut exhaust gas mixture pipe in place of the V20's 100% angle-cut exhaust gas mixture pipe. No improvement in maximum speed was achieved, however. The Fw 190 V21 achieved a maximum speed of 540 km/h at low level. On 5 May 1944 it was transferred to the *E-Stelle Rechlin* for testing.

The V25, *Werknummer* 0 050, was also completed in 1944 and was subsequently sent to Tarnewitz as a weapons test-bed. There it was experimentally fitted with engine-mounted MK 108 and MK 103 cannon. Little else is known about the aircraft.

Although the four prototypes did not reveal any serious problems during testing, the new Ta 152 A did not enter production.

Summary of Fw 190 C / Fw 190 D / Ta 152 A Prototypes

Designation	WNr.	Man. Code	First Flight
Fw 190 V19	0 041	TI+IF ?	07/07/1943

Remarks: Jumo 213 testing, not fitted withstandard power plant, D tail, later C tail, later extended fuselage. 70% damage in forced landing on 16 Feb. 1944

Designation	WNr.	Man. Code	First Flight
Fw 190 V20	0 042	TI+IG	23/11/1943

Remarks: Jumo 213 standard power plant, engine test-bed for the Ta 152 A series, initially equipped with flame damper system, later removed, lengthened fuselage. Destroyed in bombing raid on Langenhagen on 5 Aug. 1944.

Designation	WNr.	Man. Code	First Flight
Fw 190 V21	0 043	TI+IH	13/03/1944

Remarks: Jumo 213 standard power plant, engine test-bed for Ta 152 A series with flame damper system, extended fuselage, later converted to DB 603 E for Ta 152 C from 9 Nov. 1944.

Designation	WNr.	Man. Code	First Flight
Fw 190 V25	0 050	—	Apr. 1944

Remarks: Jumo 213 standard power plant, weapons test-bed, tested at Tarnewitz, centrally-mounted MK 108 installed, later MK 103, equipped with flame-damper system.

With the adoption of the Ta 152 A, which received the Focke-Wulf project designation Ta 152 Ra-1, the Ta 152 was developed independently as a new type. In December 1943 Focke-Wulf delivered a complete technical

Focke-Wulf drawing of the Ta 152 A.

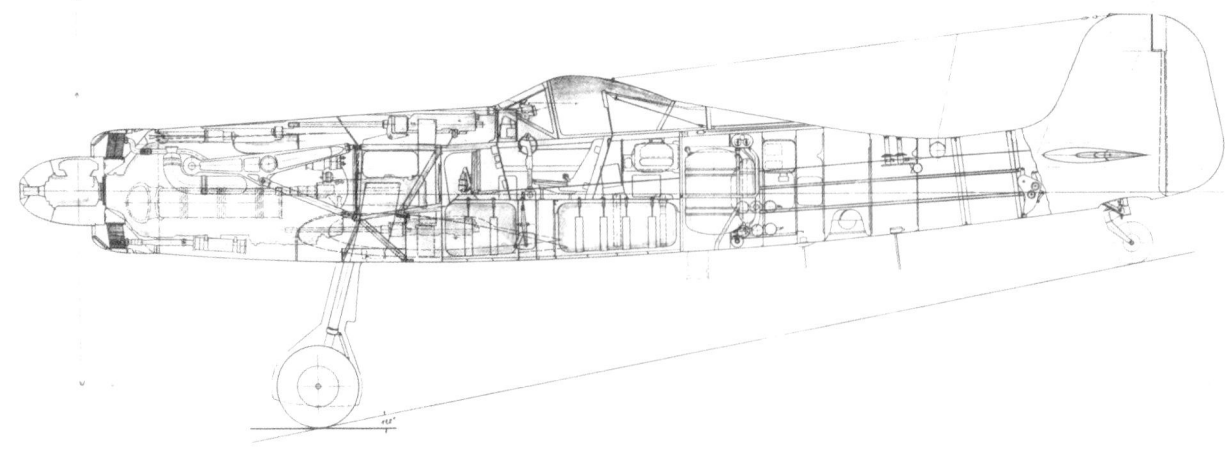

Jagdflugzeug Ta 152 A (Längsschnitt)
mit Jumo 213 A ETW und GM1-Anlage,
und Fla.V. Anlage

The Fw 190 V21 was also equipped with the Jumo 213 standard power plant fitted with a slightly modified flame-damper system. Visible on the left is the tail section of a Ta 154.

description of the Ta 152 A and B. The Ta 152 A was to be fitted with the Jumo 213 A standard power plant, the Ta 152 B with the improved Jumo 213 E. Both types could also accept the Daimler Benz DB 603 G, which was the back-up engine for both versions.

The following list provides a very interesting overview, revealing which prototypes were actually equipped with the Jumo 213 or DB 603 and under test by Focke-Wulf in April 1944.

Prototypes with Jumo 213/DB 603 In-Line Engines with Focke-Wulf			
Fw 190 V17	(0 039)	Jumo 213	Engine trials 4/44.
Fw 190 V18/U1	(0 040)	DB 603	Experimental high-altitude fighter with exhaust-driven turbosupercharger.
Fw 190 V19	(0 041)	Jumo 213	Jumo 213 test-bed, MK 103, forced landing 16/2/44, 70% damage.
Fw 190 V20	(0 042)	Jumo 213	Testing Jumo 213 standard power plant.
Fw 190 V21	(0 043)	Jumo 213	Testing Jumo 213 standard power plant.
Fw 190 V25	(0 050)	Jumo 213	Testing Jumo 213 standard power plant.
Fw 190 V30	(0 055)	DB 603 S-1	Testing as high-altitude fighter with pressurized cockpit, wing area 20.3 m^2
Fw 190 V32	(0 057)	DB 603 S-1	Converted to high-altitude fighter, DB 603 engine, wing area 20.3 m^2, turbosupercharger not installed.
Fw 190 V33	(0 058)	DB 603 S-1	Converted to Ta 152 H with Jumo 213 standard power plant, wing area 23.5 m^2.

Rear view of the Fw 190 V21 at the Langenhagen test center.

As the above list reveals, no other planned Fw 190 C / Ta 152 A prototypes were present at Focke-Wulf in April 1944. The focus of development had begun to shift to the new Ta 152 H high-altitude fighter. The Fw 190 V33 was already at the Adelheide prototype works for conversion into the first prototype of the Ta 152 H.

3.5 Installation Experiments with the V19

In 1942 the engine manufacturers BMW, Daimler Benz and Junkers were working on a variety of aero-engine projects, most of which existed only on the drawing boards. It was important, however, to determine whether they were suitable for installation in existing fighter aircraft such as the Fw 190. In April 1942, therefore, Focke-Wulf completed an exhaustive study on the technical feasibility of installing these proposed power plants in the Fw 190. The basis for this study was the design of the Fw 190 V19. The technical differences between the V19 and the Fw 190 A series will be examined in detail in the original text which follows. This study is interesting in that it reveals the full potential of the Fw 190. It has been suggested that the Fw 190 V19 was used as a flying test-bed to test these various engines, however this is incorrect.

Results of Research into the Installation of Various Power Plants in the Fw 190 Fighter Aircraft

In order to further improve the performance and armament of the successful Fw 190 aircraft powered by the BMW 801 C and D engines, provision must be made for the installation of more powerful engines. For this reason, a redesign of the airframe was undertaken, resulting in the following changes compared to the Fw 190 A-2 on which it was based:

The outline and design of the wing was changed to produce a straight leading edge. The entire wing, including the main spar and rear wing attachment points, was moved forward 120 mm. The undercarriage was modified so that, when retracted, the wheels occupy the same position relative to the main spar as before, and were thus moved forward 120 mm relative to the fuselage. For center-of-gravity reasons, however, in the extended position the mainwheels had to be moved forward 220 mm relative to the fuselage.

The remaining modifications were of little design significance and were undertaken in part to improve the equipment (armament, radio) and in part to incorporate lessons learned in flight testing and operations (modified tail surfaces).

The prototype for the new series bore the designation Fw 190 V19 and was fitted with the Jumo 213 engine. In addition to the Jumo 213, which is to be the standard engine, this new airframe can accept the following power plants with minor modifications:

BMW 801 J   DB 603
BMW P 8028   DB 614

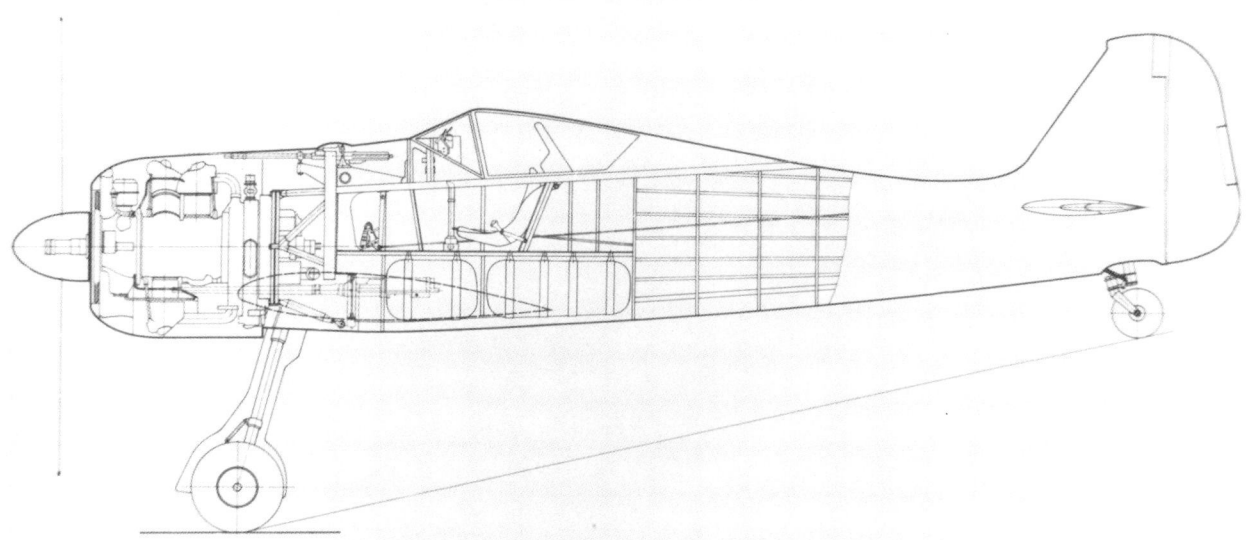

The starting point: the Fw 190 A-2 powered by the BMW 801, which was in production at the time of the Focke-Wulf study.

Research has shown that the DB 623 is not suited for the new airframe.

As well, to determine the performance limits of the new airframe, the possibility of installing the DB 609 and DB 624 engines was examined. The results were negative, partly because of weight and c.g. considerations, partly for reasons of space.

Following are the results of the research concerning all potential power plants for the Fw 190:

Power plants for the Fw 190 V19 airframe:
Power plants already installed in the Fw 190 A-2 airframe:

1.) Fw 190 with BMW 801 C – existing production version
2.) Fw 190 with BMW 801 D – existing production version
3.) Fw 190 V19 with BMW 801 J

Author's note: The BMW 801 J was not a totally new variant, rather it was a production BMW 801 D with a BMW turbosupercharger. At the time of the study, development of the BMW 801 J was proceeding rather slowly. Not until 21 October 1942 was BMW able to deliver two BMW 801 J engines for experimental installation in a Ju 88 airframe. Some modifications were necessary to install the BMW 801 J in the Fw 190 airframe.

Necessary engine modifications:
To prevent fouling of the windscreen by the upwards-facing exhaust stubs, it is necessary to move the stubs to the right side of the fuselage. However, this will mean lowering the turbosupercharger, which is attached to the engine, by at least 50 mm. It has been calculated that this will cause the stream of exhaust gases to flow beneath the canopy along the right side of the fuselage. As well, a favorable diversion of the exhaust gas stream can be expected as a result of the right-hand spiral of the propeller vortex.

Necessary airframe modifications:
An additional attachment point will have to be added to the bottom strut of the engine bearer frame. As the installation of an engine-mounted cannon is not possible, the lowering of the floor in the forward area could be dispensed with, which would allow installation of a larger fuel tank. The cannon ammunition boxes would likewise be deleted

Fw 190 with BMW 801 J.

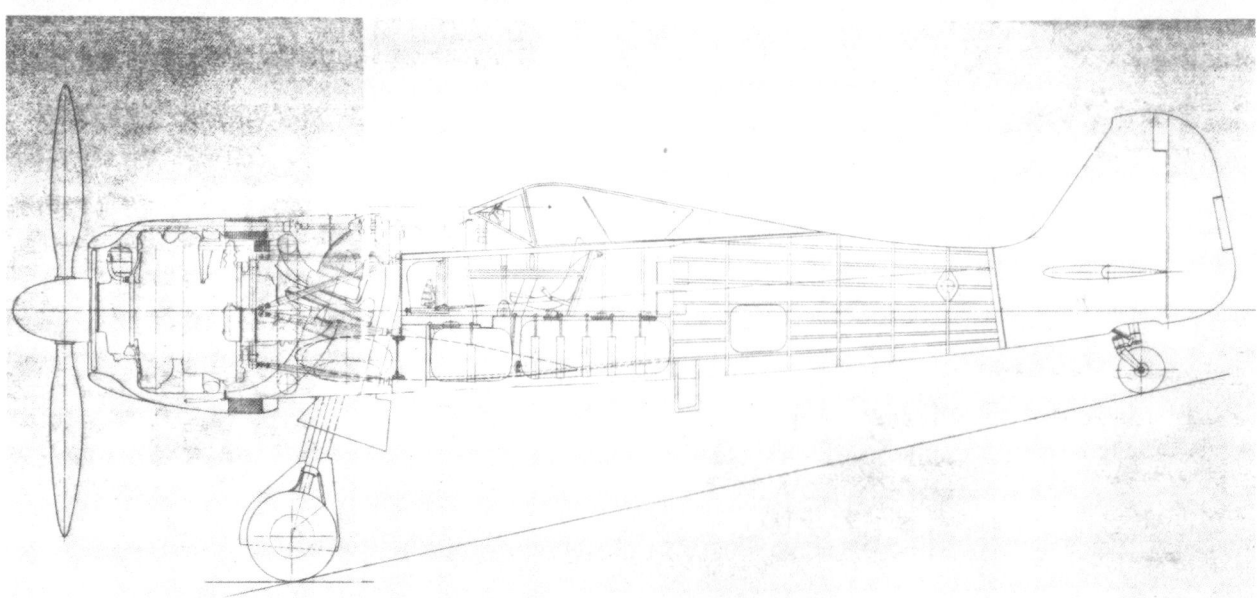

4.) Fw 190 V19 with BMW P 8028

Necessary engine modifications:
As the centrally-located supercharger air pipe makes it impossible to install a central strut at the bottom of the engine bearer frame, the proposed attachment points in the BMW engine installation diagram cannot be used. The circular engine bearer frame will therefore have to be changed.
Design of the power plant forward of the firewall:

In order to achieve sufficient clearance between the undercarriage and the supercharger air pipe, minimum engine spacing is 1745 mm, measured from Frame 1 to the center of the rear bank of cylinders. The installation of cooling gills in the area of the retracted mainwheels will not be possible, therefore it will be necessary to dispense with cooling air control in this area. To keep the forces on the struts of the engine bearer frame within acceptable limits, provision has been made for a secondary engine bearer frame, to which is attached a heat-insulated barrier to prevent heat damage to the ammunition boxes.

Necessary airframe modifications:
No major changes to the airframe are required, however as in the installation of the BMW 801 J, it will not be necessary to lower the floor in the forward area, making it possible to increase the size of the forward fuel tank. The ammunition box for the cannon may also be deleted. The installation is satisfactory in respect to center of gravity.

Fw 190 project with the BMW P 8028.

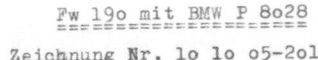

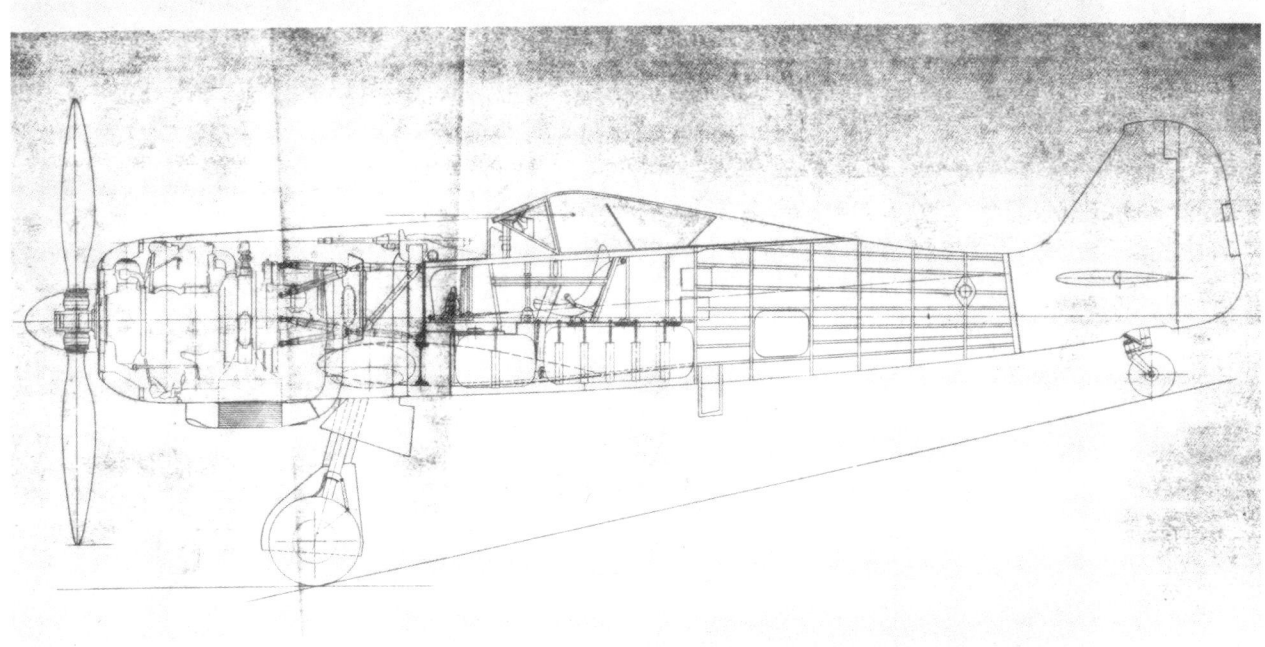

Author's note: the Jumo 213 engine was seen as a primary power plant whose design was seen as secure. It therefore only received mention in the installation investigation and no further research was carried out.

Opposite
Fw 190 with the new Junkers Jumo 213 A-2 engine.

5.) Jumo 213*   single-stage without axial first stage, no intercooler
Primary power plant for Fw 190 V19 airframe

6.) Jumo 213 A-2   single-stage without axial first stage, no intercooler
Primary power plant for Fw 190 V19 airframe

7.) Jumo 213   two-stage with intercooler
Primary power plant for Fw 190 V19 airframe

8.) DB 603

Necessary engine modifications: none.
Installation of the MK 108 made it necessary to mount the engine rather far forward, however this provided generous clearance between the engine and the undercarriage. Therefore no modifications to the engine are necessary.

Necessary airframe modifications: none.
As the engine installation is similar to that of the Jumo 213, the same attachment points can be used. The position of the engine-mounted cannon is the same as in the Jumo 213, therefore no modifications to the airframe are necessary.
Center of gravity is almost the same as with the Jumo 213.

Author's note: The estimated performance of the DB 603-powered Fw 190 included a maximum speed of 723 km/h at a height of 8000 m. Speed at ground level was 595 km/h, while low-level climb rate was 16.4 m/s. With C3 fuel, the DB 603 was supposed to produce 1,800 h.p. at 7000 meters. These performance calculations were based on a gross weight of 4366.5 kg, which included an armament of two MG 131s, two MG 151s and one MK 108 Motorkanone. Service ceiling was 11900 m.

9.) DB 614

Necessary engine modifications:
In order to achieve an engine location which provides adequate clearance from the mainwheels while remaining within c.g. limits, it is proposed that the heat exchanger mounted on the engine be altered by rotating the two superchargers by 45 degrees.

Necessary airframe modifications:
The high power plant weight may make it necessary to strengthen the attachment fittings. The most forward center of gravity position is relatively nose heavy and is close to the CG position of the Fw 190 V1 and V2.

Author's note: The estimated gross weight of the Fw 190 with the DB 614 and an armament of two MG 131s, two MG 151s and one MK 108 was

Fw 190 mit Jumo 213 bzw. 213 A-2
Zeichnung Nr. lo 13 141-11

Bewaffnung Fw 190 mit Jumo 213	Normalfall		Sondereinsatz 1		Sondereinsatz 2		Sondereinsatz 3	
Waffen-Einbau	Waffen	Schuß	Waffen	Schuß	Waffen	Schuß	Waffen	Schuß
MG 131 im Rumpf	2	2x300	2	2x300	2	2x300	2	2x300
MG 151 in Flügelwurzel	2	2x250	2	2x250	2	2x250	2	2x250
MG 151 (Gurt) im Flügelaußen	—	—	—	—	2	2x140	2	2x140
Motorkanone MK 108	1	75	—	—	—	—	1	75
Motorkanone MK 103	—	—	1	75	1	75	—	—

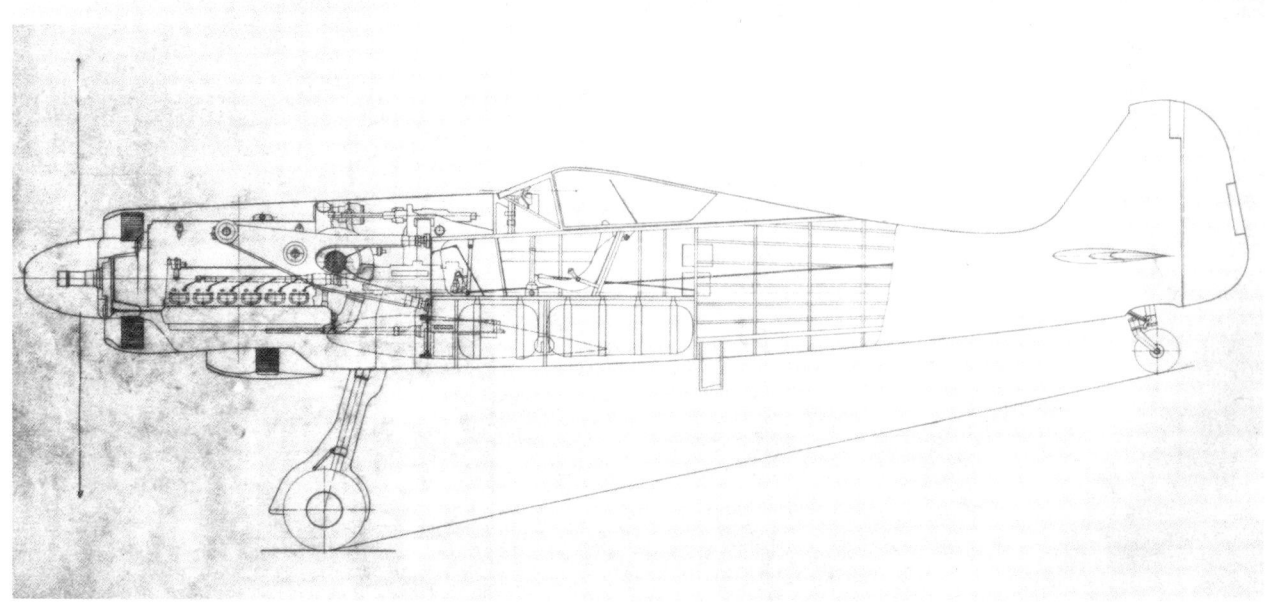

Fw 190 with DB 603 engine.

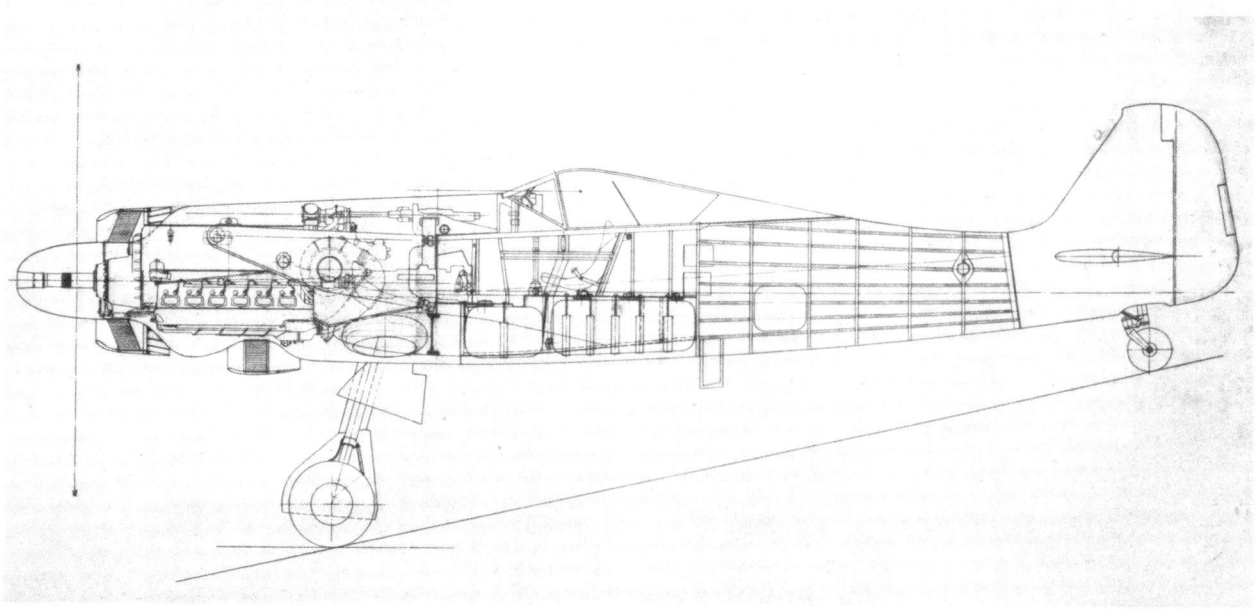

Fw 190 with DB 614.

4506 kg. Maximum speed was 580 km/h at ground level and 730 km/h at heights of 7700 and 9700 meters. At takeoff and emergency power, the DB 614 produced 1,810 h.p. at 7700 meters. Output at climb and combat power at 7700 meters was 1,535 hp. The aircraft achieved a service ceiling of 12500 m.

10.) DB 623 A

Necessary engine modifications: none.
No engine modifications were required, however conditions for the motor mount were very unfavorable. Because of poor clearance from the turbosupercharger, the engine bearer strut had a very small attachment area on the motor mount. The result was very high weights.

Necessary airframe modifications:
The wing must be lowered considerably to achieve adequate clearance between the undercarriage and the turbosupercharger, resulting in a deepening of the fuselage. This results in a change in the fuselage profile at least to the area of the aft fuselage. As a result, the DB 623 A appears thoroughly unsuitable for installation.

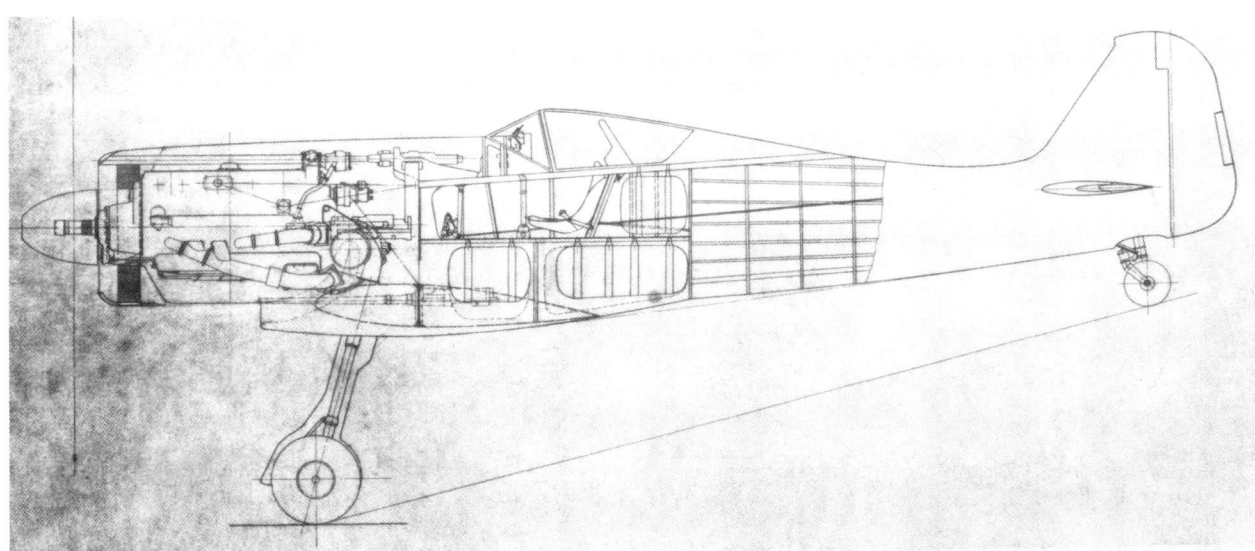

Fw 190 with DB 623A.

11.) DB 609 – Unsuitable for installation.

Necessary engine modifications:
The engine will require similar modifications to those of the DB 614. As in the case of the DB 614, it has been proposed that the heat exchanger be raised with a simultaneous rotation of the superchargers by 45 degrees, in order to achieve sufficient clearance from the mainwheels.

Necessary airframe modifications:
For CG reasons, neither the installation of the radiator in a ventral position

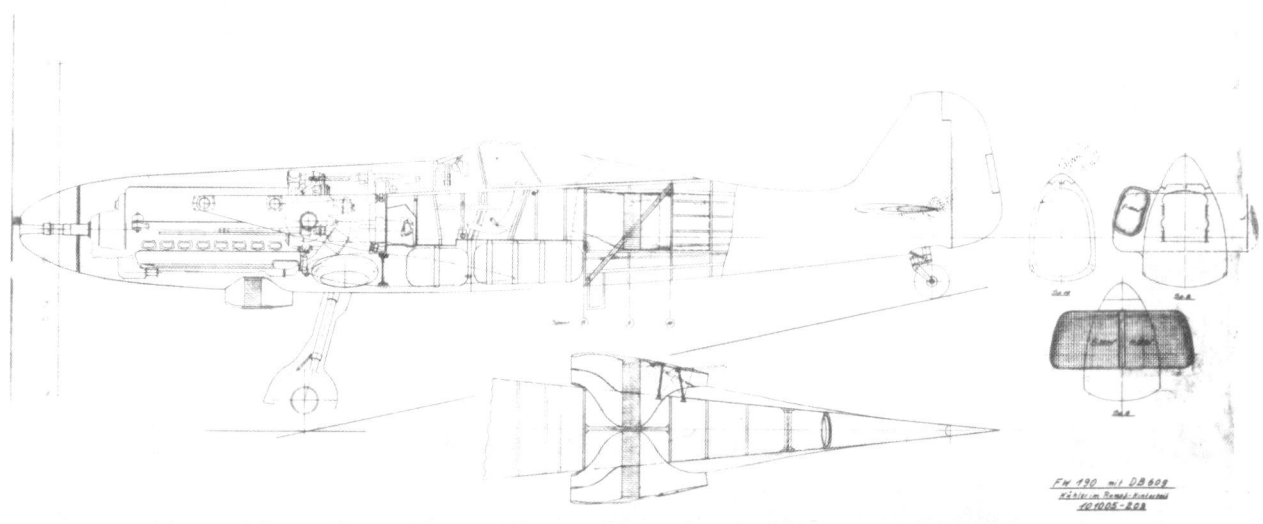

Fw 190 with DB 609.

beneath the wing nor as an annular radiator in the nose is acceptable. For this reason two radiators with a frontal area of 40 dm2 each will have to be mounted in the rear fuselage. The necessary cutouts in the fuselage will result in a considerable weakening of the entire fuselage structure, especially the lateral load bearing structure, which will have to be compensated for by strengthening of the fuselage which will in turn increase weight.

Because of the exhaust gas stream flowing over the wings, the radiator intakes will have to be placed as high as possible, however some exhaust gas must be expected to enter the left intake on account of the right-hand spiral of the propeller vortex. It is to be expected that the unfavorable shape of the intake diffuser will result in partial flow separation and thus insufficient air flow to the inner half of the radiator. To achieve a satisfactory airflow behind the outlet, it will be necessary to install a large metal fairing outside the fuselage shell, however this will disrupt considerably the flow over the horizontal stabilizer. The oil cooler, with a frontal area of 14 dm^2, is located ventrally beneath the engine. With a takeoff weight of 4965 kg, the undercarriage of the Fw 190 V19 is by far insufficient. Without reinforcement of the existing wing, structural strength will sink to an unacceptable level. For this and the other reasons stated above, the DB 609 does not appear suitable for installation in the Fw 190 V19 airframe.

12. DB 624

Installation of this engine is not possible for reasons of weight and space, especially because of the ventral exhaust ports. A drawing was therefore not produced.

Comparison and Assessment of the Performance of the Fw 190 Fighter Aircraft with Various Engines

An examination of the comparison graphs for speeds and rates of climb at different altitudes immediately shows that the optimal speeds, rates of climb and service ceiling – assuming similar armament – cannot be achieved with one and the same engine. In assessing operational worth, however, all three factors must be included simultaneously. To avoid creating an unrealistic rating value, for example through simple multiplication, the value was established on the following basis:

If one assumes that the maximum speed and armament of the fighter are superior to those of the enemy, then the operational value of the fighter depends on its ability to locate and engage an enemy aircraft whose position has been reported only in general terms. The amount of time available for this is limited by the requirement to effectively prevent the enemy bombers from dropping their bombs. The fighter aircraft can only achieve its mission if it is capable of engaging the enemy quickly, because the longer it takes to reach the enemy's last reported position, the less likely it is that it will find the enemy. For this reason, the assessment of the fighter aircraft must include both its rate of climb and time to climb to the bombers' altitude, and its maximum level speed at that altitude, so as to be able to quickly find and overtake the enemy bombers. It can be assumed that the maximum amount of time a fighter can use to search for the enemy is approximately twenty minutes after takeoff. If the bomber is not found in this time, in most cases it will have already reached its target or flown away on an unknown course.

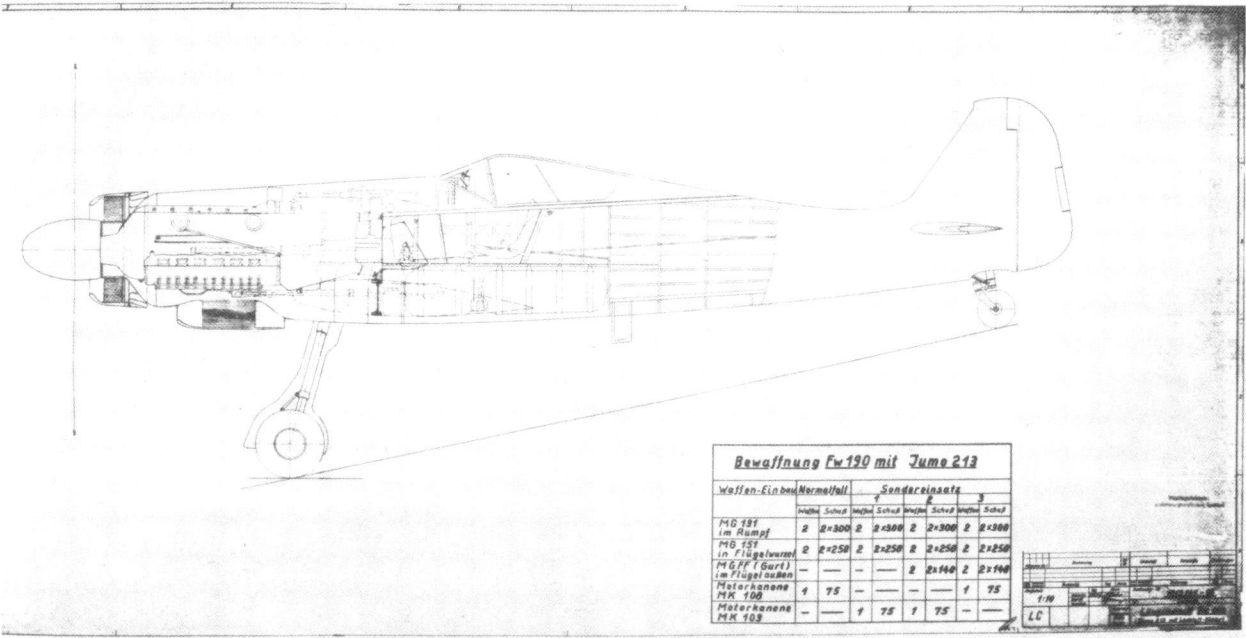

Fw 190 V19 with Jumo 213 with intercooler.

In this way the problem of rating fighter aircraft is simplified to the question of which of the fighters under consideration can cover the greatest amount of airspace in 20 minutes flying time – measured from takeoff – with the proviso that the airspace covered must extend at least to the enemy's cruising altitude.

This rating at first seems disputable and primitive. Closer examination of the area covered by a fighter aircraft in 20 minutes shows it to be a body of revolution, whose base circle radius is represented by the distance the fighter can fly in 20 minutes at low altitude, its height by the altitude that can be reached in 20 minutes, and its apex radius the horizontal distance flown in 20 minutes of climbing flight. In the intervening heights it was assumed that the limiting point of the area will be reached by climbing to the desired height at the best rate of climb with subsequent horizontal flight at that height. A mathematical derivative of this "covered area" does not produce a uniform formula, as the performance characteristics of high-altitude engines do not allow themselves to be compressed into a simple relationship, however the covered airspace may be derived simply from the usual performance figures of the aircraft. This provides a scale for the probability of being able to engage the enemy and expressed as a rating number it realistically includes the aircraft's speed and rate of climb.

The evaluation of the various engines resulted in the following ranking list:

Combat Height	6000 m	10000 m	11000 m
	DB 603	DB 603	DB 603 (reduced armament)
	Jumo 213 with initial stage	DB 614	DB 614
	Jumo 213 A 2	Jumo 213 with initial stage	DB 623
	DB 614	Jumo 213 A 2	BMW 801 J
	Jumo 213 with intercooler	Jumo 213 with intercooler	
	Jumo 213 A 2 (OZ 87)	DB 623	
	BMW 801 D	BMW 801 D	
	DB 623	Jumo 213 A 2 (OZ 87)	
	BMW 801 C	BMW 8028	
	BMW 8028	BMW 801 J	
	BMW 801 J		
Combat height was not reached in 20 min. by:	—	BMW 801 C	DB 603 with standard armament
			all Jumo 213
			BMW 8028
			BMW 801 D
			BMW 801 C

This tabular overview ended the comparison of engines for the Fw 190 V19. The ratings clearly show that the Daimler Benz DB 603 would have been the best choice to power the Fw 190 V19.

CHAPTER FOUR

The Fw 190D becomes the Ta 153

With the Fw 190 C program facing considerable delays as a result of the adoption of the Jumo 213 standard power plant, development of the series now designated the Fw 190 D continued, at least at the planning level. The Focke-Wulf designation for this project was Fw 190 Ra-4. Compared to the previous layout, the new Fw 190 D's most significant changes were its greater wing area (20 m^2), extended fuselage and the installation of a total of seven weapons. Just when it seemed certain that the Fw 190 D would be built with the Jumo 213, the RLM changed its mind again. On 6 April 1943 it decided that the Fw 190 D series would be powered by the new BMW 8035 engine. The BMW 8035 was based on the 2,000-h.p. BMW 801 E with turbosupercharger. The maximum boost altitude of the BMW P 8035 was 14000 meters. At an air armaments conference held in September 1943, it was stated that the BMW P 8035 was to begin replacing the BMW 801 J

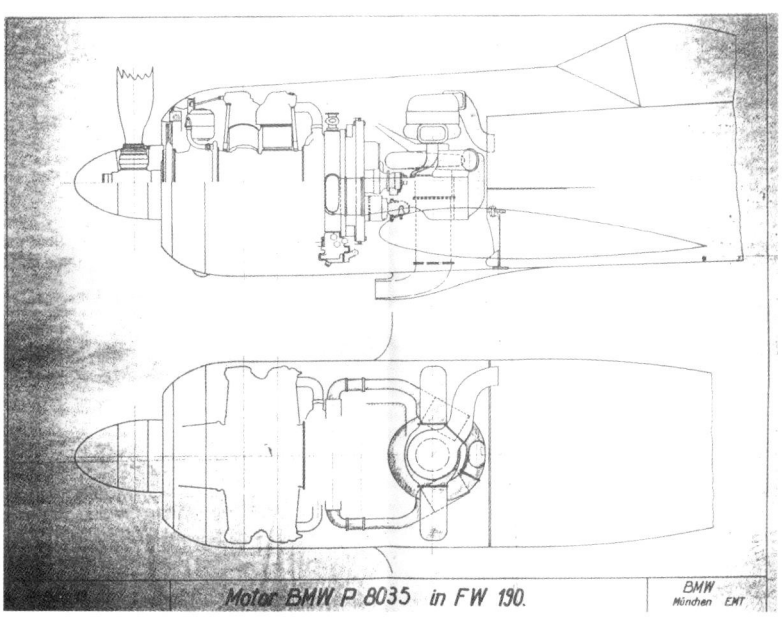

BMW project drawing of the Fw 190 with the BMW P 8035 engine.

in September 1945. Thus the BMW P 8035 would arrive too late for installation in the Fw 190 airframe. The engine never went into production and planning for the Fw 190 D turned once again to the Jumo 213. One month later, in May 1943, Focke-Wulf published a type survey which predicted that the Fw 190 D powered by the Jumo 213 would enter production in 1944.

4.1 The Renaming

Just as the developed version of the Fw 190 C was renamed the Ta 152, in mid-1943 the revised Fw 190 D was renamed the Ta 153. The adoption of the Ta prefix was in recognition of Kurt Tank's success as an aircraft designer. From 31 July 1943, therefore, Focke-Wulf continued development of the Fw 190 Ra-4 as the Ta 153 Ra-1. The Ta 153 was thus a direct competitor for the Messerschmitt Me 209. Following the demise of the Me 309, the RLM initially favored the M2 209, which was to replace the increasingly obsolescent Bf 109.

4.2 Performance Comparison with the Me 209

The performance values obtained from the Fw 190 V17 allowed Focke-Wulf to make a direct comparison between the new Ta 153 V1 and the Me 209 A. One of these two fighters was to be the last piston-engined fighter aircraft to be built in quantity and would bridge the gap to the Me 262 jet fighter. The decision as to which of the two fighters was the right choice was so contentious that the RLM ordered direct performance comparisons. The result was a number of meetings between representatives of Messerschmitt and Focke-Wulf. Weights were compared, as were estimated performance figures. Comparison of these estimates revealed that there was no significant difference in performance between the two

The Me 209 V5 flew for the first time on 3 November 1943. The Me 209 was intended to replace the Bf 109 and was a direct competitor of the new Ta 153.

Focke-Wulf used the Fw 190 V17 to determine the performance of the Ta 153.

designs, although the Ta 153 was 145 kg heavier. Furthermore, Focke-Wulf specified that, in order to save, time, both sides would make their performance calculations based on combat power. Had the calculations been based on takeoff and emergency power, the differences in favor of the Me 209 would have been much greater. The decision as to which fighter was the right one and should be built was postponed repeatedly, with the result that ultimately neither of the two aircraft entered production.

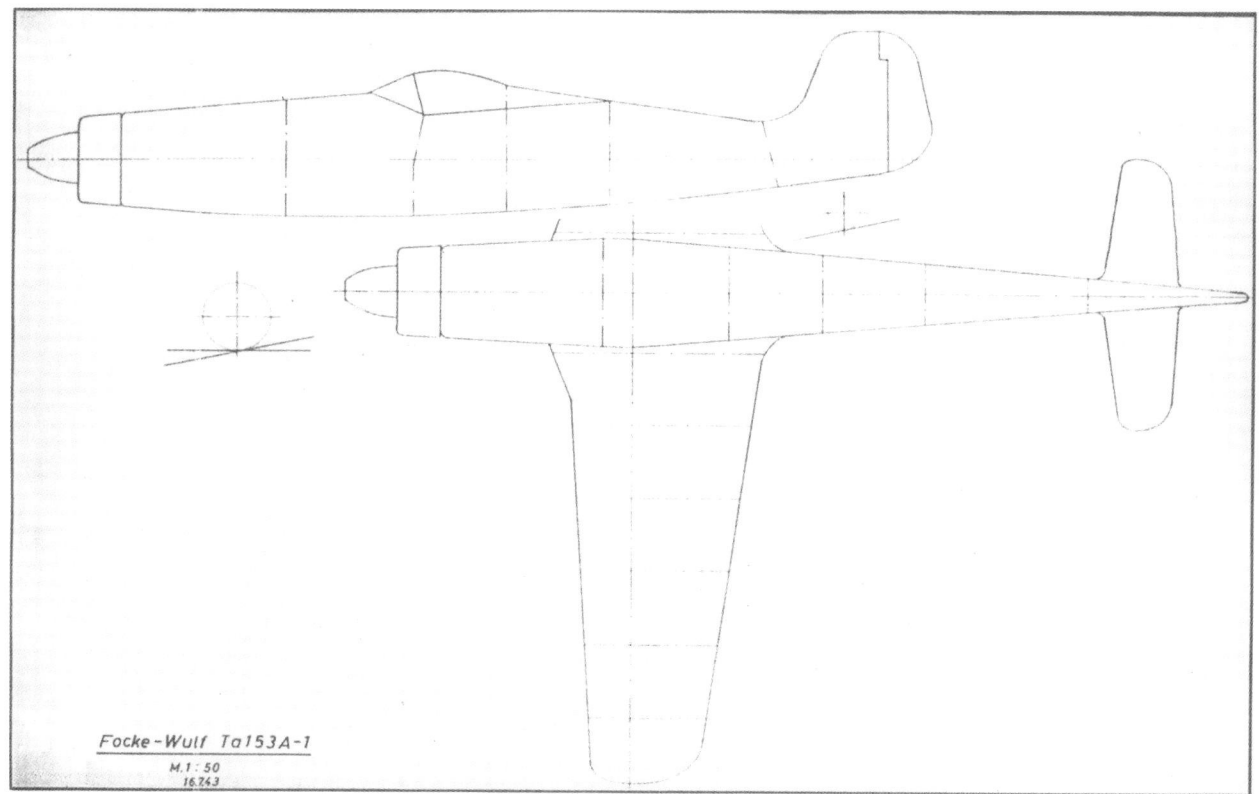

Focke-Wulf Ta 153 A-1.

CHAPTER FIVE

The Fw 190 D-9 Finally Enters Production

The fierce air battles being waged over the Reich and the resulting heavy losses in aircraft and pilots finally forced the RLM to act. Too late the RLM recognized the need for a new high-performance fighter. The radial-engined Fw 190 A serving in the *Reichsverteidigung* was unable to effectively deal with the incursions by Allied fighters and bombers. In the spring of 1944 new long-range escort fighters, the North American P-51 Mustang and Republic P-47 Thunderbolt, appeared in the skies over Germany. Not only could they carry an enormous amount of fuel, they were also capable of outperforming the Fw 190 A and Bf 109 G in many respects.

This finally resulted in a production variant of the Fw 190 powered by the Jumo 213 engine. Based on the Fw 190 A-9, which was in the planning stage, the project was designated Fw 190 Ra-8 internally and had nothing to do with the earlier Fw 190 D series (Ta 153). In keeping with the A-series aircraft from which it was derived, the new type was

Model of the new Fw 190 D-9. The anticipated extent of modifications compared to the A-8 series was made apparent. (Griehl)

assigned the designation Fw 190 D-9. The first detailed information on the Fw 190 D-9 appeared in a Focke-Wulf development report dated 23 February 1944.

The new Fw 190 D-9 was essentially a development of the Fw 190 A-8 airframe with the Junkers Jumo 213 in-line engine. It was never intended to be a major production variant, instead it was viewed as an interim type to fill the gap until the Ta 152 could enter large-scale production. All changes compared to the Fw 190 A-8 airframe will be examined in detail in the technical description which follows.

Since 1942 Focke-Wulf had developed the Jumo 213 A into the 9-8213 E standard power plant for the Fw 190. The Jumo 213 offered a significantly better high-altitude performance than the 14-cylinder BMW 801 D radial engine. It was hoped that the new Fw 190 D-9 would enable the *Jagdflieger* to once again gain the upper hand over Allied fighters, however production was not scheduled to begin until August 1944. Until then the German fighter arm would have to face the Allies in fighters with an inferior performance.

5.1 Focke-Wulf Technical Description No. 268: The Fw 190 D-9

A. General

The Fw 190 D single-seater is the result of a requirement to install the Jumo 213 A in the Fw 190 A-8 airframe with the minimum possible modifications to the fuselage. It is intended that the Jumo 213 A standard power plant should find the widest possible use. There is no engine-mounted cannon, however the engine is designed in such a way as to allow the later installation of the MK 108 (but not the MK 103!). A 0.5-meter fuselage extension required for reasons of stability partly compensates for the aircraft's nose-heaviness resulting from the installation of the heavier engine. Depending on the equipment installed in the aircraft, 10 to 30 kg of ballast has to be affixed in the vertical stabilizer.

The Fw 190 D-9 represents an interim solution pending the introduction of the Ta 152 and will be delivered in limited numbers, hence the requirement to minimize changes and associated costs. For reasons of engine availability, the large production numbers planned for the Fw 190 make it necessary to introduce as soon as possible a version powered by the Jumo 213 A to complement those powered by the BMW 801 TH engines. As well, the Fw 190 D represents a back-up solution in the event that deliveries of the BMW 801 engine are halted for reasons associated with the war.

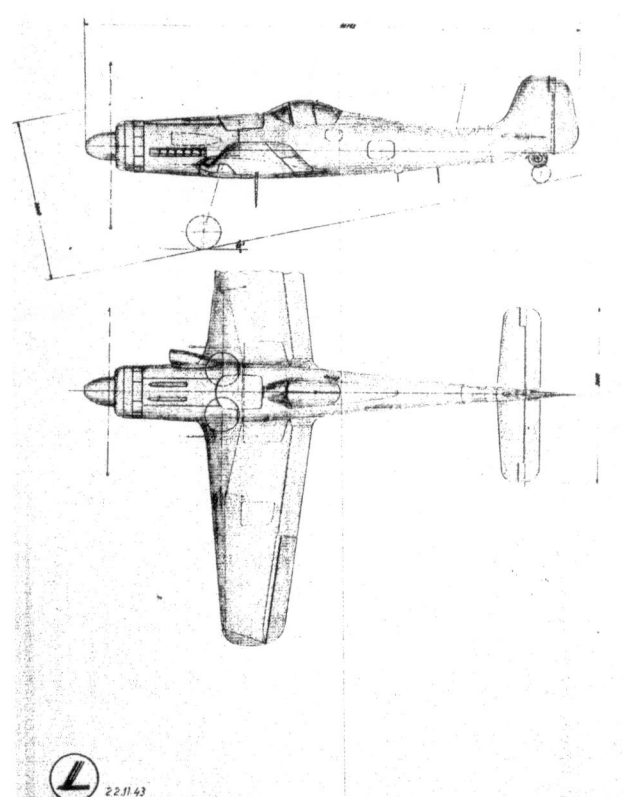
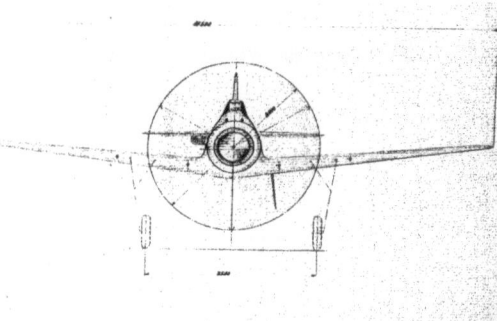

B. Technical Description

Fuselage

The fuselage is that of the Fw 190 A-8, however the following changes are necessary as a result of the fundamentally different engine mounting:

Of the radial engine's five attachment points, the bottom support strut is eliminated together with the associated attachment point.

The considerable increase in engine attachment forces makes it necessary to strengthen the attachment fittings and the bulkhead behind them. The latter consists of sheet steel of tapered thickness.

The lengthened engine area compared to that of the BMW 801 has a very destabilizing effect on flight characteristics, especially on directional stability. To compensate for this, the rear fuselage was lengthened by inserting a cylindrical section 0.5 meters in length. This also serves to accommodate the oxygen bottles, which have been moved to the rear for CG reasons.

The considerable increase in fuselage moment resulting from the lengthening of the fuselage made it necessary to strengthen the structure of the rear fuselage. This reinforcement followed the pattern of the Ta 152 and in part involves the installation of steel sections in place of the Dural sections used previously.

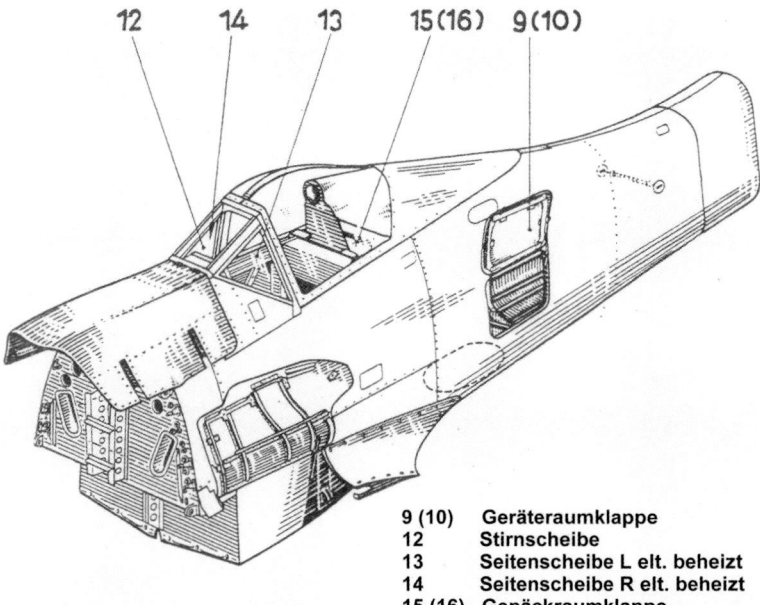

9 (10)	Geräteraumklappe
12	Stirnscheibe
13	Seitenscheibe L elt. beheizt
14	Seitenscheibe R elt. beheizt
15 (16)	Gepäckraumklappe

Fuselage structure of the Fw 190 D-9.

Undercarriage

The electrically-actuated undercarriage has been adopted unchanged from present production. The installation of larger 740x210 wheels instead of the present 700x175 wheels is not possible within the terms of the present contract, therefore overload weight must remain limited to 4900 kg (see table of weights).

Tail Section

The tail surfaces have been adopted from present production unchanged. A standard tail with a larger vertical stabilizer of 1.77 m^2 is under development, and as soon as this is available it will be installed. The design provides for the installation of ballast plates on the vertical stabilizer main spar. 10 to 30 kg of ballast can be fitted depending on the equipment installed in the aircraft.

Control Linkages

The control linkages are essentially unchanged, however the extended rear fuselage makes it necessary to lengthen the control rods.

Wing

The wing is also taken from current production, with only one minor change between the wheel covers resulting from the deletion of the bottom engine support strut.

Power Plant

Jumo 213 A engine. An effort is being made to use the Jumo 213 A standard power plant to the maximum extent possible.

Focke-Wulf Fw 190 "Long Nose" - An Illustrated History of the Fw 190D Series

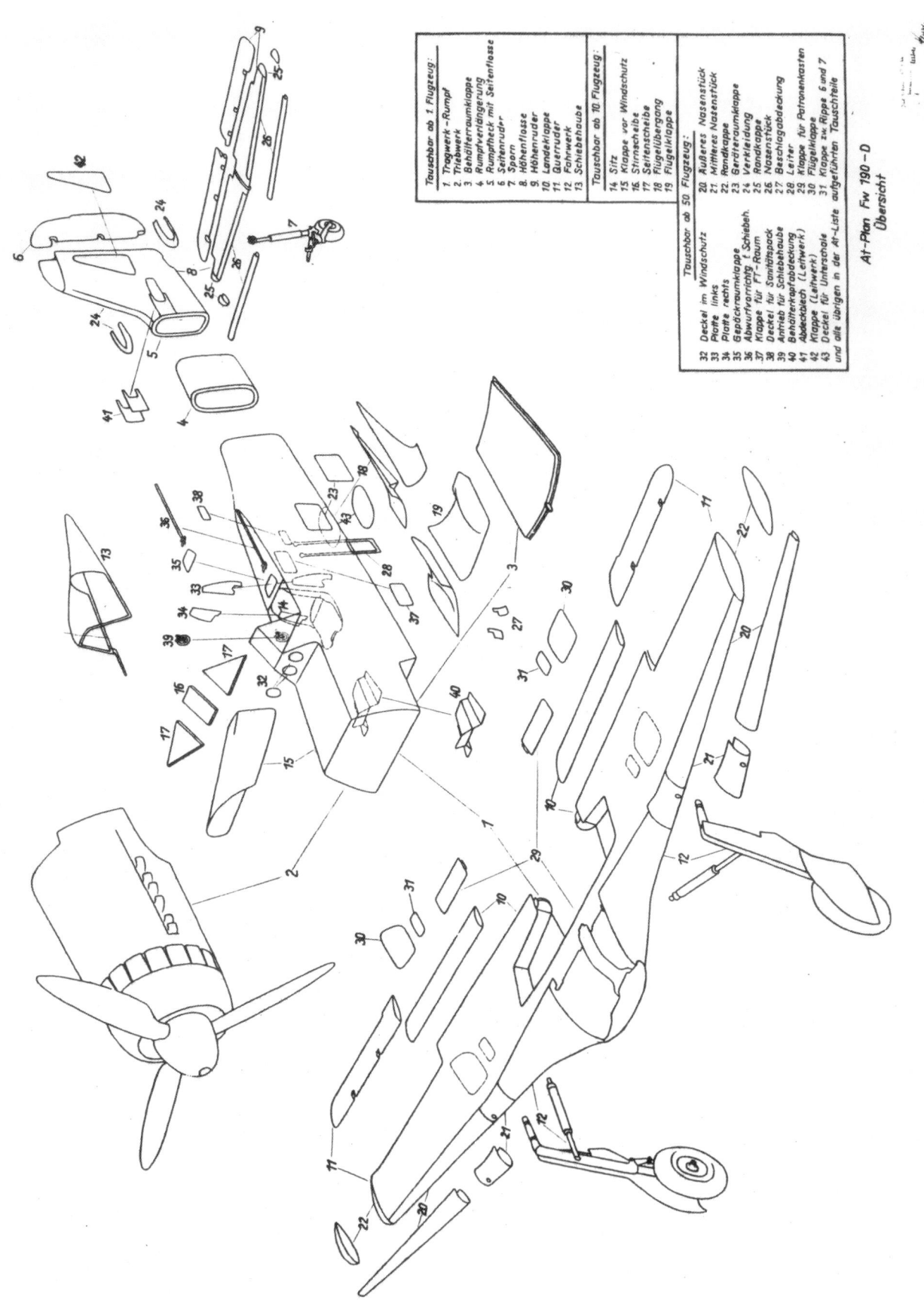

Two Fw 190As were converted to Fw 190 D-9 prototypes. Shown here is *Werknummer* 170 003, as Fw 190 V53.

The radiator block and the entire coolant system have been retained unchanged. On the other hand it was necessary to redesign the oil system and motor mounts: the oil supply of approximately 60 liters is contained in the left engine bearer, which was designed to also serve as an oil tank, the so-called "Tank Bearer". The right engine bearer is taken from the Ju 188. The structural strength of this bearer meets all requirements and also makes possible a suitable location of the engine in terms of CG and other design factors. Accessibility at the air intake is, however, restricted by a curved support strut. In order to keep the engine mounting as short as possible, without having to mount the engine so high as to hamper visibility, with the agreement of Jumo the two fuel filters were relocated to the engine underside. The engines are delivered unmodified and are then modified by Fw during installation. The exhaust system consists of conventional exhaust stubs. No flame damper system is planned.

For <u>increased high-altitude performance</u> an 85-liter GM 1 tank may be installed in the rear fuselage. At an average rate of consumption of 100 g/sec, this provides for approximately 17 minutes of operation.

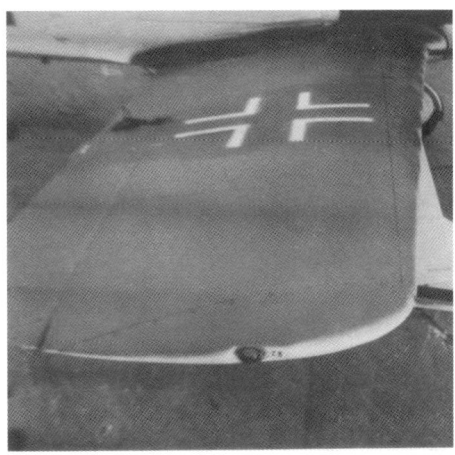

Wing profile of the Fw 190 D-9.

For <u>increased range</u> a "metal-protected" 115-liter tank may be installed in the fuselage in place of the GM 1 tank described above. To further increase range a 300-liter auxiliary tank may be carried beneath the fuselage. The tank is mounted on an ETC 503 bomb rack. As the oil system is designed only for use with the 115-liter tank, part of the cold-start mixture will have to sacrificed when the 300-liter tank is installed.

Opposite
Component breakdown drawing of the Fw 190 D-9.

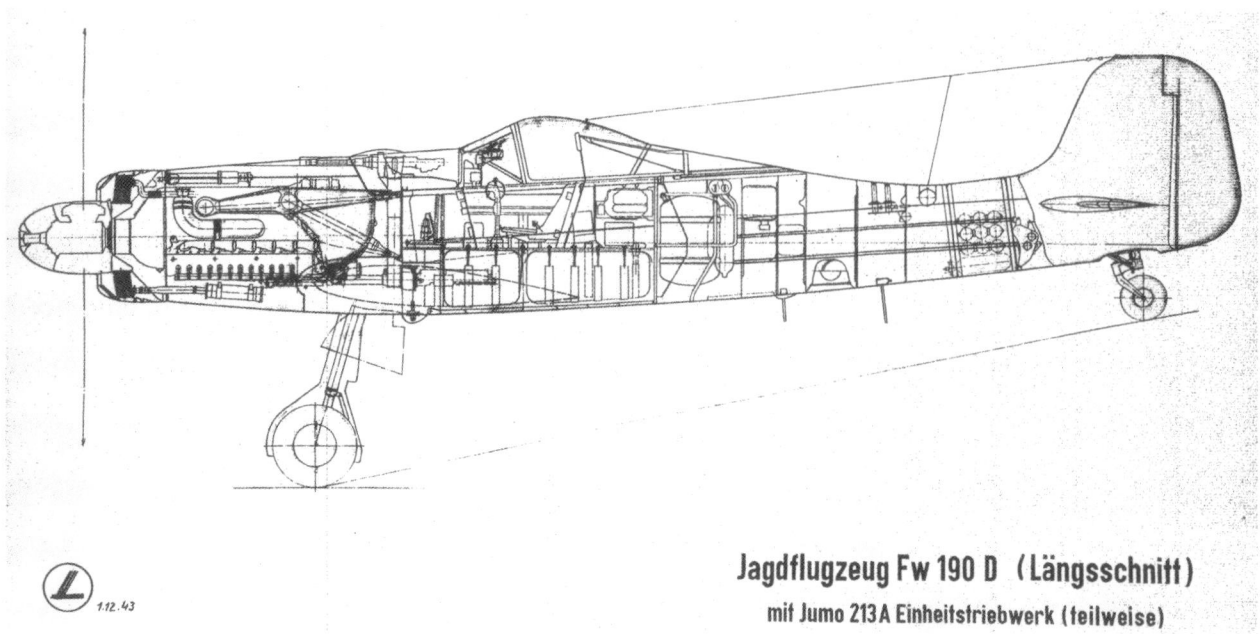

Jagdflugzeug Fw 190 D (Längsschnitt)
mit Jumo 213A Einheitstriebwerk (teilweise)

Equipment

The equipment was taken from the A-8 series with minor changes associated with the installation of the Jumo 213.

Armament

Guns (see armament sketch).

The weapons installed in the airframe are essentially taken from the A-8 series. The spacing between the two MG 131s had to be increased from 260 to 308 mm on account of the position of the synchronizer on the Jumo 213.

Possible Armament Combinations:

Standard Armament:
    2 MG 131 with 475 rounds per gun in fuselage
    2 MG 151 with 250 rounds per gun in wing roots

Additional Armament:
    2 MK 108 with 55 rounds per gun in outer wings, or,
    2 MG 151 with 140 rounds per gun in outer wings, or,
    2 MK 103 with 40 rounds per gun beneath the outer wings

Available space at the firewall is such that the MG 131s may be replaced by one engine-mounted MK 108 with 75 to 100 rounds or two MG 151s in the upper fuselage with 200 rounds per gun. There is also sufficient space to accommodate the following armament: one MK 108 as described above plus one MG 151 in the upper fuselage with a maximum of 200 rounds. The extent of the modifications required for this will require a new variant, however.

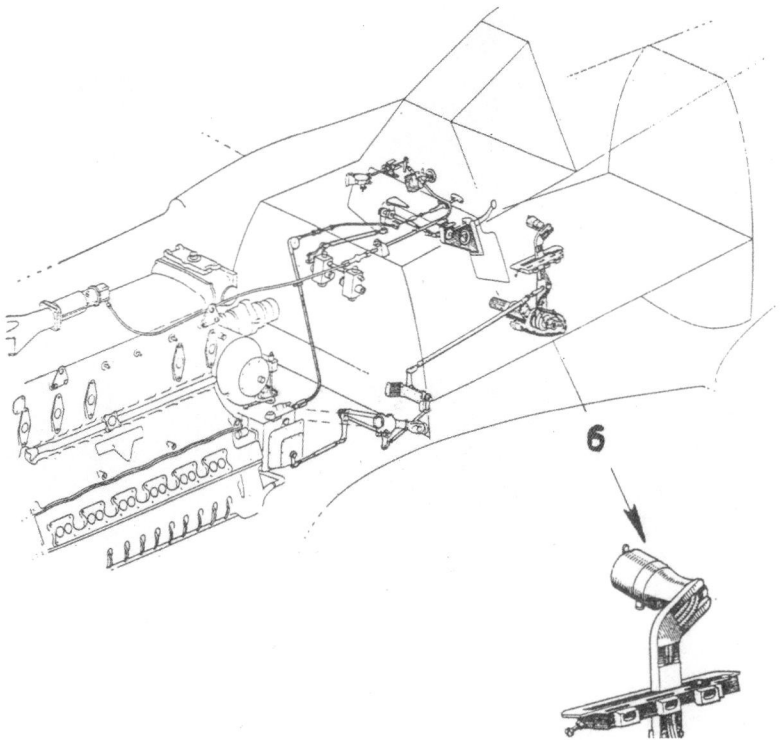

Fw 190 D-9 throttle lever.

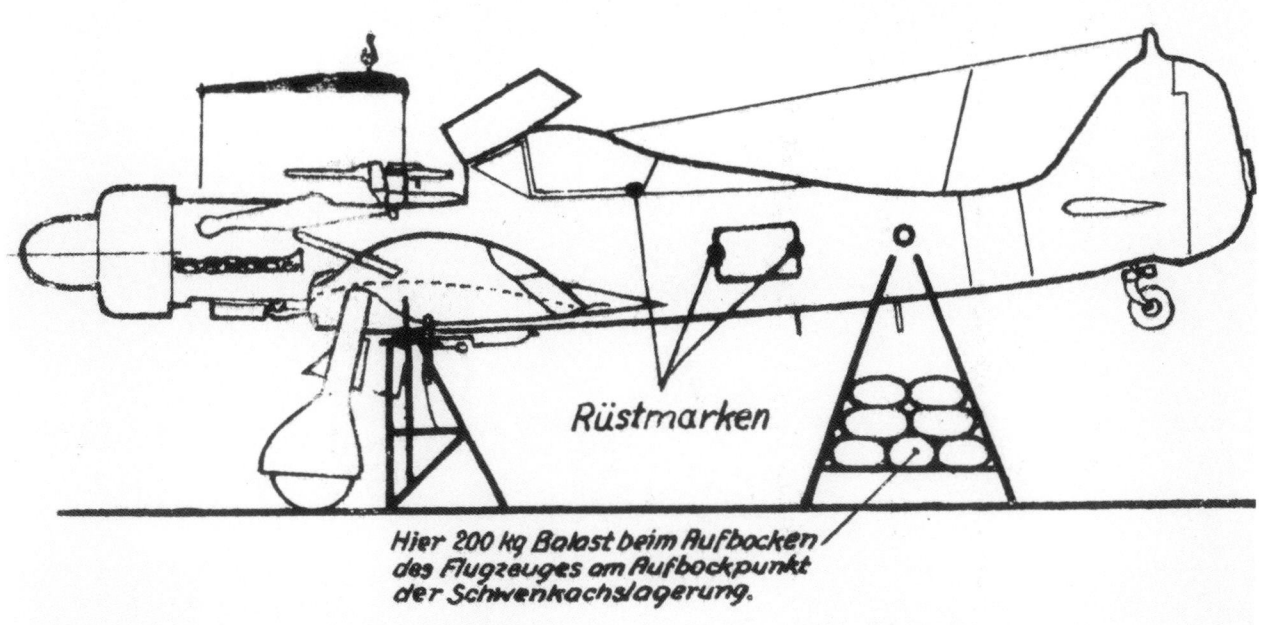

D-9 on jacks.

The two 13-mm MG 131 machine-guns mounted above the engine of the D-9.

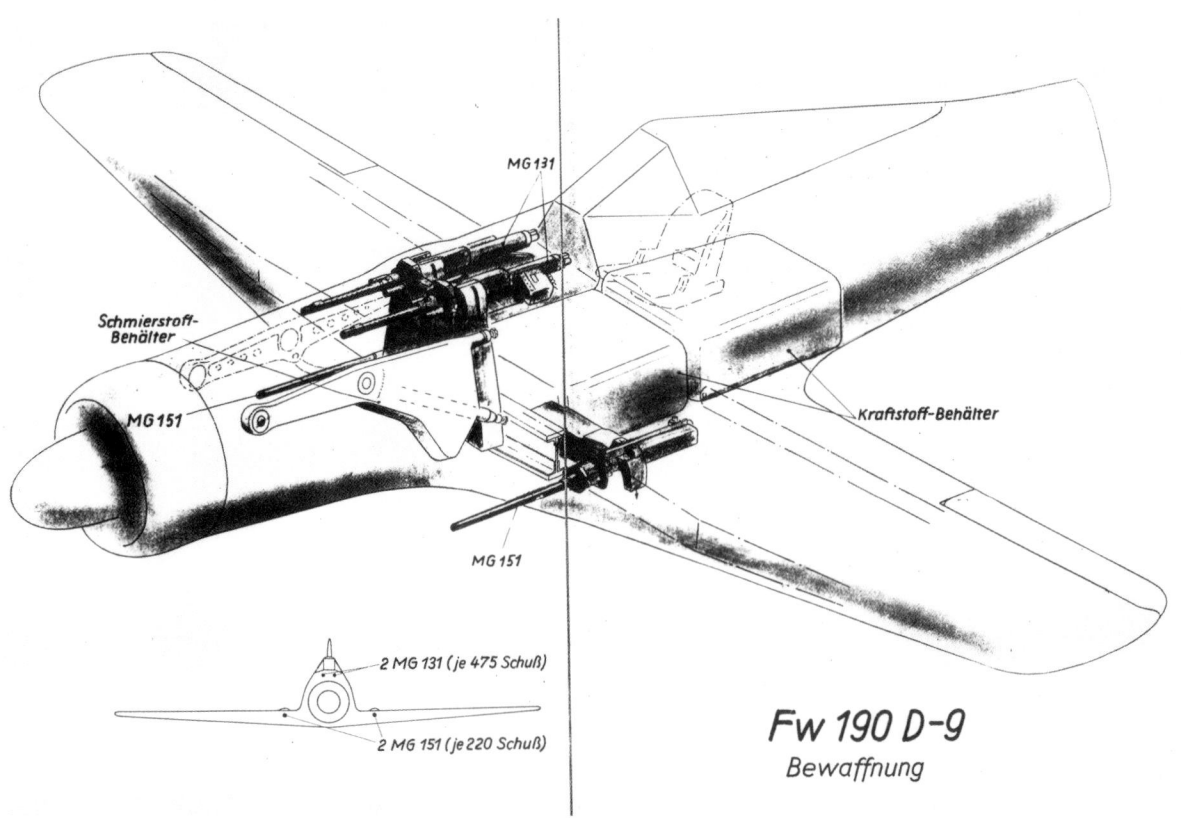

Top: left Visible above the control stick grip is the fuel contents gauge. To the left is a cover plate; this was the intended location of the pressure gauge for the MW 50 system.

Above: On the far right is the engine rpm indicator. Above it is the boost pressure gauge, repeater compass and the vertical speed indicator (from left to right). Directly below is the handwheel used to adjust the position of the cooling gills.

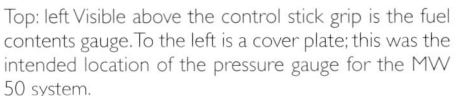

Left: This photograph clearly illustrates the equipment in and beneath the main instrument panel. At the top left is the SZKK 4 round counter, and beside it the reflector sight. The row of instruments below consists of the airspeed indicator, combined turn-and-bank indicator and artificial horizon, vertical speed indicator, the repeater compass and the boost pressure gauge.

Left: Additional equipment was housed in two consoles to the right and left of the pilot's seat. Visible in front of the seat is the control stick with firing buttons for the fixed weapons. Directly in front of it is the bomb release selector panel which was installed in fighter-bombers.

Fw 190 D-9 instrument panel.

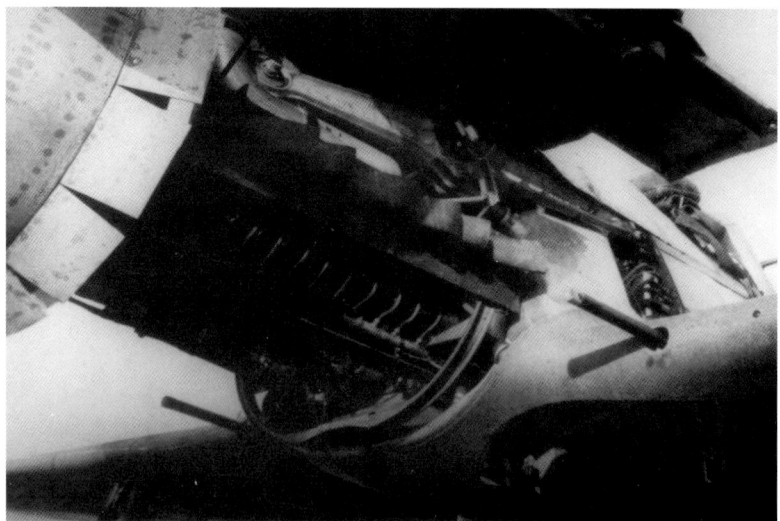

This photograph depicts the major components of the Fw 190 D-9 from the annular radiator to the wheel wells in the wing. The two MG 151 cannon in the wing roots are clearly visible.

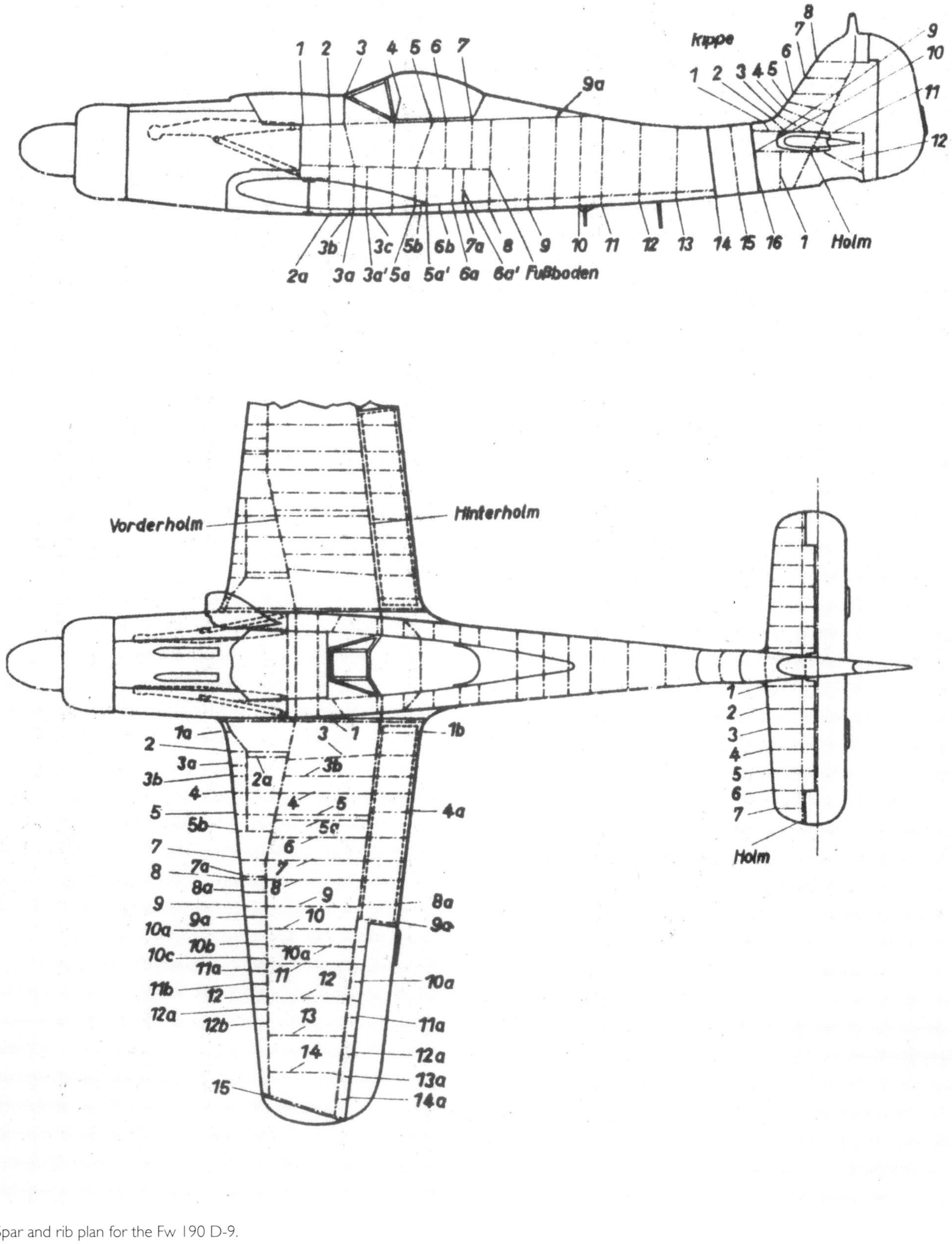

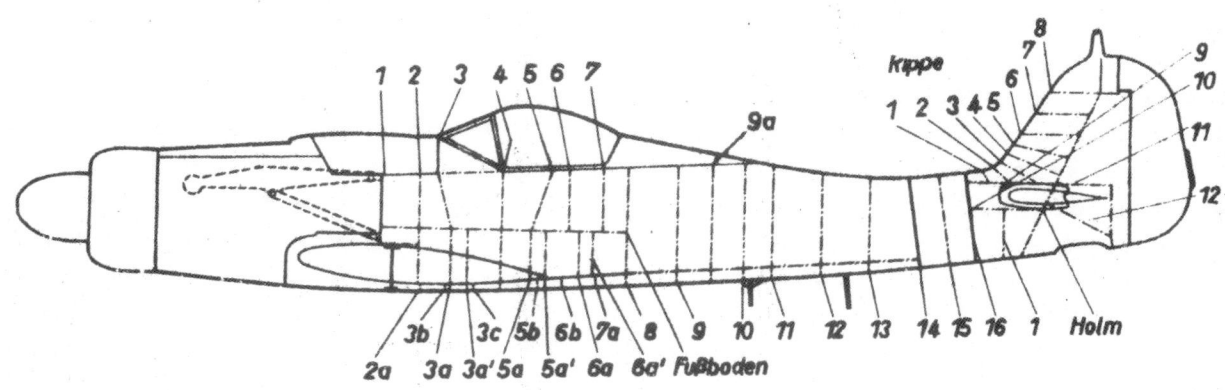

Spar and rib plan for the Fw 190 D-9.

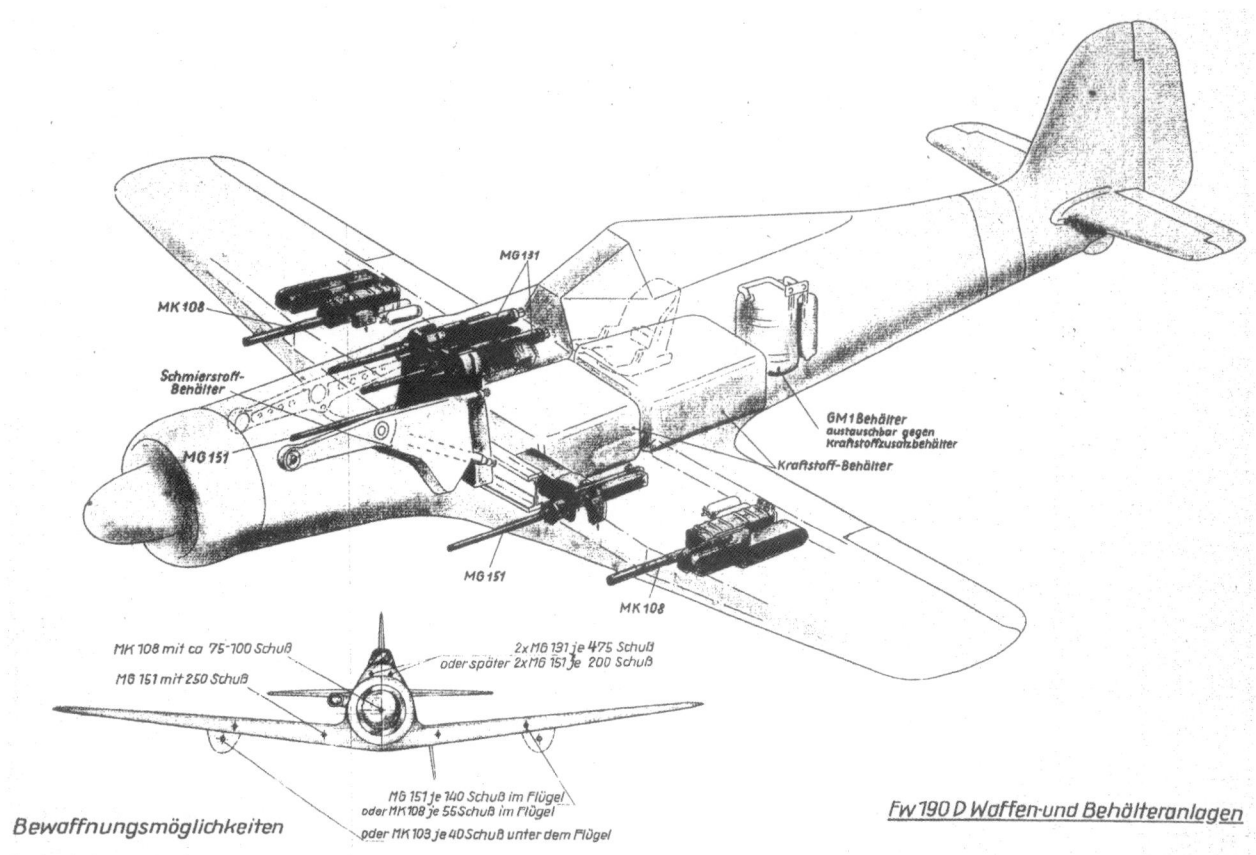

Above: It was originally planned that the Fw 190 D-9 should also carry MK 108 cannon in the outer wings.
Below: Plans showing possible cannon placement.

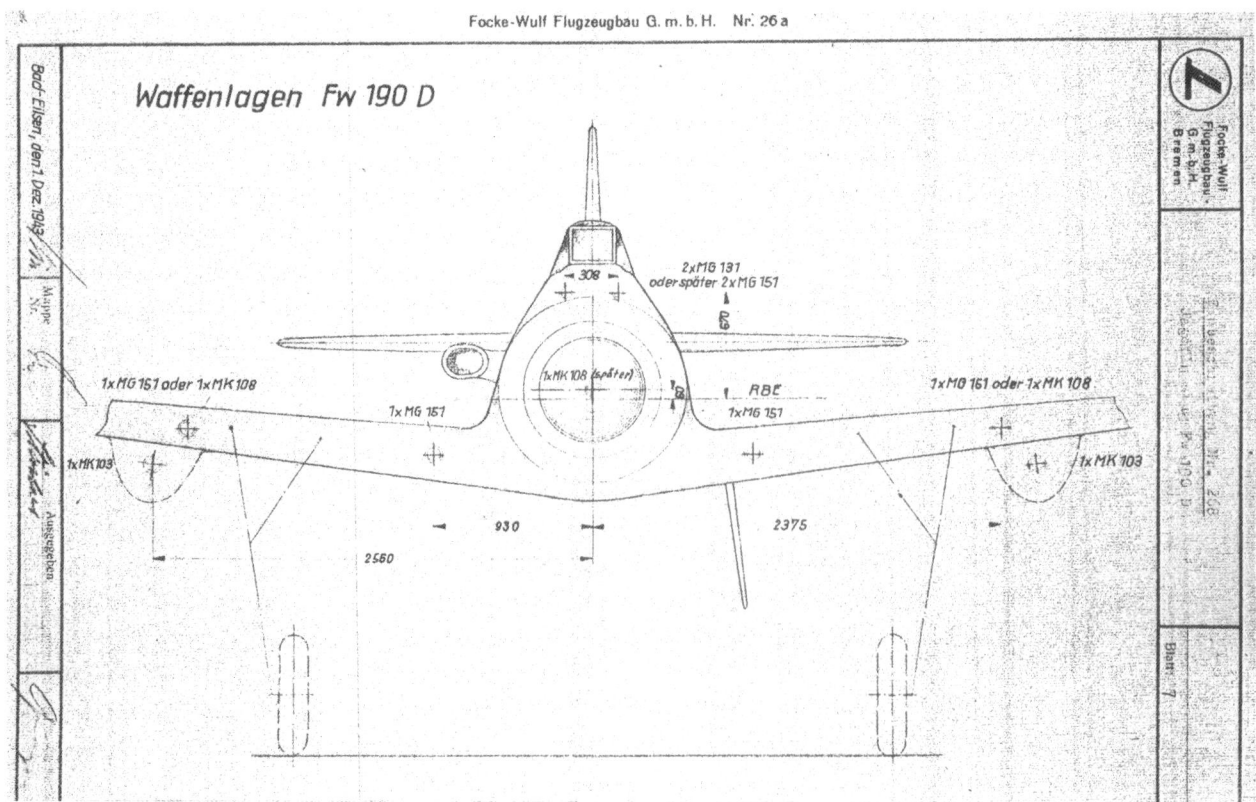

External Weapons

It is intended that the Fw 190 D should be delivered as a pure fighter aircraft at first. It is possible, however, to install the ETC 503 external stores carrier (8-190.8093) in conjunction with a sub-carrier. The carriage of external loads (210-mm air-to-air rockets, etc.) beneath the wings is possible to the same extent as with the Fw 190 A-8.

Structural Strength

A safe wing load factor of 6.20 was established for the designed gross weight of 4250 kg. The engine mounts were designed for a load factor of 6.5. The structural strength of the reinforced rear fuselage is somewhat greater than that of the wing.

Table of Weights

Fuselage	325 kg
Undercarriage (electric)	278 kg
Tail assembly (without ballast)	124 kg
Control linkages	32 kg
Wing	453 kg
Airframe	1212 kg
Power plant with 115-l fuel tank (40 kg)	1878 kg
Normal equipment	180 kg
Special equipment	220 kg
Equipped weight	3490 kg
One pilot	100 kg
Fuel - 525 liters	410 kg
Residual fuel in empty aux. tank (90 kg)	—
Oil	40 kg
Ammunition MG 131 (2 x 475 rounds)	80 kg
Ammunition MG 151 (2 x 250 rounds)	110 kg
Ballast in vertical fin	20 kg
Normal load	760 kg
Gross weight – fighter with standard armament and empty auxiliary tank (design gross weight)	4250 kg
Equipped weight 1	3490 kg
Bomb-dropping equipment	60 kg
Equipped weight with bomb-dropping equipment and auxiliary fuel tank	3550 kg
One pilot	100 kg
Fuel – 525 liters	410 kg
Residual fuel – empty 115-l tank	90 kg
Oil	40 kg
Ammunition MG 131 (2 x 475 rounds)	80 kg

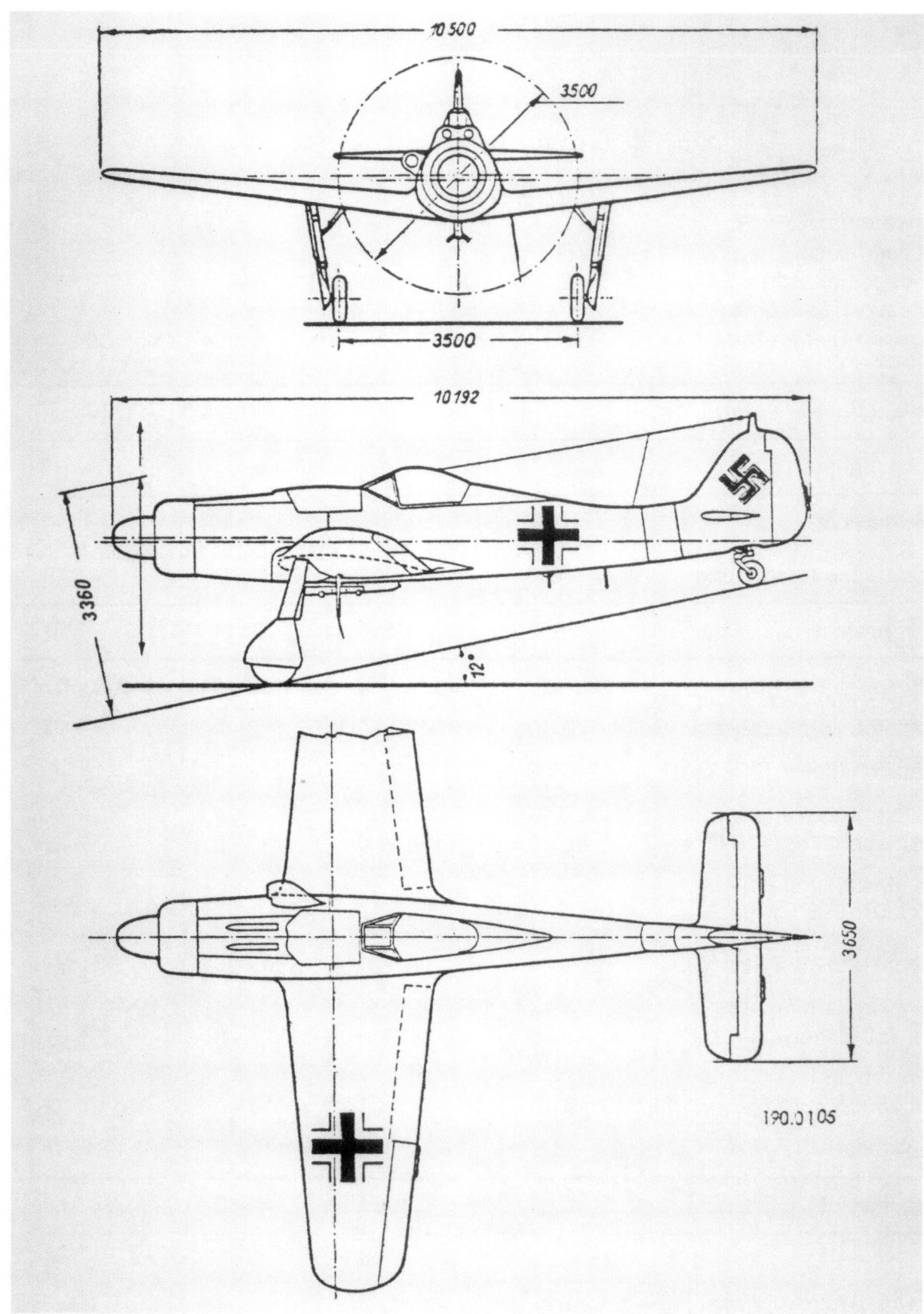

Ammunition MG 151 (2 x 250 rounds) .... 110 kg
Ballast in vertical fin .... 20 kg
External payload .... 500 kg
Load .... 760 kg
Gross weight – fighter-bomber with 500-kg .... 4900 kg
bomb and 115-l auxiliary fuel tank (overload
gross weight)

Gross weight 1 .... 4250 kg
Removal of 115-liter tank .... - 40 kg
Removal of 5 kg ballast .... - 5 kg
GM 1 system .... 41 kg
GM 1 charge .... 104 kg
Gross weight 3 – fighter with standard .... 4350 kg
armament and GM 1 system

Additional weight of 2 MG 151 in outer wings
with 140 rounds per gun .... 175 kg
Additional weight of 2 MK 108 in outer wings
with 55 rounds per gun .... 240 kg

Addendum
The above technical description is dated 18 December 1943. Since then, the following change was made and will be included in a subsequent technical description:
Instead of the previously-planned Focke-Wulf tank-bearer of welded sheet steel construction, the Ju 188 engine bearer previously used only on the right side of the engine will also be used on the left side. The oil will be contained in two tanks, with the larger 35-liter tank built around the left support strut, while the smaller 25-liter tank will be placed atop the engine next to the left engine bearer.

5.2 The First Prototypes

The first development report for the D-9 series is dated 23 February 1944. Originally only two prototypes, the Fw 190 V17/U1 and the Fw 190 V53, were planned for the series. Then, on 31 May 1944, a third prototype was ordered. Focke-Wulf thus had three prototypes with which to prepare for production of the Fw 190 D-9: the Fw 190 V17/U1, Fw 190 V53 and Fw 190 V54.

The Fw 190 V53, WNr. 170 003, was a converted Fw 190 A-8 airframe which was fitted with the new Junkers Jumo 213 C engine in Adelheide. Unlike the Jumo 213 A, the new engine was designed to accommodate an engine-mounted cannon. The V53, manufacturer's code DU+JC, was also fitted with two MG 151 cannon in the outer wings. This armament had originally been planned for the Fw 190 D-9 series. The converted machine

The Fw 190 V53 was converted from a Fw 190 A-8.

took to the air for the first time on 12 June 1944. By the end of September 1944 the V53 had completed more than 100 test flights. Once production of the Fw 190 D-9 was well established, the aircraft became the Fw 190 V68 and served as an armament test-bed for the Ta 152 B-5 with two MK 103 cannon in the wing roots.

The Fw 190 V17 had been the very first Fw 190 to be fitted with the Jumo 213 A in-line engine, in the summer of 1942. Powered by the Jumo 213 A-0, the Fw 190 V17 flew for the first time on 26 September 1942. Now the aircraft was to be converted to Fw 190 D-9 standard. On 13 April 1944 test pilot Bernhard Märschel flew the V17 from Langenhagen to Adelheide. There, in Focke-Wulf Branch Plant 8, the prototype works, all of the necessary modifications were completed in one month.

On 17 May 1944 Märschel flew the prototype, which was now designated the Fw 190 V17/U1, back to Langenhagen. On 6 June the machine was flown to Rechlin for initial flight trials there. The V17/U1 was tested thoroughly at Rechlin between 11 June and 6 July 1944. The last information concerning the Fw 190 V17/U1 comes from Focke-Wulf. According to the company test program, in August 1944 there was no test program for the V17/U1. It was stated, however, that the V17/U1 could be readied for testing again within two weeks.

The third prototype, the Fw 190 V54, was also a converted Fw 190 A-8. In February 1944 the RLM thought that two prototypes would suffice, but then it changed its mind, and in May a third prototype for the D-9 series was ordered. The V54 was converted from *Werknummer* 174 924, BH+RZ, in Adelheide and was the first prototype to have the methanol-water injection system planned for production aircraft.

The V54's role was to test the functioning and performance of the MW 50 system. The aircraft first flew at Adelheide on 26 July 1944. That

The only known photograph of the Fw 190 V17 after conversion to D-9 standard with provisional weapons installation.

same day Bernhard Märschel flew the V54 to Langenhagen. He subsequently test flew the aircraft there on 29 July and 2 August. Chief test pilot Hans Sander probably made the last flight in the V54 on 4 August 1944. Then disaster struck: on 5 August Langenhagen was heavily bombed by aircraft of the American 8th Air Force.

The V54 sustained 80% damage, sufficient for it to be written off. Other important Focke-Wulf prototypes, such as the Fw 190 V20, TI+IG, which was earmarked for the Ta 152 C program, were also destroyed. The effects of the bombing on the Ta 154 program were catastrophic. All but one of the aircraft of the test detachment EK 154 were destroyed. The Ta 154 V1, V2 and V3 prototypes were also destroyed, while the Ta 154 V7, V15 and V22 were seriously damaged. The Fw 190 V53 sustained minor damage (5%) in the raid but was subsequently repaired.

The Fw 190 V54, BH+RX, was to have been the third prototype equipped with the Jumo 213 A.

Copy of the Fw 190 D-9 Development Report

Development Report

Fw 190 D Fighter Aircraft

Journal XV b 2 and 3 of 31 May 44 are invalid as a result of the changes adopted on 14 June

Subject: Fw 190 D-9 with Jumo 213 A

Purpose: After construction of the second prototype Fw 190 D-9, V54, was delayed contrary to Development Report Journal XV b 1 of 23 Feb. 1944, the program for prototypes for the Fw 190 D-9 was expanded as follows:

1st Prototype: V53 WNr. 170 003 flying since 12 June 44 (see Journal XV b 1 of 23 Feb.)

2nd Prototype: Fw 190 V17/U1 – Werk-Nr. 0 039

    This prototype was equipped with the power plant for the D-9 series for engine trials.

    Fit to fly since 17 May 44

    For comparative flight experiments the V17/U1 is being fitted with provisional armament.

    Committee 10 13 328

3rd Prototype: A third Fw 190 A-8 is to be converted to D-9 series standard.

    Designation: Fw 190 V54, WNr. 174 024
    Ready to fly date: 30 July 1944

    One 213 A engine (9-8213) will be delivered complete.

    Instead of GM 1, the system for methanol including switch (8-4365) is to be installed for testing.

    Committee 10 13 336

B-Series: 1.) Start of Fw 190 D-9 Production

    Fw   August 1944

    Arbg.   September 1944

    Ago   "

    Fieseler "

2.) Note:

The present panel in front of the windscreen (Component 190.168) still has two bulges for two MG 151s, however the series is to be delivered with two MG 131s. After consultation between Herr Kaether and Herr Steinbach, the management has promised that a modified panel for two MG 131s, i.e. with smaller bulges, will be introduced into production as quickly as possible.

Design bureau changes: delivered by 10 July 44

3.) After clarification by the RLM on 14 and 17 June, the following now applies for the equipment and delivery standard of the Fw 190 D-9 series:

Armament

Fuselage   2 MG 131
Wing roots   2 MG 151
(Outer wing armament will normally not be installed.)

Design bureau changes of 26 June – 27 July 44

ETC 504 on every aircraft leaving the factory with

170- or 300-liter auxiliary tank installed beneath the fuselage.

115-liter long-range tank installed in every aircraft, <u>however provision to be made for use with methanol-water as well.</u> MW 50 system to be installed in every aircraft.

      Design bureau changes by 30 July 44

As a rule, the previously-planned GM 1 system will not be installed.

Radio set FuG 16 ZY

700 x 175 mainwheels with electrically-actuated undercarriage and landing flaps.

4.) <u>Manuals for the Fw 190 D-9 series are to be completed by the time production begins.</u>

Author's Note: Committee: indicates the official RLM contract number for the various prototypes.

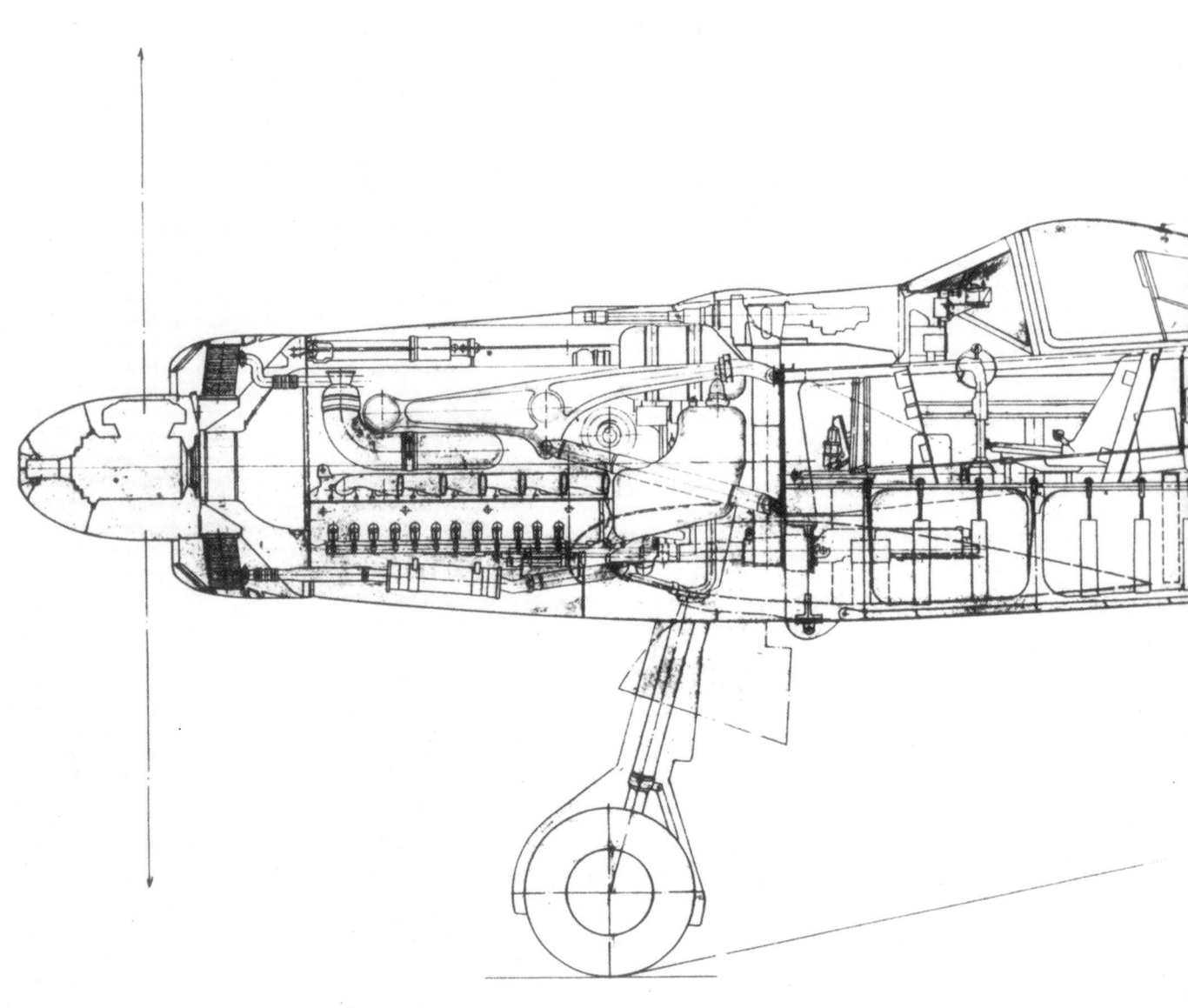

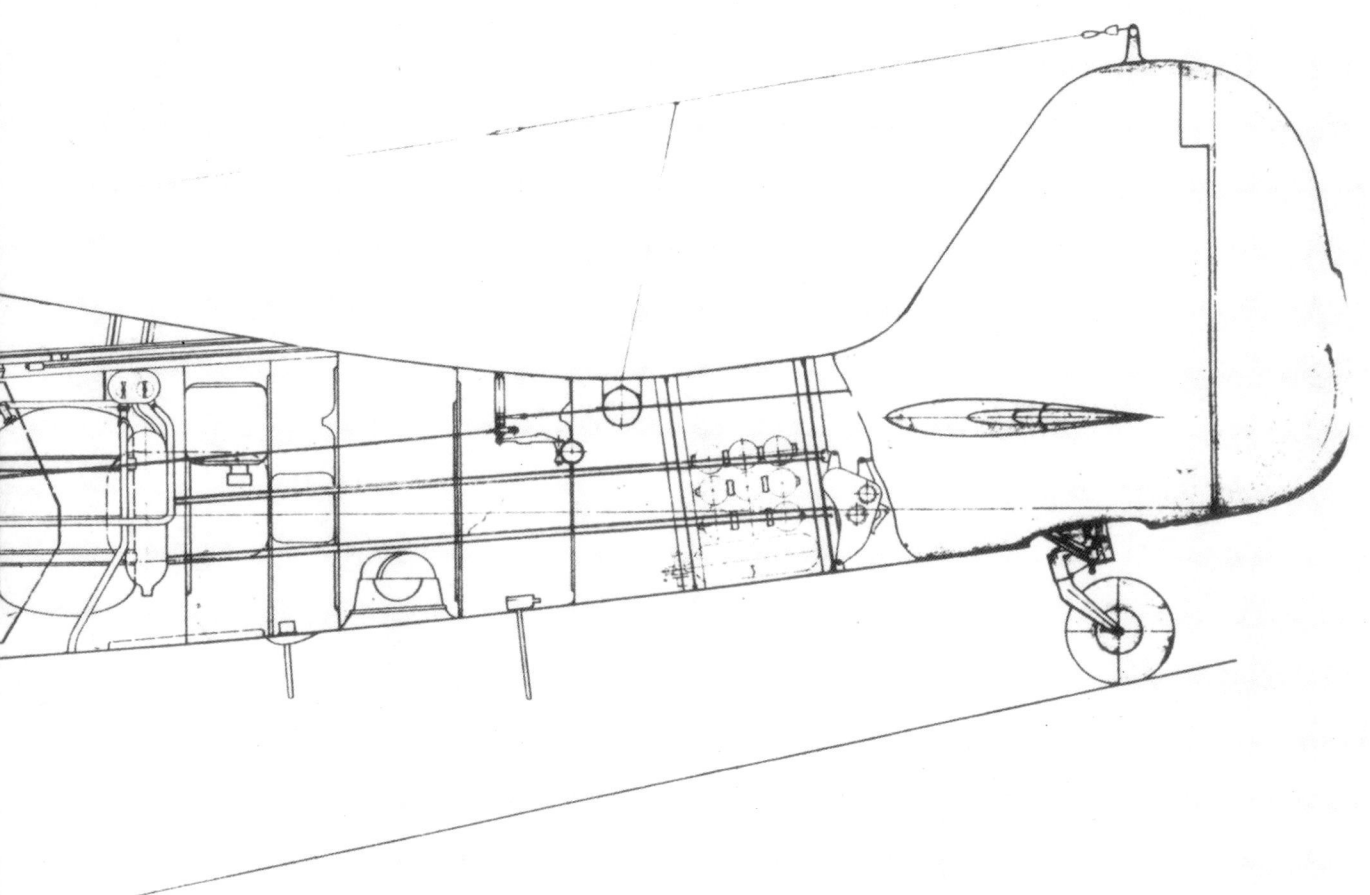

Fw 190 D-9

Motor: Jumo 213 A
Fläche: F = 18,3 m²
Bewaffnung:

This page and opposite: Three views of the Fw 190 V53, the first prototype of the Fw 190 D-9.

5.3 The Fw 190 V17/U1, Fw 190 V53 and Fw 190 V54 in Detail

The three Fw 190 D-9 prototypes will be examined in detail below. While the second machine was a conversion of the Fw 190 V17, which in 1942 had become the first Fw 190 prototype to be equipped with the Jumo 213, the other two were Fw 190 A-8s which were taken from the production line and converted to D-9 standard in the Adelheide prototype works.

Fw 190 V53

Werknummer 170 003

Manufacturer's code DU+JC

The converted Fw 190 first flew in D-9 form on 12 June 1944. Unlike the Fw 190 V17/U1, the V53 was equipped with the Jumo 213 C. This

The Fw 190 V53 performed the bulk of the Fw 190 D-9 production testing. During performance measuring flights the V53 achieved a maximum speed of 554 km/h at low level.

The Fw 190 V17, seen here prior to conversion, is refueled and made ready for another flight.

prototype's role in the Fw 190 D-9 program was that of armament and equipment test-bed. Unlike later production aircraft, the Fw 190 V53 was initially fitted with two MG 151 cannon in the outer wings. These were later removed, however. The V53 logged the most air time of all the D-9 prototypes, completing its 100th test flight on 26 September 1944.

When production of the Fw 190 D-9 began in August 1944, the V53's role as experimental aircraft was essentially over. It was rebuilt as a weapons test-bed for the Ta 152 B-5, which was to replace the Fw 190, and was equipped with two MK 103 cannon in the wing roots. Thus modified, the V53 was redesignated the Fw 190 V68. In this form it took to the air for the first time on 13 December 1944.

Fw 190 V17/U1

Werknummer 0 039

Manufacturer's code CF+OX

On 13 April 1944 test pilot Bernhard Märschel flew the "old" Fw 190 V17 from Langenhagen to Adelheide for conversion to Fw 190 D-9 standard. The work was completed in just one month and the aircraft was fitted with provisional armament. On 17 May 1944 test pilot Märschel flew the modified aircraft, now designated Fw 190 V17/U1, back to Langenhagen. On 6 June the V17/U1 was transferred to the *E-Stelle Rechlin* for testing.

Fw 190 V54

Werknummer 174 024

Manufacturer's code BH+RX

The Fw 190 V54 made its first flight at Adelheide on 26 July 1944 and was flown to Langenhagen the same day. The V54 was scheduled to go to the test center at Tarnewitz as a weapons test-bed. The V54 was also to have been the first to receive the new MW 50 system which was planned for the Fw 190 D-9 series. Chief test pilot Hans Sander made the last flight in the V54 at Langenhagen on 4 August 1944. By this time, however, the Allies suspected that important combat aircraft development was taking place at Langenhagen, and on 5 August the facility was heavily bombed. A number of twin-engined Ta 154s were destroyed and the V54 was extensively damaged (80%). Other aircraft which had sustained minor damage were repaired, but not the V54.

5.4 Production Begins

As originally planned, production of the Fw 190 D-9 began in August 1944 at the Focke-Wulf factory in Sorau. The first forty Fw 190 D-9s were delivered in September. A further 70 D-9s followed in October and in November no less than 142 machines left the Sorau production line. October also saw the start of Fw 190 D-9 production by Fieseler and the *Roland Arbeitsgemeinschaft* (Roland Consortium). Fieseler delivered its first D-9 in October, followed by 40 more in November. Including production by the consortium, a total of 366 Fw 190 D-9s were delivered by the end of November. According to Industry Delivery Plan SA F 4 of 25 February 1945, a total of 1,030 Fw 190 D-9 were delivered by 31 January 1945. Of these, Focke-Wulf had delivered 569, the *Roland Arbeitsgemeinschaft* 281 and Fieseler 180. The peak production month was January 1945, when 304 Fw 190 D-9s were completed.

Page 92
The Fw 190 V53 was later converted into a weapons test-bed for the Ta 152 B series and was renamed the Fw 190 V68. Armed with two MK 103 cannon mounted in the wing roots, the aircraft was sent to Tarnewitz for further testing at the end of December 1944. When this photograph was taken the aircraft was still equipped with two MG 151 cannon in the wing roots.

Page 93
Two more interesting views of the Fw 190 V53. As the Fw 190 V68, on 12 December 1944 it received a clean bill of health and was equipped with two MG 131 machine-guns mounted in the fuselage and two synchronized MK 108 cannon in the wing roots. Thus equipped, the aircraft flew for the first time on 13 December 1944. According to chief test pilot Hans Sander, the Fw 190 lost 50 km/h of airspeed when the MK 103 cannon were fired.

Fw 190 D-9 production at Sorau. In the foreground *Werknummer* 210 210 is in final assembly. Behind it is the fuselage of *Werknummer* 210 211.

The Fw 190 D-9 Finally Enters Production

	September	October	November	December	January	Total to 31 Jan.
Fw 190 D-9 Production Breakdown to 31 January 1945						
Focke-Wulf	40	70	142	145	172	569
Consortium		18	55	100	108	281
Fieseler		1	40	105	34	180
Total Production	40	129	366	716	1030	

Opposite
Composition of the Fw 190 consortium.

In this photograph the V53 already shows clear signs of wear and tear.

Focke-Wulf delivered another 172 Fw 190 D-9s in January 1945, of which 76 were equipped with *Rüstsatz* (equipment set) R11 for operations in bad weather. According to the Aircraft Distribution Plan of the *Genst.Gen.Qu.6 Abt. (III C)*, another 287 D-9s followed in February 1945 plus 28 aircraft equipped with the new EZ 42 reflector gunsight, while production in March amounted to 165 standard D-9s and 7 with the EZ 42. No concrete figures are available for April 1945. Total production by the end of March 1945 was thus more than 1,500 aircraft, while total production by war's end must have been in the area of 1,700 machines. Copies of Focke-Wulf accounts confirm 498 Fw 190 D-9s with serial numbers from that company alone. Of the approximately 20,000 Fw 190s built from 1940 to 1945, the percentage of Fw 190 D-9s is a not inconsiderable 8.5%. Converting to production of the Fw 190 D-9 proved much less complicated than the introduction of the Focke-Wulf Ta 152. This is shown very clearly by the high production rates that were achieved within a short time. Production of the Fw 190 D-9 was to have continued until April 1945, by which time 2,825 machines were to have been built.

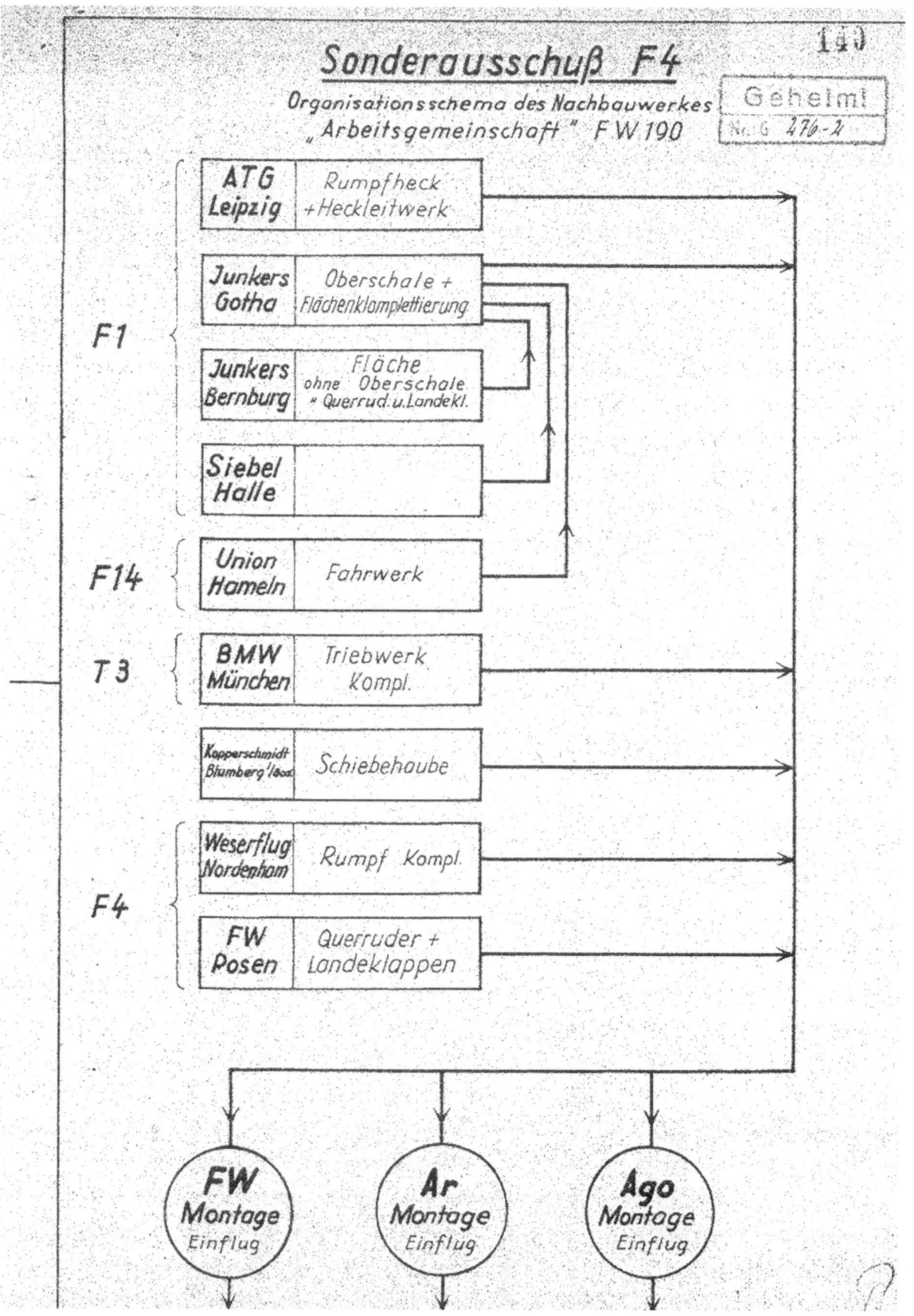

5.5 Testing the D-9

In the beginning only the Fw 190 V17/U1 and Fw 190 V53 prototypes were available for extensive flight testing. The V53 was used for performance trials at Langenhagen. For the most part these confirmed the estimated performance figures. The V53's armament initially consisted of two MG 131 machine-guns in the fuselage, two MG 151 cannon in the wing roots and two MG 151s in the outer wings. This was the armament originally planned for the production D-9. The outer wing cannon were later removed. The V53 was painted in a standard camouflage finish. At a gross weight of 4070 kg with ETC 503 external stores rack, the V53 achieved 555 km/h at ground level at 3,250 rpm (emergency power). During flight trials the V53 was involved in a heavy forced landing. It was subsequently repaired, but for safety reasons it was limited to low-level flights.

When production began, aircraft from the production line joined the test program. The first and second aircraft from the Sorau production line were flown to Langenhagen to participate in series testing. *Werknummer* 210 001, manufacturer's code TR+SA, made its first flight on 31 August with chief test pilot Hans Sander at the controls. On 7 September 1944, just a few days after the D-9 arrived in Langenhagen, the first case of engine trouble was encountered after just four hours flying time. This aircraft underwent four engine changes by 9 January 1945. Even the Jumo 213 A had teething troubles. The second aircraft, *Werknummer* 210 002, TR+SB, followed on 15 September 1944. The aircraft was piloted by *Hauptmann* Schmitz on its initial flight. These two production aircraft were used by Focke-Wulf at Langenhagen for long-term testing until

Opposite
Performance graphs for the two Fw 190 D-9 production aircraft during testing by Focke-Wulf. In standard configuration with a takeoff weight of 4100 kg, the aircraft achieved a maximum speed of 664 km/h at a height of 6000 meters using takeoff power. According to Focke-Wulf documents, the Jumo 213 A engines from the first batch delivered had a maximum boost altitude 400 meters lower than specified.

Delivery standard for production aircraft from Sorau.

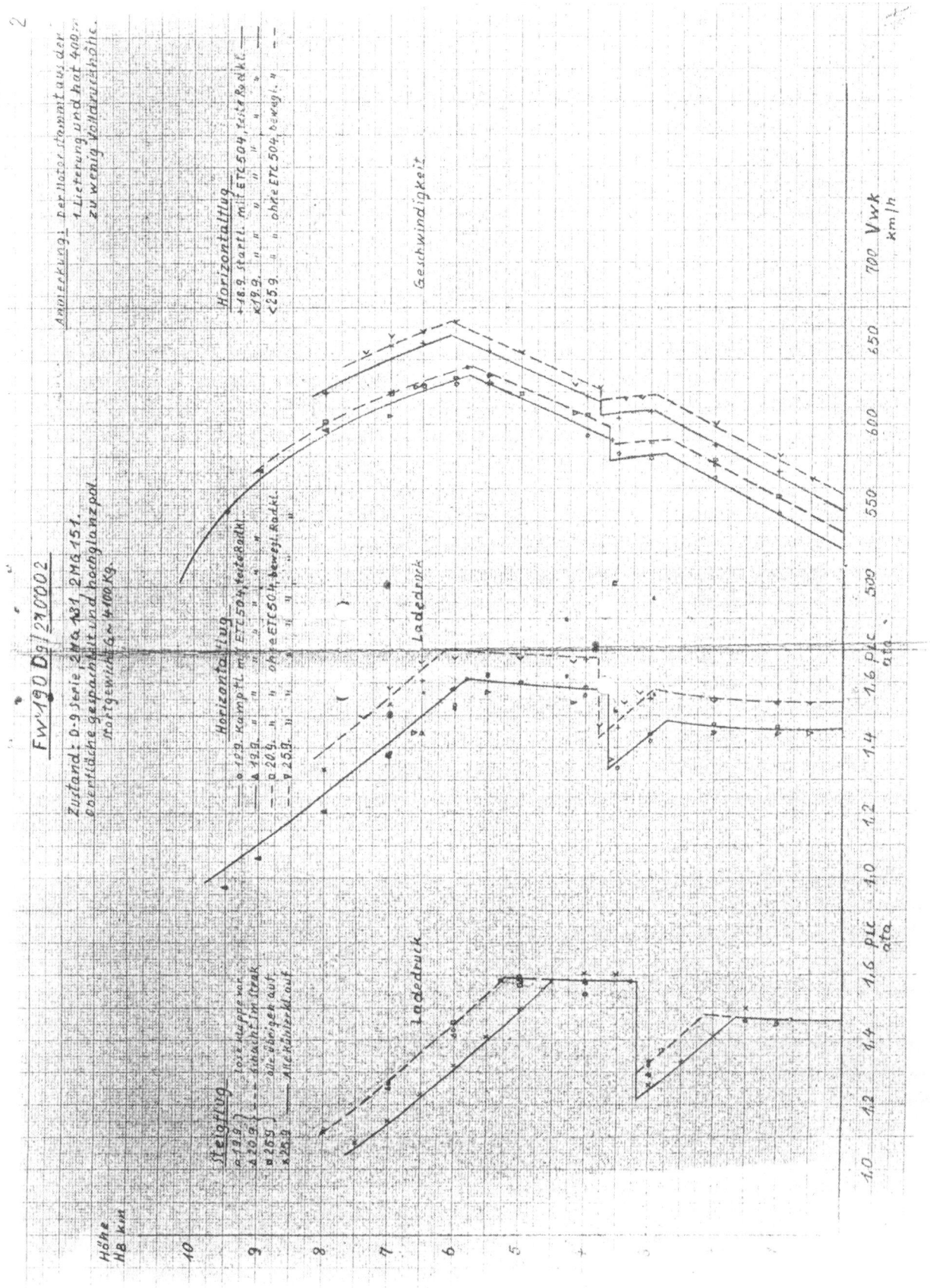

March 1945. While 210 001 was to have been made ready for delivery to the *Luftwaffe* in March 1945, 210 002 was scheduled to take part in further performance trials.

The fourth production machine, *Werknummer* 210 004, TR+SD, was assigned to the *E-Stelle Rechlin*, but crashed there on 25 September 1944. The exact cause of the crash remains a mystery. Another Fw 190 D-9, *Werknummer* 210 007, TR+SG, which had been used for static and air gunnery trials at Tarnewitz, was assigned to Rechlin as a replacement. On its arrival at Rechlin, however, 210 007 made a crash-landing (10% damage) and subsequently had to be repaired. Rechlin was subsequently assigned the sixth production aircraft for further testing.

The ninth production aircraft, *Werknummer* 210 009, TR+SI, was flown from Sorau to Langenhagen on 18 September 1944. After just a few test flights, on 26 September this D-9 was transferred to Jumo in Dessau to serve as an engine test-bed. Flight tests were still being carried out there in March 1945, including some with the four-blade VS 19 propeller that was to be used on the Ta 152 H.

Three views of the newly-completed *Werknummer* 210 051.

It was originally intended that two aircraft should be converted to test the Fw 190 D-9 with the MW 50 system. The company planned to convert *Werknummer* 210 002 at Langenhagen and *Werknummer* 210 043 at Cottbus, however nothing came of this. Instead, *Werknummer* 210 048 was equipped with the system in Sorau. The machine was supposed to go to Rechlin for testing of the MW 50 system, however it crashed at Sorau while on its third flight. Pilot Finke was killed. In spite of this, testing of the MW 50 system continued on the ground. Interestingly, the special tank was filled with water only, as no methanol was available. Estimated maximum speed at ground level without methanol-water was 540 km/h at 3,300 rpm and 1.5 atm of boost. With methanol-water, maximum speed at ground level was 585 km/h at 3,300 rpm and 1.76 atm of boost. In production aircraft it was planned that the MW 50 system could be used to draw fuel or methanol/water from the 115-liter tank. On account of delivery difficulties, however, it was decided to use the tank with methanol-water only, and this was dubbed the "Oldenburg System" (see III./JG 54). This system was installed in production aircraft beginning in November 1944

5.6 Fw 190 D-9 Testing Report by the *E-Stelle Rechlin*

Summary: The stated performance figures are for the Fw 190 D-9 (production version). The high-altitude speeds were measured using *Werknummer* 006. During the course of long-term testing various aircraft were checked at 3,000 rpm. The achieved speeds were 520 and 530 km/h at ground level, and between 625 and 635 km/h at a height of 6500 m (roughly maximum boost altitude, depending on engine tuning).

At 3,250 rpm speeds of between 645 and 655 km/h were achieved at 6600 m and from 540 to 550 km/h at low level. Low-level rate of climb at 3,250 rpm was 17 m/sec, and 2.0 m/sec at 10200 meters. Takeoff weight 4300 kg (Group E2c, 2 March 1945)

General: Aircraft Fw 190 D-9, *Werknummer* 210 006
- Wing area: 18.3 m2
- Wingspan: 10.46 m
- Aspect ratio: 6.0
- Power plant: Jumo 213 A (B4 fuel)
- Allowable engine speed for 30 min.: 3,250 rpm
- Continuous speed: 3,000 rpm
- Intake system: external scoop without filter
- Exhaust system: ejector ports
- Pitot system: Bruhn 5 d
- Heine propeller, three-blade, 3.5 m diameter

Condition of Aircraft:
Production version ETC 504 (without fairing)

Engine without aerodynamic seal
Standard external surface, puttied and sprayed
Weapons: in fuselage 2 MG 131 with 475 rounds per gun
　　　　　 in wings (inner) 2 MG 151 with 200 rounds per gun
Antennas for FuG 16, FuG 25, equipment and DF loop
Gross weight: 4350 kg
Fuel capacity: 640 l, of which 115 l in auxiliary tank in fuselage
　　　　　　　Weight 4640 kg with 300-l external tank

Performance Measurements: Speeds were determined by pressure head measurement (pitot). Calibrated measuring instruments were used. The interesting V (a) range was measured by flight calibration on the calibrating range. Rates of climb were measured with a carbon recorder.

Measurement Results: Horizontal speeds were measured at various rpm settings. It is interesting to note that the speeds achieved earlier by *Werknummer* 006 at 3,000 rpm were approximately 15 km/h higher (see report of 15 Nov. 44). The current speeds were measured following installation of a new engine, after proper engine tuning and installation of the standard propeller. The speeds listed in the report of 15 Nov. 44 were achieved with an untuned engine, a D-12 propeller, and were measured during long-term testing. The loss of speed is therefore due to differences in the engine and propeller (D-9 and D-12 propellers).

Horizontal Speeds: Valid for the nominal weight of 4200 kg.

Climbing Speeds:　　0 – 7000 m　　280 km/h
　　　　　　　　　　　8000 m　　　270 km/h
　　　　　　　　　　　9000 m　　　260 km/h
　　　　　　　　　　　10000 m　　 255 km/h

Cooling gill influence: The influence of the cooling gills on speed (with empty tank) was measured at a height of 2000 m at 2,700 rpm. The entire range of movement was divided into 10 equal segments, with 0 completely closed and 10 completely open. Measurements showed that the highest speed, and therefore the lowest drag, was achieved with the gills in position 2.8 (roughly corresponding to most streamlined position). This position should always be selected in horizontal flight.

The maximum speeds achieved by WNr. 210 006 were:

3,250 rpm	3,000 rpm (15 Nov. 44)	2,700 rpm
537 km/h at sea level	521 km/h at sea level (527)	489 km/h at sea level
643 km/h at 6600 m	623 km/h at 6500 m (638/6200)	580 km/h at 6300 m
600 km/h at 9000 m	580 km/h at 9000 m (623/7500)	524 km/h at 9000 m

Rates of climb were measured with cooling gills fully open.

3,250 rpm:	16.6 m/sec at sea level	3,000 rpm:	14.8 m/sec at sea level
	15.2 m/sec at 3250 m		13.2 m/sec at 3250 m
	14.6 m/sec at 3300 m		12.6 m/sec at 3300 m
	12.2 m/sec at 6300 m		10.4 m/sec at 6100 m

5.2 m/sec at 9000 m		3.2 m/sec at 9000 m
2.0 m/sec at 10200 m		2.0 m/sec at 9450 m
0 m/sec at 11000 m		0 m/sec at 10250 m

To 1000 m:	1 min.	1.2 min.
To 3000 m:	3.2 min.	3.6 min.
To 5000 m	5.4 min.	6.4 min.
To 6000 m:	6.8 min.	8.0 min.
To 8000 m:	10.2 min.	12.4 min.
To 10000 m:	17.8 min.	27.2 min.

Table of all known Fw 190 D-9 prototypes and test-beds

Prototype	Series	WNr.	Code	First Flight	Remarks
Fw 190 V17/U1	D-9	0 039	CF+OX	17/05/44	Jumo 213 A engine test-bed for Fw 190 D-9 series
Fw 190 V53	D-9	170 003	DU+JC	12/06/44	First Fw 190 D-9 prototype, converted from Fw 190 A-8
Fw 190 V54	D-9	174 054	BH+RX	26/07/44	Second Fw 190 D-9 prototype, converted from Fw 190 A-8, initially planned for GM 1 system, later supplanted by MW 50, destroyed at Langenhagen on 5/8/44.
Production	D-9	210 001	TR+SA	31/08/44	Used by Focke-Wulf for long-term testing of the Fw 190 D-9 series
Production	D-9	210 002	TR+SB	15/09/44	Used by Focke-Wulf for long-term testing of the Fw 190 D-9 series
Production	D-9	210 004	TR+SD	09/44	Fw 190 D-9 test-bed in Rechlin, crashed there on 25/09/44
Production	D-9	210 006	TR+SF	09/44	Fw 190 D-9 test-bed in Rechlin, used for performance-measuring flights.
Production	D-9	210 007	TR+SG	09/44	Weapons testing in Tarnewitz, then to Rechlin for further testing.
Production	D-9	210 009	TR+SI	18/09/44	To Jumo on 26/09/44 for use as engine test-bed.
Production	D-9	210 048	—+—	17/10/44	Planned for MW 50 trials in Rechlin, crashed in Sorau on 17/10/44

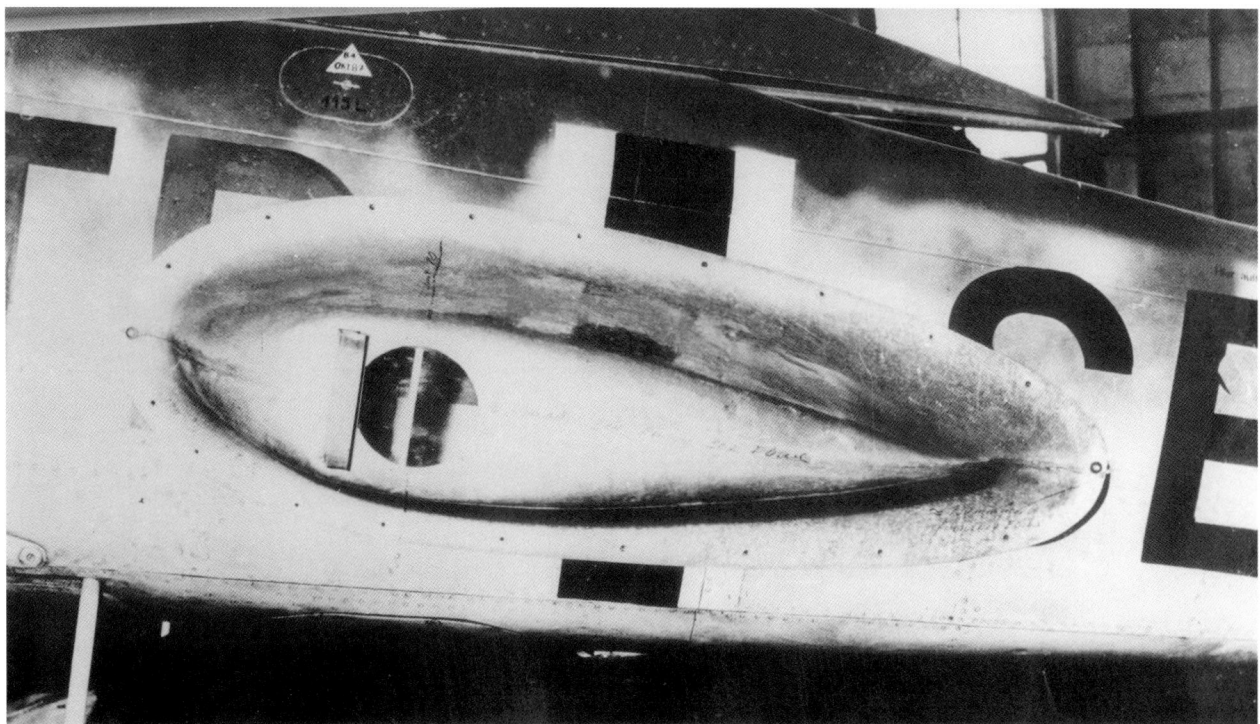

This photograph clearly shows that *Werknummer* 210 002 bore the manufacturer's code TR+SB. No known photograph shows all of the second prototype. Here the aircraft has been used to test the new fairing for the oblique camera to be mounted in the Ta 152 E-1/R1 reconnaissance aircraft.

5.7 The Jumo 213 A Engine in the Fw 190 D-9

The Fw 190 D-9 powered by the Jumo 213 A engine provided the fighter pilots of the *Luftwaffe* with an aircraft whose performance was significantly better than those which preceded it. The installation of the 12-cylinder in-line engine radically altered the shape of the Fw 190. The BMW 801 radial engine used previously gave the Fw 190 a rather beefy appearance. The true aerodynamics of the Fw 190 first became apparent with the new Jumo 213. The pleasing shape of the D-9 suggested an excellent performance, and its pilots were not disappointed. Although there was little to choose between the Jumo 213 A and the BMW 801 in terms of power, the D-9 was 28 km/h faster than the A-8 at low level and 41 km/h faster at the maximum boost altitude of 6600 m. The Fw 190 D-9's maximum speed was 685 km/h at 6600 m. A program to increase boost, the so-called *"Sonderaktion 1900 PS"* (Special Action 1,900 h.p.), was introduced before the aircraft entered service. As a result of this, emergency power was increased to 1,900 h.p. at altitudes to 5000 m. This was intended to give German pilots a performance advantage over Allied fighters at low level and thus improve the chances of survival for the *Luftwaffe*'s many young pilots. What was even more important against the Allied bombers was the improved high-altitude performance of the Jumo 213 A above maximum boost altitude. Unlike units equipped with the Fw 190 A, those with the Fw 190 D did not require an escort of Bf 109s.

Another performance-enhancing option was MW 50 injection, which increased the performance of the standard Fw 190 D-9 to 702 km/h at 5700 meters, an improvement of 17 km/h. The graph on the following page shows clearly the D-9's impressive performance. The Fw 190 D-9 had a phenomenal rate of climb with MW 50 injection. At low level the

This photograph of a crash-landed Fw 190 D-9 clearly illustrates the compactness of the Jumo 213 A in the D-9 airframe. The engine bearers with the two oil tanks are clearly visible. Visible on the far right are the engine attachment points on the firewall.

D-9 was capable of 22.5 m/sec, compared to 17.8 m/sec without MW 50. Previously only the Spitfire was capable of such a climb rate. With MW 50 the D-9's rate of climb was clearly superior to that of aircraft without the power boosting system.

Although it was originally planned that the aircraft built by Fieseler should be equipped with GM 1 boost, this was inexplicably cancelled by the RLM a short time later. The injection of an oxidizer (nitrous oxide) would have further enhanced the D-9's performance at higher altitudes. Although a D-9 so equipped would not have been comparable to the Ta 152 H, lacking a pressurized cockpit, this variant would have given its pilots the performance advantage they needed to escape from dangerous situations. Instead the RLM decided to wait for the Fw 190 D-12/D-13 series then under development. Powered by the Jumo 213 F, these variants were expected to have improved high-altitude performance, however production was delayed until March 1945.

General Adolf Galland was an outspoken critic of GM 1. He argued that on hot summer days, with aircraft and pilots waiting at readiness, the GM 1 mixture could evaporate quickly in spite of its insulated tank. Production of the Fw 190 D-9 began in the autumn of 1944 and was supposed to end in the summer of 1945; by then, however, the days of German fighters being parked in the open on their bases were long over.

Focke-Wulf conducted experiments with a Fw 190 D-9 (WNr. 210 002, TR+SB) in an attempt to further increase the performance of production aircraft. Gaps in the engine cowling fore and aft were sealed with rubber. In the course of these experiments an increase in speed of 17 km/h was achieved at combat power. Focke-Wulf subsequently advised the manufacturing plants to pay special attention to proper sealing of the engine compartment pending approval by the *E-Stelle Rechlin*. Rechlin rejected the idea of rubber seals for the engine compartment, however.

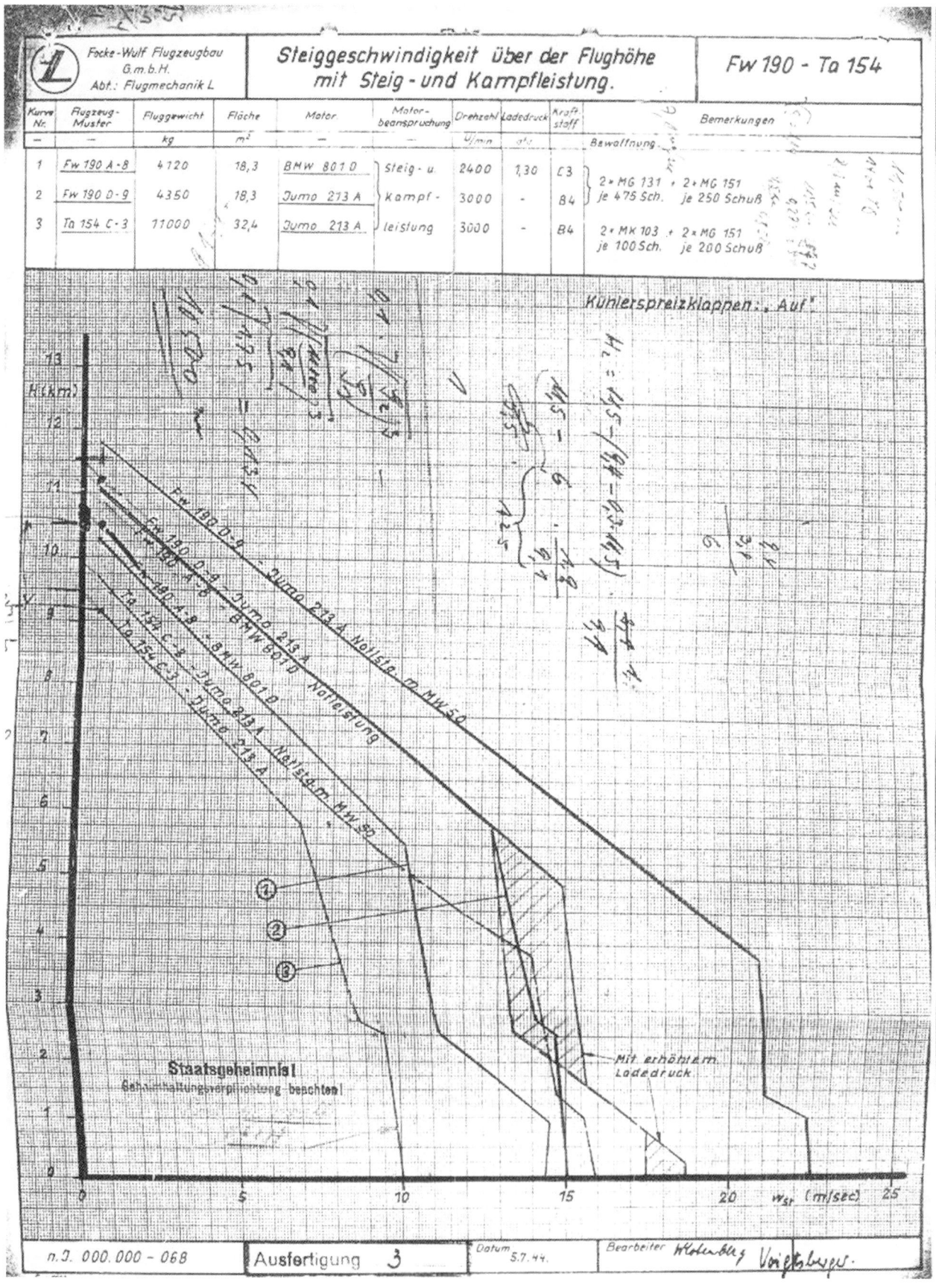

Opposite: This Focke-Wulf performance sheet underlines the outstanding climb rate of the Fw 190 D-9 (Curve 2) compared to that of the Fw 190 A-8 (Curve 1). With the increased boost modification, which was carried out on all Fw 190 D-9s before they joined combat, the aircraft's maximum climb rate was 18.7 m/sec at low level at normal combat power. The use of MW 50 injection as emergency power increased this to 22.5 m/sec.

Above: Engine installation in the Fw 190 D-9. Note the sturdy engine bearer with lower bracing strut and the L-shaped oil tank. Below: Prototype construction at Focke-Wulf. The Jumo 213 has already been installed. In the background is the Ju 88 which served as engine test-bed for the all-wood Focke-Wulf Ta 154.

Two views of the new cowling for the Jumo 213 A with bulges for the twin MG 131 machine-guns. Also clearly visible is the new supercharger air intake.

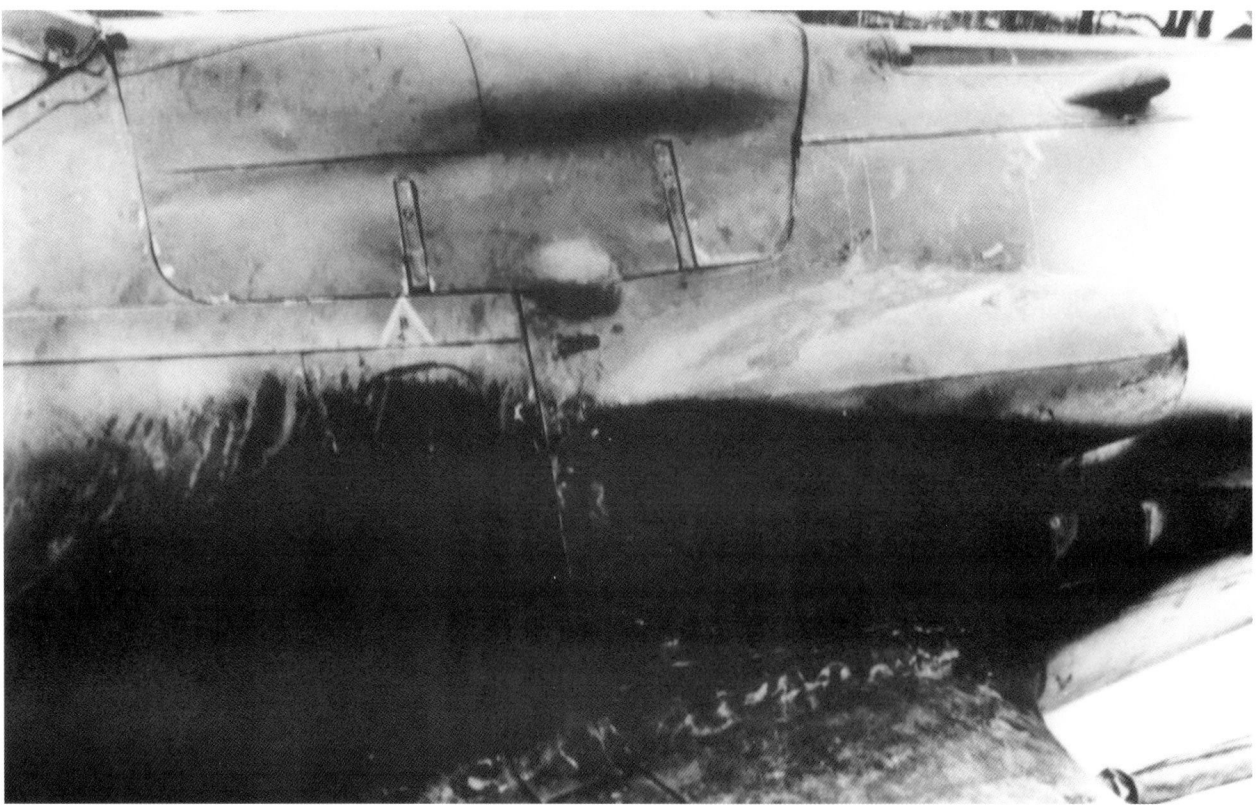

Planned Rüstsätze for the Fw 190 D-9

Fw 190 D-9/R2	MK 108 cannon in the outer wings
Fw 190 D-9/R3	MK 103 cannon beneath the outer wings
Fw 190 D-9/R11	Bad weather equipment consisting of PKS 12 autopilot, FuG 125, heated windscreen and backup turn-and-bank indicator.
Fw 190 D-9/R14	Torpedo-carrying aircraft with *Schloss 504* rack for LT I B aerial torpedo.
Fw 190 D-9/R15	Carrier for BT 1400 bomb-torpedo with *Schloss 504* rack.

Abb. 1: Fw 190 mit 21 cm BR

Left: Illustration from the Fw 190 D-9 handbook showing the aircraft equipped with tubes for launching 210-mm rockets.

Below: Original Fw 190 V53 below and retouched V53 above.

5.8 Fw 190 D-9/R14 Torpedo-Carrying Aircraft

On 30 December 1944 Focke-Wulf completed a study to determine the suitability of various versions of the Fw 190 and the new Ta 152 for the carriage of torpedoes. The study compared the Fw 190 F-8 and F-9 powered by the BMW 801 engine, the Fw 190 D-9 and D-12 with the Jumo 213, and the Ta 152 C-1 with the DB 603.

It was determined that under the existing conditions the Fw 190 D-9 was best suited as a torpedo carrier. The order was given for the experimental installation of an aerial torpedo carrier built by MWN (Neubrandenburg Mechanical Workshops) to be carried out as quickly as possible. As the aircraft production program called for production of the Fw 190 D-9 to end in May 1945, the Fw 190 D-12 was suggested as a replacement. The Jumo 213 F high-altitude motor was poorly suited for this role, however, and it was proposed that the Jumo 213 A be installed instead. Calculations were made for a standard Fw 190 D-9 and a version of the aircraft equipped with two 220-l fuel tanks beneath the wings, the so-called "*Doppelreiter*" system.

Silhouette of the Fw 190 D-9 from the aircraft handbook Part 0.

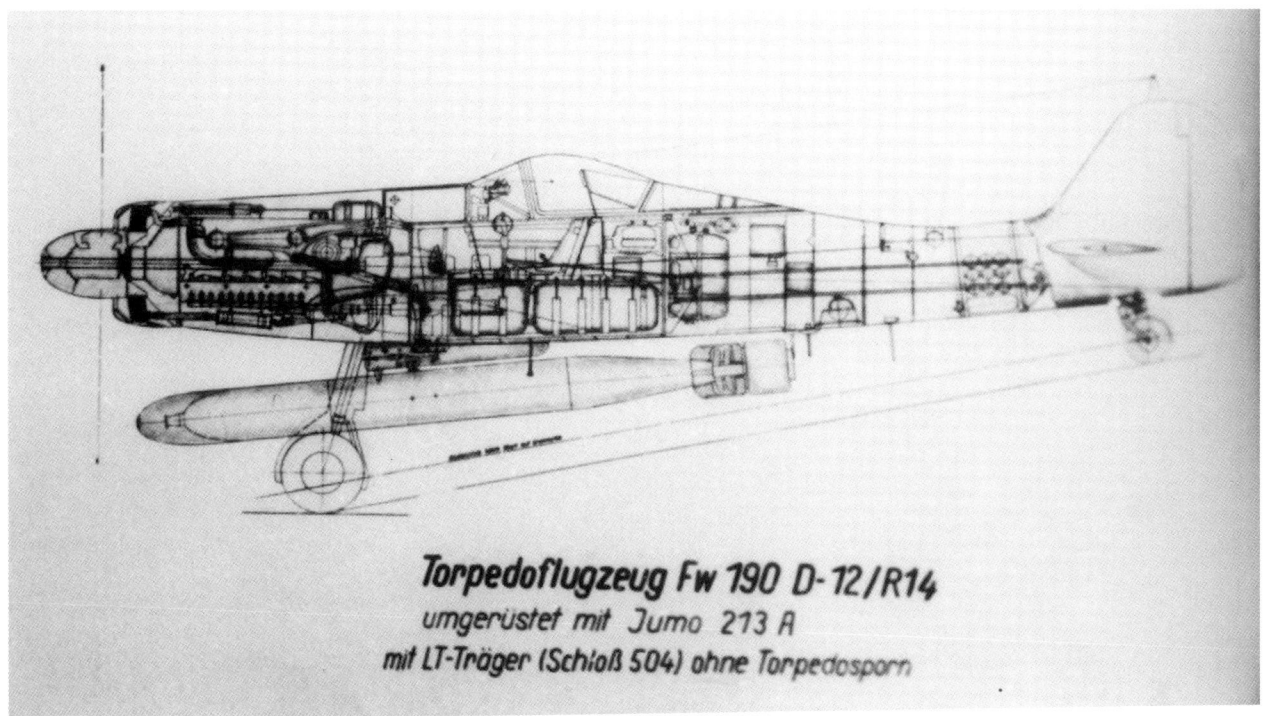

Torpedoflugzeug Fw 190 D-12/R14
umgerüstet mit Jumo 213 A
mit LT-Träger (Schloß 504) ohne Torpedosporn

Fw 190 D-9/R14 Torpedo-Carrier Specification

Power Plant: Jumo 213 A, armament two MG 151/20 (250 rounds per gun)

Payload: *LT I B kurz* (short) torpedo weighing 780 kg or *LT 1 B lang* (long) torpedo weighing 850 kg

	D-9/R14	D-9/R14 with 2 x 220 l Doppelreiter
Weight with short torpedo:	4970 kg	5260 kg
Weight with long torpedo:	5040 kg	5330 kg
Fuel capacity:	639 l B4	964 l B4
To/from target at height of 3000 m:	560 km/h/605 km/h	544 km/h/555 km/h
Range at combat power:	665 km	1000 km
To/from target at height of 3000 m:	510 km/h/555 km/h	497 km/h/555 km/h
Maximum range at cruising power:	1000 km	1350 km

The fuel system of the Fw 190 D-9 normally consists of two standard fuel tanks containing 524 liters plus an auxiliary tank in the fuselage with 115 liters. The torpedo rack (*Schloss 504*) is also designed to carry the BT 1400 (Fw 190 D-9/R15).

CHAPTER SIX

Operational History of the Fw 190 D-9

The first production Fw 190 D-9s left the Focke-Wulf factory in Sorau at the beginning of September 1944. Factory trials continued, however an operational unit was needed to assess the type's value as a combat aircraft. The *III. Gruppe* of the fighter wing *JG 54* was chosen as an operational trials unit. *III./JG 54 Grünherz* (Green Heart) thus became the first unit of the *Luftwaffe* to reequip with the new Fw 190 D-9. The first thirty production aircraft were delivered to the unit at the beginning of October 1944. *Junkers Motorenbau* assisted in the introduction of the Fw 190 D-9 and its Jumo 213 A power plant. As the engine was just entering service, the manufacturer initially maintained a close working relationship with the fighter units. Precise data still exists today, as Junkers filed monthly reports on the fighter units visited.

Hauptmann Weiss (left) was a major advocate of the new Fw 190 D-9. (via Urbanke)

6.1 Conversion of III./JG 54

III./JG 54 converted to the Fw 190 D-9 at the unit's base in Oldenburg. At that time the *Gruppe* was commanded by *Hptm*. Robert Weiss. Space makes it impossible to examine in detail the interesting story of the *Gruppe*'s experiences with the new fighter in the early weeks.

6.1.1. Extract from the *Luftwaffe* TAM-Gruppe's Monthly Report for September 1944:

...Another visit was made to III./JG 54, the first Gruppe to be equipped with the Fw 190 D-9 with the Jumo 213 A engine. The unit's opinion of the quality and performance of the Jumo 213 A was not exactly confident. This bias can be traced to an unsatisfactory directive by a Gen. T.T. traveling staff. The engine expert failed to satisfactorily address the concerns of the commander and the technical officer. The commander's request to approach the company directly was approved. With the arrival of the first machines the TAM

On 1 January 1945 *Lt.* Nibel of 10./JG 54 was forced to put his Fw 190 D-9 "Black 12" down near Brussels after the aircraft's engine failed. The forced landing caused little damage and the D-9 was subsequently taken to Farnborough for closer examination. According to the English report the D-9 had received the 1,900 h.p. modification.

assumed responsibility for instruction and technical support and thus completely restored trust in the Jumo 213.

During a subsequent discussion the commanding officer emphasized the increased speed of the enemy fighters at low altitude and at the same time characterized the improved low-level speed of the new machines as vital.

As the MW 50 system will not now be introduced until December, it was determined in consultation with Dr. Lichte that an immediate increase in output to 1,900 h.p. could be achieved by increasing boost pressure. The installation is being undertaken by the TAM before the

Photographs of force-landed D-9s are quite common. Here is *Werknummer* 212 133.

A most unusual photograph. A Fw 190 D-9 flies beneath a formation of American bombers just as they release their bombs.

Gruppe begins operations. At the present time the Gruppe is retraining with about 30 aircraft.

One engine had to be replaced on account of oil leaks in cylinders 5 and 7. The engine is being sent to Dessau for examination. One engine failed during the ferry flight because of a broken connecting rod. Three other machines had to make forced landings, allegedly because of engine trouble. Investigations have been initiated.

The impression exists that the ferry crews were insufficiently familiar with the aircraft, least of all the engine. To prevent further incidents the replacement training/ferry wing has been thoroughly briefed by the TAM ...

As the above extract shows, the increased low-level speed of the enemy fighters posed a particular threat to the German fighters. Consequently, after consultation with Jumo's head of development, Dr. Lichte, in September 1944 an equipment kit was installed which raised boost pressure

Fw 190 D-9 of II./JG 26 taking off on a fighter-bomber sortie. Note the bomb beneath the fuselage.

and increased the Jumo 213 A's emergency output from 1,750 to 1,900 h.p. The installation was carried out on-site by Junkers' Technical Field Service (TAM). This increased emergency power could be used at altitudes to 5000 meters. At the same time, use of takeoff power (1,750 h.p.) was extended to 30 min., while authorization was given to use combat power (1,620 h.p.) without restriction.

The Junkers technical field service visited *III./JG 54* monthly. In October the total number of Fw 190 D-9s on strength with the *Gruppe* rose to 68. Of these, 53 had been converted to 1,900 h.p. and one was delivered by Focke-Wulf with the MW 50 system. The remaining 14 were in the process of being converted and completion was imminent. The *Gruppe* declared itself satisfied with the performance of the aircraft and praised the excellent rate of climb and high-altitude capabilities of the D-9, which they had jokingly dubbed "*Langnase*" (long-nose). The *Gruppe* had also gained confidence in the Jumo 213, and subsequent engine problems were of a minor nature. The average number of hours logged by the D-9s was fifteen. One area which came in for criticism was the engine's tendency to leak oil from the ventilation ports during the cold-start procedure.

In November 1944 other *Gruppen* began converting to the Fw 190 D-9. Among them were *III. Gruppe* of *JG 2 Richthofen*, *II./JG 26*

Fw 190 D-9 *Werknummer* 601 007 after a crash-landing near Frankfurt. The fuselage band indicates that the aircraft was employed in the Defense of the Reich, probably with JG 4.

Fw 190 D-9, Werknummer 601 444.

Schlageter and *II./JG 301 Wilde Sau*. That same month *III./JG 54* reached its authorized strength of 80 aircraft. In its November report, Junkers noted that all the aircraft of the three new *Gruppe* were being converted to 1,900 h.p., and that the conversion work was significantly more difficult at front-line airfields where there were no hangars. Frequent rain hindered the conversion operations.

To solve the problem of leaking oil during cold starts, the November report ordered a temporary fix: the ventilation ports were to be sealed with two layers of canvas cloth. The proposed permanent solution was to use the hydraulic tank, which was no longer needed, as an oil separator. The necessary experiments were begun. In December 1944 more *Gruppen* converted to the Fw 190 D-9.

With few exceptions the Jumo 213 A proved to be a reliable power plant, nevertheless in its reports Junkers noted the not inconsiderable operational losses. Pilot casualties were also significant. One of the greatest advocates of the Fw 190 D-9, *Gruppenkommandeur* of *III./JG 54* and wearer of the Knight's Cross with Oak Leaves *Hptm*. Weiss, was killed in action while flying the Fw 190 D-9. By the end of December 1944 there were 183 Fw 190 D-9s in operation with the increased performance modification, and 60 more had been delivered with the MW 50 system and were at the point of entering service. The systems were not checked before the aircraft were delivered, and consequently Junker's technical

Photograph of a captured Fw 190 D-9. Just visible through the cockpit canopy is a P-47 Thunderbolt. This aircraft, *Werknummer* 600 651, probably belonged to I./JG 2.

Operational History of the Fw 190 D-9

Fw 190 D-9, Werknummer 600 578.

Fw 190 D-9 captured by Canadian units. Note the number 2 painted on the mainwheel fairing. (Robert Bracken)

A number of Fw 190 D-9s and F-8s were captured at airfields near Prague. The parked aircraft appear to be in good condition. (Eberhard Weber)

The Fw 190 D-9 "Red 13" belonged to the "Protection Staffel" of JV 44. The latter unit was equipped with the Me 262 and the role of the D-9 Staffel was to protect the jet fighters during landings and takeoffs, when they were extremely vulnerable. This D-9 was flown by *Hauptmann* Klaus Faber.

field service had to carry out these system checks before the aircraft could enter service.

The problem of oil leaking onto the engine during the cold-start procedure was overcome through the use of cloth inserts. Because of the limited number of breakdowns, in December Jumo proposed that the time between overhauls be increased from 120 to 150 hours. Five Fw 190 D-9s had been lost as a result of engine fires in a short space of time. In each case the pilot was able to parachute to safety, but the aircraft were completely destroyed, making it impossible to determine the cause of the fires. According to the pilots, the fires had begun on the left side of the engine. It was accepted that the fires had started after the radiator compensating line burst, causing coolant to run onto the exhaust stubs, which ignited the glycol in the coolant. This theory was confirmed by two cases which occurred on the ground during engine run-ups. A directive was issued which ordered the compensating line cut through and reattached with rubber sealant, providing the line with some flexibility. At the same time, a search was begun for a better mounting for the line. In one eight-week period ending February 1945 *JG 2* experienced a total of 18 engine failures. The new problem was caused by failure of the fuel pump drive

resulting from seizure of the pump. The cause was found to be water in the fuel lines. An examination of the fuel tanks revealed as much as five liters of water mixed with the fuel. How the water came to be in the fuel tanks was never explained.

In March 1945 *General der Jagdflieger* Gordon Gollob issued a list of aircraft types from the Emergency Fighter Program to be assigned to the Fw 190 units. The Fw 190 units were to convert from the Fw 190 D-9 and D-12 to the new Ta 152 C and H. The list appears below:

The Fw 190 D-9s of the so-called "Papageistaffel" (Parrot Staffel), whose correct name was actually "Würgerstaffel" (Butcher Bird Staffel), have become quite well-known. Their most striking feature was the special paint schemes worn on the underside of the aircraft, in this case red with white stripes. (Griehl)

Unit	Current Equipment	New Equipment
I./JG 2	Fw 190 D-9	unchanged
II./JG 2	Fw 190 D-9	unchanged
III./JG 2	Fw 190 D-9	unchanged
IV./JG 2	Fw 190 A-8/A-9	Fw 190 D-9
II./JG 4	Fw 190 A-8/A-9	Fw 190 D-9
I./JG 6	Fw 190 A-8/A-9	Fw 190 D-9
II./JG 6	Fw 190 A-8/A-9	Fw 190 D-9
I./JG 11	Fw 190 A-8/A-9	Fw 190 D-9
III./JG 11	Fw 190 A-8/A-9	Fw 190 D-9
I./JG 26	Fw 190 D-9	Fw 190 D-12
II./JG 26	Fw 190 D-9	Fw 190 D-12
IV./JG 26	Fw 190 D-9	Fw 190 D-12
I./JG 54	Fw 190 A-8/A-9	Fw 190 D-9
II./JG 54	Fw 190 A-8/A-9	Fw 190 D-9

III./JG 54	Fw 190 A-8/A-9	Fw 190 D-9
II./JG 300	Fw 190 A-9/R11	to Fw 190 D-9/R11 to Me 262
I./JG 301	Fw 190 A-9/R11	to Fw 190 D-9/R11 to Ta 152
II./JG 301	Fw 190 A-9/R11	to Fw 190 D-9/R11 to Ta 152
III./JG 301	Ta 152 H	unchanged
III./KG(J) 27	Fw 190 A-9/R11	Fw 190 D-9/R11

By the end of the war may fighter units were equipped with the Fw 190 D-9, including all the *Gruppen* of *JG 2* and *JG 26*. Since 1941 these two units had borne the brunt of the battle against Allied fighters in the west. In 1941 they had reequipped with the Fw 190 A-1 and A-2, which were superior to the Spitfire Vb, the best Allied fighter of the day. At the end of the war they were flying the Fw 190 D-9 or D-12, which were equal, if not superior to the latest versions of the Spitfire. The times of great successes by the German fighter arm were over, however. The Allied fighters were superior in number and they maintained a constant watch over the German fighter bases. To avoid detection, the German fighter aircraft had to be hidden in camouflaged dispersals in the forests which lined their airfields. The situation became so bad that German fighters had to fly defensive patrols over their own airfields to cover takeoffs and landings. Heavy casualties forced the *Luftwaffe* to commit young, inadequately-trained pilots. They proved easy prey for the better-trained Allied fighter pilots. Although their aircraft were equal in performance to those of the enemy, they were not up to the task and their sacrifices were in vain.

6.2 A Fighter Pilot's Opinion of the Fw 190 D-9

We began converting to the Fw 190 D-9 in Fürstenau on 24 December 1944. From then until 31 December we had the opportunity to familiarize ourselves with the new machine and fly training

This well-known photograph depicts Focke-Wulf D-9, WNr. 210 194, which was flown by *Oberfeldwebel* Werner Hohenberg, wingman to the *Gruppenkommandeur* of I./JG 2 *Richthofen, Hptm.* Hrdlicka. The aircraft was hit by flak while making a second pass over St. Trond airfield in Belgium during Operation Bodenplatte. His engine damaged, Hohenberg force-landed the aircraft in enemy territory. He was taken prisoner. Here American soldiers are seen inspecting the downed aircraft.

missions. *The first problems cropped up when the machines were test flown. In several cases the ignition cut out during a steep banking turn to the left. There was general consternation: "What are we to do with such a bird?" It was inevitable that the pilots should have reservations about the new machine. Civilian engineers from Junkers soon came to the rescue. When filled with belted ammunition for the left MG 131 above the engine, the metal ammunition tank located in front of the firewall pressed on the system of cables from the generator to the engine. The problem had obviously not made itself felt during unarmed factory test flights. The field workshop came up with a solution: a metal spacer which was riveted in place. I don't know if the Junkers people submitted a modification report to the BAL (Construction Supervisory Board, Air), that was not my concern. All I know for sure is that it is a dangerous affair to have a fighter strapped to your behind whose engine sputters or stops every now and then. Once this problem was cleared up there were scarcely any complaints about the new bird.*

While on a comparison flight during the familiarization phase between Christmas and New Year, I achieved an indicated airspeed of 605 km/h in a Sorau-built machine at "Beer Bottle Height" (10 to 20 meters above the ground), at about minus 4 to 5 degrees C, with no external tank, but with full load and MW 50. (As a joke, we used to say: with ears laid back, fire extinguisher on, downhill, tailwind, cooling gills closed.) In the process, I slowly passed my Gruppenkommandeur, Major Borris. That was something!!! As the technical officer of 2. Staffel, I had picked out the machine for myself on Christmas Eve. The finish of aircraft from Sorau was especially good, particularly in respect to the flush riveting of the panel joints, which resulted in a smooth external surface. The ground crew then polished the bird with Simonize wax, and I gained another 5 to 6 km/h as a result of the reduction in boundary layer turbulence. After the flight Major Borris asked if I was willing to trade. I said no and he understood. I kept this machine, "Black 8", until it was destroyed in an 8th Air Force bombing raid at the end of March.

In general, I should say that we of the I./JG 26 "Schlageter" were very satisfied with the D-9 and regretted that this aircraft had not appeared at the front much sooner. The old Fw 190 A-8 that we flew until 24 December 1944 was surely no feast for the eyes compared to the Bf 109, the Spitfire or the P-51 D Mustang, with their elegant lines. The A-8 was powered by a bulky BMW 801 radial engine and tapered to the rear like a tadpole. The lengthened fuselage of the Fw 190 D-9 transformed the aircraft and placed it in the same class as the above-mentioned machines.

Lt. Ossenkop summarized the differences between the Fw 190 D-8 and the Fw 190 A-8 as follows:

When the Fw 190 D-9 was introduced into service by the I. *Gruppe* of JG 26 *Schlageter*, *Leutnant* Karl Heinz Ossenkop was the technical officer of that unit's 2. *Staffel*. The *Geschwader*'s I. *Gruppe* continued flying the Fw 190 A-8 until 24 December 1944, when it began converting to the new D-9. Ossenkop is seen here in December 1944 as a *Leutnant* in the 2. *Staffel*. On 17 April 1945 *Lt*. Ossenkop's D-9 was shot down in combat with Spitfires near Ratzeburg. He bailed out successfully and returned to the *Staffel* on 30 April. I./JG 26 surrendered in Flensburg on 5 May 1945.

Lt. Ossenkop (left) with two comrades in February 1945. In the middle is *Lt.* Söffing (KIA) and right *Oblt.* Littelmann (KIA).

A Fw 190 D-9 parked at the edge of a forest.

1. Larger vertical fin.

2. The Junkers VS 11 propeller was new. While the propeller had the same diameter, the blades had a stronger profile and increased chord. The propeller, which was made of laminated plywood, thus appeared more massive. It was also lighter than the aluminum propeller and, because of its improved aerodynamic profile, produced more thrust at the same revolutions. The tendency for the aircraft to swing on takeoff and landing was reduced.

3. The Jumo 213 A with annular radiator and cooling gills had a reduced frontal area and therefore created less drag. It produced 40 to 50 horsepower more at the crankshaft. The heavy engine vibrations which were typical for the A-8 almost disappeared with the new engine.

4. The cockpit canopy was new. Possibly inspired by the latest Mustangs, Typhoons, Thunderbolts, Tempests and Spitfires, it provided a significantly better view all around and to the rear.

5. The fuselage had been lengthened through the insertion of a 50-cm section at the break point in front of the tail section. This was obviously to compensate for the longer engine section and improve the leverage of the elevator and rudder forces.

6. Handling characteristics on the ground and in the air were much better than those of the A-8. As in the A-8, forward view while taxiing was poor, however the narrower forward fuselage made it easier to see the marshaller while following the required zigzag course.

7. Takeoff and climb were rather better than in the A-8. It was possible to make tighter turns before the onset of flow separation. In a dive, the D-9 was far superior to the A-8 with its drag-producing radial engine.

8. At a height of approximately 3500-4000 meters the A-8 began showing the performance weaknesses of the BMW 801; however, with its single-stage supercharger with automatic boost control, the D-9 was the equal of most enemy aircraft at altitudes above 4000 meters up to its maximum boost altitude, I estimate 6000-7000 meters. The engine burned B4 fuel instead of the high-grade C3 fuel used by the BMW 801.

Compared to our opponents:

Spitfire: the D-9 was better in level flight, climb and dive. It was slightly inferior in turns.

Tempest: almost equal in level flight, a lengthy pursuit was usually fruitless. The D-9 climbed and turned better, but was inferior in a dive.

Mustang: the two aircraft were about equal in normal combat maneuvers, which was an advantage for us compared to the A-8. The Mustang was rather faster in a dive.

Thunderbolt: with the Dora-9 we had advantages in level flight, climb and turn. We were hopelessly inferior in a dive. (Never try to dive away from a Thunderbolt.)

In closing, I can only say that we pilots of JG 26 were very satisfied with the new machine. Although some doubts were expressed in the beginning, we found that we were equal, and in some cases superior, to our opponents. We were unable to turn the tide, but we flew to the bitter end.

6.3 The D-9 Compared to Fighter Aircraft of the Allies

In terms of numbers produced, the D-9 was one of the most significant variants of the Fw 190 series. As well, the D-9 had the highest performance of any production variant of the Fw 190, apart from a few examples of late D-series aircraft. Many consider the Fw 190 D-9 to have been the most capable German fighter aircraft of the late war period. A comparison with British and American fighters from the same period therefore seems appropriate.

Performance Comparison between the Fw 190 D-9, P-51 D Mustang and Spitfire Mk. XIV			
Designation	**Focke-Wulf Fw 190 D-9**	**North American P-51 D Mustang**	**Supermarine Spitfire Mk. XIV**
Purpose	*Fighter/fighter-bomber*	*Fighter*	*Fighter*
Empty weight	3,490 kg	3,232 kg	2,994 kg
Gross weight	4,250 kg	4,581 kg	3,856 kg
Wingspan	10.50 m	11.28 m	11.23 m
Length	10.20 m	9.83 m	9.96 m
Height	3.36 m	3.71 m	3.87 m
Wing area	18.30 m²	21.66 m²	22.48 m²
Wing loading	225 kg/m²	211 kg/m²	310 kg/m²
Power plant	Junkers Jumo 213 A	Packard V1650-7 Merlin	Rolls-Royce Griffon 65
Takeoff power	1,750 HP	1,490 HP	2,050 HP
Fuel	B4/87 Octane	100 Octane	100 Octane
Fuel capacity	525 l	1185 l[4]	510 l
Range	980 km	1,529 km	740 km
Range with auxiliary tanks	1,450 km[5]	3,348 km	1,368 km
Speed at low level	572 km/h 612 km/h[6]	581 km/h	584 km/h
Maximum speed	685 km/h 702 km/h[7]	699 km/h	717 km/h
at maximum boost altitude	6.6 km 5.7 km	7.6 km	7.742 km
Landing speed	170 km/h	160 km/h	120 km/h
Low-level climb rate	16.8 m/s 22[8] m/s	17.6 m/s	23.1 m/s
Time to climb to 2000 m	2.3 min	2.30 min (2438 m)	1.75 min (2438 m)
Time to climb to 4000 m	4.9 min	4.00 min (4267 m)	3.40 min (4267 m)
Time to climb to 6000 m	7.7 min	6.10 min (6096 m)	5.10 min (6096 m)
Service ceiling	10.8 km	12.7 km	13.1 km
Armament	2 x MG 151/20, 2 x MG 131	6 x 12.7mm Browning	2 x 20mm Hispano - MK 2 x 12.7mm Browning MG
Bomb load	max. 500 kg	none	max. 454 kg

Table footnotes:
4. Two 92 U.S. gal. wing tanks, one 85 U.S. gal. fuselage tank.
5. With 300-liter drop tank beneath fuselage.
6. With MW 50 injection.
7. With MW 50 injection.
8. 22 m/sec. with MW 50 injection.

This comparison immediately reveals the amazing performance of the British Spitfire XIV. At the end of the war it represented the technical standard by which piston-engined fighters were measured. In a then secret report by the Air Fighting Development Unit dated 5 June 1944, the Spitfire XIV and other aircraft were compared with the already obsolescent Fw 190 A powered by the BMW 801 radial engine. This report also predicted the appearance of a Fw 190 with an in-line engine, although it named the DB 603 as power plant, not the Jumo 213.

Four Mustang escort fighters of the American 8th Air Force.

Combat Trial against Fw 190 (BMW 801 D)

Maximum Speeds

From 0 – 5000 ft (1500 m) and 15000 to 20000 ft, the Spitfire XIV is only 20 mph (32 km/h) faster, at all other heights it is up to 60 mph (100 km/h) faster than the Fw 190 (BMW 801 D). It is estimated to have about the same maximum speed as the new Fw 190 (DB 603) at all heights.

Maximum Climb

The Spitfire XIV has a considerably greater rate of climb than the Fw 190 (BMW 801 D) or (estimated) the new Fw 190 (DB 603) at all heights.

Dive

After the initial part of the dive, during which the Fw 190 gains slightly, the Mk XIV has a slight advantage.

Turning Circle

Spitfire XIV can easily turn inside the Fw 190, though in the case of a right-hand turn the difference is not so quite pronounced.

Rate of Roll

The Fw 190 is very much better.

Conclusion

In defense, the Spitfire XIV should use its remarkable maximum climb rate and turning circle against any enemy aircraft. In the attack it can afford to "mix it" but should be aware of the quick roll and dive. If the maneuver is used by the Fw 190 and the Spitfire follows, it will probably not be able to close the range until the Fw 190 has pulled out of his dive.

As this English assessment shows, by mid-1944 the Fw 190 A with the BMW 801 D engine was outclassed by Allied fighters in almost every

The Fw 190 D-9 reserve flight in Prenzlau, led by *Oblt.* Romm.

respect. Its technical inferiority, especially in terms of maximum level speed, was unacceptable. Even a well-trained pilot flying the Fw 190 A would have had serious difficulty in combat against the Spitfire. The statements concerning the DB 603, which was in the same performance class as the Jumo 213, must be seen as incorrect, however. The Fw 190 with in-line engine was clearly superior in performance to the radial-engined Fw 190.

The Fw 190 D-9 with the Jumo 213 A was able to reduce the Spitfire's speed advantage to a maximum of 30 km/h. Thus the Fw 190 D-9's performance was useful against western opponents. At lower altitudes the Fw 190 D-9's performance was equal to that of Allied fighters. Only when equipped with increased boost or MW 50 injection did the Fw 190 D-9 gain a performance advantage. With methanol-water injection the Fw 190 D-9s maximum speed was 612 km/h at ground level and 702 km/h at 5500 meters. At the latter altitude the Spitfire XIV's performance was poorer (663 km/h) on account of the Rolls-Royce Griffon's performance characteristics.

The Mustang's legendary reputation was not built on its excellent performance alone. Its greatest advantage was its tremendous range. The first P-51 B Mustangs entered service with the American 8th Air Force in late 1943. Beginning in the spring of 1944, P-51s escorted the American heavy bombers to Berlin, providing effective fighter cover to the target and back. This took the *Luftwaffe* command completely by surprise. The heavy Messerschmitt twin-engined fighters which were being used against the heavy bombers were inferior to the Mustang in every respect. The same applied to the German single-seat fighters. Neither the Bf 109 G-6 nor the Fw 190 A could match the performance of the Mustang. Once engaged, however, the Mustangs were forced to jettison their long-range tanks. Tests at Boscombe Down revealed that a Mustang equipped with two 75 U.S. gallon drop tanks lost 87 km/h at low level and 93 km/h at 6100 m.

Romm's aircraft "1" and that of his wingman, "2", of 15./JG 3 in January 1943. (Weber)

The performance of the Fw 190 D-9 was absolutely comparable with that of the Mustang. It could have been made available much sooner. Not until February 1944, by which time the Mustangs were appearing over the German Reich, did the RLM order the D-9 series into production as an interim type pending the arrival of the Focke-Wulf Ta 152.

6.4 The Fw 190 D-9 with R4M Air-to-Air Rockets

In the final weeks of February 1945 a complete *Staffel* of the *Erprobungskommando Jagdgruppe 10* at Parchim was equipped with Fw 190 D-9s armed with R4M air-to-air rockets. Each Fw 190 D-9 was capable of carrying a total of twenty-four R4M rockets on two racks mounted beneath the wings. *JGr. 10* had been specially assigned to test the R4M. The R4M was the only purposely-designed air-to-air rocket to see service with the *Luftwaffe* and the warhead carried an explosive charge of 540 grams. The designation R4M stood for *Rakete* (rocket), 4 kg (the rocket's weight), *Minenkopf* (warhead).

The testing resulted in an immediate order for the Me 262, Fw 190 D-9 and Ta 152 to be equipped to carry the R4M. The R4M system was to have been installed in the Fw 190 D-9 on the production line, while modification directives were planned for the retrofitting of those aircraft already in service. The R4M's effectiveness as an anti-bomber weapon was demonstrated by the first operational Me 262 A-1a jet fighters. The degree of success achieved by *Jagdgruppe 10* is not known, although the immediate order to install the R4M system would suggest that it achieved some measure of success. On 2 April 1945 orders were issued for *Jagdgruppe 10* to disband. The order specified that all of the D-9s equipped to carry the R4M, which were assigned to 2. *Staffel/Jagdgruppe 10*, were to be transferred to *I. Gruppe/JG 301*. It is not known if this order was in fact carried out.

This Fw 190 was equipped to carry a maximum of four 50-kg bombs beneath the wings. The underwing racks were supposed to become standard equipment as of March 1945.

The same machine viewed from the rear. The aircraft bears no manufacturer's code on the fuselage or visible unit marking. It may have been a Focke-Wulf test machine.

6.5 The Fw 190 D-9 with *Panzerblitz* and Underwing Bomb Racks

It was also intended that the Fw 190 D-9 series should be equipped to carry the *Panzerblitz* anti-tank rocket and underwing bombs. Several production aircraft were modified to carry bombs beneath the wings. Racks were fitted for the carriage of two 50 kg bombs beneath each outer wing. These were similar to the racks fitted to the Fw 190 F-8/F-9 and F-16 close-support aircraft.

No proof exists that the Fw 190 D-9 was equipped to carry the *Panzerblitz*, although plans existed to install the necessary equipment as carried by the Fw 190 F. The *Panzerblitz* saw limited use by close-support units equipped with the Fw 190 F. Two different systems were used, *Panzerblitz 1* and *Panzerblitz 2*. Aircraft fitted with *Panzerblitz 1* carried seven 73-mm rockets on rails beneath each wing. While *Panzerblitz 1* proved unsuccessful, some local successes were achieved with *Panzerblitz 2*. The problem with *Panzerblitz 1* was that the aircraft had to reduce speed drastically to score hits, even to the extent of lowering its undercarriage, which was impractical in combat situations.

Panzerblitz 2 consisted of two wooden racks beneath the wings, each capable of carrying twelve R4M rockets. For use against surface targets the rocket was fitted with an armor-piercing warhead, which proved effective against armored vehicles. Toward the end of the war the *Panzerblitz 2* was used with effect on a number of occasions.

CHAPTER SEVEN

The Fw 190 D-10 is Stillborn

The RLM continued to insist that every fighter aircraft be equipped with a large-caliber centrally-mounted weapon. This was not possible with the Jumo 213 A, however. To at least partially meet this requirement, the two fuselage-mounted MG 131 machine-guns of the Fw 190 D-10 were to be deleted in favor of a single 20-mm cannon mounted asymmetrically in the forward fuselage. The RLM rejected this proposal, however, and the D-10 proceeded no farther than the drawing board.

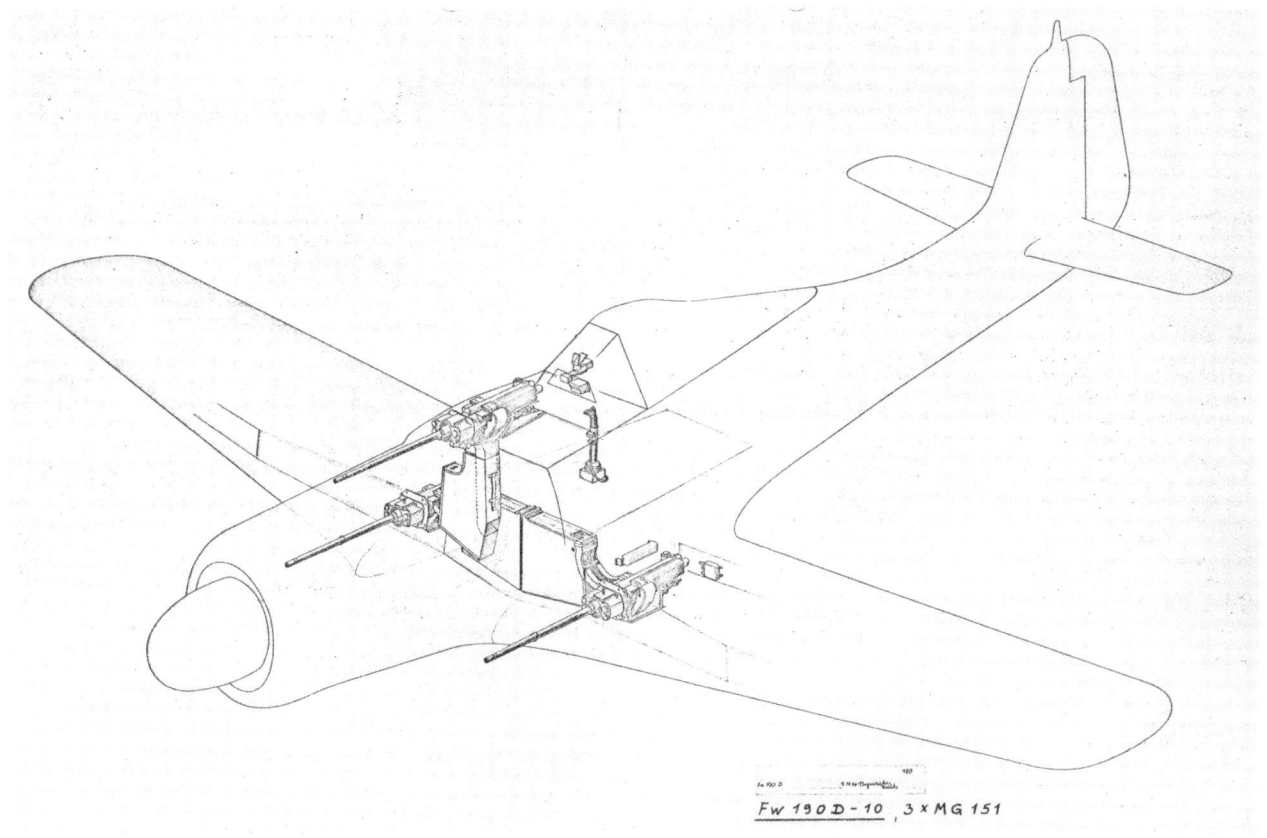

CHAPTER EIGHT

The Fw 190 D-11 - The Last Minute Fighter

In May 1944 the OKL[1] first called for the installation of the more powerful Jumo 213 F engine in the production airframe of the Fw 190 A. The Jumo 213 F, power plant designation 9-8213 H, was derived from the Jumo 213 A and was therefore suitable for use in the Fw 190 airframe. The Fw 190 D-11 was intended for use by the *Luftwaffe* as a fighter-bomber and close-support aircraft.

Unlike the Jumo 213 E installed in the Ta 152 H, the Jumo 213 F had no intercooler, as there was no room for it in the Fw 190 D-9 airframe. Instead, the supercharger air was cooled by means of MW 50[2] injection. The Jumo 213 F was based on the Jumo 213 A, which was built in large numbers, powering the Fw 190 D-9 and bombers such as the Ju 188. The liquid-cooled, 12-cylinder in-line engine had a capacity of 34.97 liters and was equipped with a two-stage supercharger with three-speed geared drive (the Jumo 213 A had a single-stage supercharger with two-speed geared drive). The Jumo 213 F produced 2,050 h.p. for takeoff and offered promising development potential. The supercharger's second gear engaged at 2500 m, the third gear at 7000 m.

The first engine test-bed for the D-11 series began testing even before the first production Fw 190 D-9 with the Jumo 213 A left the production

Side view of the Fw 190 V30/U1. GH+KT was the second prototype of the Ta 152 H high-altitude fighter, which was developed in parallel with the Fw 190 D-11. The V30/U1 made its first flight on the same day (6 Aug. 1944) as the Fw 190 V55, GV+CV, WNr. 170 923. (DASA)

line at Sorau. Focke-Wulf produced seven prototypes for the D-11 series, all converted Fw 190 A-9 production airframes. The seven prototypes received the designations Fw 190 V55 to V61. The production version of the D-11 was to have a revised armament compared to the Fw 190 D-9, consisting of two MG 151/20 cannon in the wing roots and two MK 108 cannon in the outer wings. The fuselage-mounted armament was dropped and the bulged fairing over the weapons was replaced by a smooth, aerodynamically cleaner panel. No engine-mounted weapon was planned. The D-11 was abandoned in favor of the Fw 190 D-12/D-13, however Focke-Wulf was not able to switch production to the D-12/D-13 series until January 1945. As a result, production of the Fw 190 D-11 (*Werknummer* block 220) began in January 1945. It was already known that Junkers' delivery capacity for the Jumo 213 E/F engine would be severely limited because of the higher priority assigned to the Jumo 004 turbojet engine program. This made it necessary to shift emphasis to the DB 603 as a replacement engine for the Fw 190 D-11, D-12 and D-13, by March 1945 at the latest. Fifteen Fw 190 D-11s were supposed to be converted to the DB 603 in January 1945. Whether these conversions were actually completed is not known. The D-11 first appears in the Gen.Qu. 6 Abt.'s aircraft distribution plans in March 1945. According to these, thirteen standard D-11s and four D-11s with the EZ 42 gunsight were delivered to operational units. It is possible that a few more were delivered in April 1945. Production Fw 190 D-11 fighters are known to have been issued to *Stab JG 300* (*Kommodore Major* Rall), *II./JG 300* (*Major* Baier) and the *JV 44* Protection *Staffel* ("*Würgerstaffel*") under Lt. Sachsenberg.

[1] OKL = Luftwaffe High Command
[2] MW 50 = Methanol-water injection with 50:50 mixture ratio

Copy of the Fw 190 D-11 Development Report

Subject: Fw 190 D-11

<u>Object:</u> The changeover from the D-9 to D-11 version cannot be accomplished on time because of the required expenditure of working capital (also see Dev. Report XV). Focke-Wulf will therefore begin deliveries of the Fw 190 D-11 in January. The MK 108 *Motorkanone* will have to be dropped. In its place two MK 108s will be installed in the outer wings.

<u>1.) Equipment State:</u>   <u>Fw 190 D-11</u>

        Airframe as Fw 190 D-9
        Power plant 9-8213 E (Jumo 213 F engine) as Fw 190 D-12/D-13
        MW 50 injection system as Fw 190 D-12, other equipment arrangement
        Armament: Upper fuselage   no weapons
                            Wing roots   2 MG 151
                            Outer wings   2 MK 108
        Smooth panel in front of windscreen
        WGR 21 system deleted

ETC 504 bomb rack for carriage of bombs or 300-l drop tank installed on every aircraft

The installation of bad-weather equipment as previously installed in Fw 190 /R11 variants is also planned here

D-11/R11 PKS 12 autopilot (like D-9)
     FuG 125 radio set
     Heated windscreen
     Backup turn-and-bank indicator

2.) Construction Drawings Fw 190 D-11/R11 delivery to series management 30/11/44

3.) Prototypes: No prototype is being built. Instead the following prototypes are already under test
     Fw 190 D-11 V55 – V61
One aircraft is to be moved into production testing.

4.) Series Delivery as per delivery plan

Fw 190 D-11/R11 Fw beginning Jan. 45
Determination by SA F4

Note: The other companies (Fieseler and Arbeitsgemeinschaft) delivering the Fw 190 D-12/D-13 series with *Motorkanone* as before

  MK 108 in D-12
  MG 151 in D-13

5. Manuals: Conversion and maintenance manuals for this variant are to be completed by 30 Dec. 1944. Fw 190 D-9 replacement parts list is to be supplemented.

6. Note: The insertion of four bag tanks in the wing is to be carried out exactly as Fw 190 D-12/D-1 as per Dev. Report XV, P. 1,2. Designation D-11/R5 (including PKS 12 autopilot). Target date to be announced by SA F4.

Copy of Addendum to Fw 190 D-11 Development Report

1. Addendum to Development Report Journal XV e 11 of 28 Nov. 44
(Cancellation of Fw 190 D-11/R5 with bag tanks in the wing)

The recipient is requested to strike Paragraph 6, Note, in Journal XV e 11, which was cancelled before the Development Report was issued.

2. Addendum to Development Report XV e 10 of 28 Nov. 44
(Cancellation of Fw 190 D-11/R11 with bad-weather Rüstsatz)

Subject: Fw 190 D-11

Contrary to previous requirements, as per SA F4 determination of 15/12 (Bad-Weather Fighter Delivery Plan), the autopilot with FuG 125 will not be installed in the D-11 variant.

The D-11/R11 designation is therefore cancelled.
The above lists for the D-11 variant are being produced as required. In the interim provisional information to the Sommerfeld working bureau by KB.

The last paragraph of Journal XV e 10 of 28 Nov. under Point 1.) is to be deleted, as well as the sections dealing with R11 under Points 2.) and 4.).

These addenda supplemented the Fw 190 D-11 development report. Both the Fw 190 D-11/R11 bad-weather fighter and the Fw 190 D-11/R5 with four additional bag-type fuel tanks in the wing were dropped.

Another version, which was to be built at a later date, was the Fw 190 D-11/R20. This version of the D-11 was to have the new and more reliable high-pressure version of MW 50, which Focke-Wulf hoped would result in improved ease of operation. The existing MW 50 low-pressure system (BNE system) was still considered to complicated and delicate.

8.1 The Prototypes

The first prototype, the Fw 190 V55, was converted from the Fw 190 A-8 *Werknummer* 170 923 at Focke-Wulf Branch Plant 9, the prototype works, in Adelheide. Bearing the manufacturer's code GV+CV, the aircraft took to the air for the first time on 6 August 1944. Another prototype made its first flight that day: the Fw 190 V30/U1, *Werknummer* 0 055, GH+KT, was the second prototype for the Ta 152 H series (see photo). In August 1944, the Fw 190 D-11 and the Ta 152 H were at a similar state of development.

The second D-11 prototype was the Fw 190 V56. Pilot Alfred Thomas took the machine into the air for the first time on 14 August 1944. The first successful test flight lasted thirteen minutes. Like many test pilots, Alfred Thomas came from the *Luftwaffe*. Thomas was to lose his life a short time later: he was killed on 23 August in the crash of the Fw 190 V30/U1, the second prototype for the Ta 152 H. He was just 32 years old.

One day after the first flight of the Fw 190 V56, the famous Focke-Wulf test pilot Hans Sander flew the D-11 prototype from the Adelheide prototype works to Langenhagen, Focke-Wulf's test center near Hanover. There the V56 was flown several times by designer Kurt Tank, who liked to fly his latest creations to judge their capabilities for himself.

The first two prototypes of the Fw 190 D-11, the Fw 190 V55 and V56, remained at Langenhagen for long-term testing. Aerodynamically, neither was in first-class condition.

The first aircraft used to determine the new variant's performance was the third prototype, the Fw 190 V57, GV+CY. It was a good 25 km/h faster than the first two prototypes and was later tested at Rechlin.

A photograph taken at the prototype works in Adelheide. In the background is the Fw 190 V56, seen during conversion to Fw 190 D-11 standard. The BMW 801 engine has already been removed and the engine mounts have been prepared to accept the Jumo 213 F.

In the initial stages there were problems harmonizing the methanol system with operation of the supercharger. Beginning on 10 September 1944, the methanol injection was moved in front of the supercharger. The short oval supercharger air intake was separated from the airframe by 100 mm. It was larger than that the supercharger air intake of the Fw 190 D-9 and similar to that of the Ta 152 H high-altitude fighter. The engine problems continued (see chapter "Report on Testing"). The most serious technical problem was the so-called "supercharger surging" in third gear. This was caused by fluctuations in boost pressure which caused the engine to vibrate badly. The phenomenon occurred in the speed range of 2,700 to 3,050 rpm, and above that speed it disappeared again.

In an attempt to correct the problem, supercharger ventilation capacity was increased and the supercharger ventilation openings were extended by means of pipes downwards through the undercarriage well. The MW 50 tank behind the D-11's cockpit had a capacity of 115 liters, which was good for 40 minutes of operation at a rate of consumption of 150 l/hr. On 4 October test pilot Friedrich Schnier was obliged to make a forced landing at Adelheide. The reason was entry of water into Cylinder 1 of the Jumo 213 F. The Fw 190 V56 suffered a total of four engine failures by 14 October 1944. The large number of engine failures delayed the introduction of the Fw 190 D-11 into *Luftwaffe* service. In spite of this, the V56 logged

21 flying hours by the end of the year. Focke-Wulf also used the V56 in experiments aimed at improving the maximum speed of the Fw 190 D-9 and D-11. Sealing the engine cowling fore and aft resulted in a speed increase of 14 km/h at combat power and 17 km/h at takeoff power. With the Jumo 213 F and performance enhancements, the Fw 190 D-11 would have been equal to any enemy fighter aircraft. The last log book entries by Focke-Wulf test pilots flying the V56 appear at the beginning of February 1945. More unrecorded test flights may have been made after this date.

Shortly before the end of the war, the Fw 190 V56 was to have served as test-bed for the improved Jumo 213 F with MW 50 high-pressure system. It was hoped that this system would significantly improve the functioning and reliability of the Jumo 213 F engine. On the Jumo 213 F1 it was possible to move the methanol-water injection equipment back behind the supercharger. This made it possible to use the system to inject water as well. At that time it was also planned to conduct a test program with the V56 at Langenhagen, like the V55.

The V55 was abandoned by a Focke-Wulf test pilot in Reinsehlen at the beginning of April 1945, however nothing is known about the fate of the Fw 190 V56.

The third prototype, the Fw 190 V57, was also a converted Fw 190 A-8. Unlike the V55 and V56, the exterior finish of the V57 was excellent. All seams were filled and polished and all protruding panels were smoothed. The V57 was 20 to 25 km/h faster than the V55 and V56 and was thus the aircraft used by Focke-Wulf to determine the type's performance. The three prototypes were initially used by Focke-Wulf for test purposes. All of the remaining prototypes were assigned to Focke-Wulf test facilities or engine manufacturers for testing purposes.

Sensibly, the D-11 prototypes were later incorporated into the test program for the Fw 190 D-12 and D-13. The V57 was still flying at Rechlin in February 1945 as part of this program.

As part of the Fw 190 D production process, complete tail sections were assembled separately and then taken to the final assembly line for installation. The 0.5-meter fuselage extension, a characteristic feature of all D-series aircraft, is clearly visible.

Three views of the Fw 190 V56, *Werknummer* 170 924, with the registration GV+CW. (Focke-Wulf)

Vergleich Fw 190$_D$ – Ta 152$_C$

	Fw 190$_D$	Ta 152$_C$
Motor	Jumo 213 E ohne Ladeluftkühler (aus Platzgründen) Einbau eines 603 Motors nicht möglich wegen Freigängigkeit am Fahrwerk.	DB 603 L mit Ladeluftkühler Einbau eines 213 Motors jederzeit möglich **Vorteile:** a) Die Ta 152 ist nicht an ein Motormuster (213g – ohne Ladeluftkühler) gebunden, sondern kann wahlweise den 213 E und 603 L oder auch 801 E schalten. Damit kann auch der jeweils stärkste Motor zum Einsatz in den Jäger gelangen. b) Verwendung von Einheitstriebwerken nur bei der Ta 152 möglich. Bei der Fw 190 D nur Einheitskühlerkopf.
Bewaffnung	1 x MG 151 150 Schuss / MK 108 85 Schuss oder MG 151 250 Schuss / MG 151 je 175 Schuß	MK 103 80 Schuss oder MK 108 90 Schuss oder MG 151 250 Schuss / 2 x MG 151 je 150 Schuss / MG 151 je 175 Schuß Flächenzusatzbewaffnung in beiden Fällen 2 x 108 oder 2 x 151 **Vorteil:** a) Stärkere Grundbewaffnung mit MK 103 als Motorwaffe. MK 103 in Fw 190 D nicht einbaubar. b) Die starke Grundbewaffnung lässt den grundsätzlichen Fortfall der Flächenzusatzbewaffnung möglich erscheinen, wodurch im Flächenzusatzteil Raum für innenliegende Kraftstoffbehälter frei wird (nächste Spalte)
Flugdauer in 7000 Höhe	ohne Außenbehälter 1,65 Std. V_m = 495 km/h mit Außenbehälter 2,70 Std. V_m = 465 km/h (300 Ltr.)	ohne Außenbehälter 2,22 Std. V_m = 484 km/h mit Außenbehälter 3,27 Std. V_m = 459 km/h (300 Liter) (Gleiche Verbräuche beim 213 und 603 angenommen. Wasser-Methanol bei Ta 152 im Innenflügel) **Vorteil:** Bei der Ta 152 lässt sich der Kraftstoffvorrat auf etwa 1000 Liter gegenüber 525 Liter bei der Fw 190 D (beides ohne Außenbehälter) erhöhen. Damit Flugzeit für die Ta 152 ohne 300 Ltr. Außenbehälter 3,1 Std. für Ta 152 mit 300 Ltr. Außenbehälter 4,0 Std. für Ta 152 (Anlage wird z.Zt. konstruiert)
Radlasten	Zulässige Radlast (700 x 175) 1200 kg Vorhandene Radlast ohne Außenbehälter 1240 kg mit Zusatzbehälter 2060 kg	Zulässige Radlast (940 x 210) 2200 kg Vorhandene Radlast mit innenliegenden Zusatzbehältern im Flügel 2150 kg mit zusätzlichen Außenbehältern 2300 kg **Vorteil:** Obschon die Ta 152 (ohne 300 Ltr. Außenbehälter) eine um 90 %, grössere Flugzeit besitzt als die Fw 190 D, sind die zulässigen Radlasten nicht überschritten. Erst bei 4,0 Std. Flugzeit = 1900 km Reichweite bei V_m = 460 km/h wird die Radlast um 4 %, überschritten.
Lastvielfaches	n_A = ~5,0	n_A = 6,5

Performance comparison between the Fw 190 D-11 and the new Ta 152. Although the Ta 152 possessed a superior performance, the Fw 190 D-11 offered certain advantages, for example less disruption to existing production.

Focke-Wulf Fw 190 "Long Nose" - An Illustrated History of the Fw 190D Series

8.2 Capsule Histories of the Other Fw 190 D-11 Prototypes

Fw 190 V58

Werknummer 170 933

Code GV+DF

First flight on 29 August 1944. On 1 September sent to the *E-Stelle Tarnewitz* for weapons trials. In Tarnewitz satisfactory results were achieved with experimental installations of one and two MG 151 cannon mounted in the fuselage in place of the MG 131s and synchronized to fire through the propeller disc. On 11 October the aircraft returned to Langenhagen. There Focke-Wulf mechanics replaced the engine and installed the latest modifications. The Fw 190 V58 was in Adelheide on 27 March 1945, probably for the last time, and on the same day was flown to Junkers Motorenbau in Dessau.

Fw 190 V59

Werknummer 350 156

Code TG+MH

First flight on 13 September 1944. On 24 September it was flown from Adelheide to Langenhagen. After logging just 1 hour and 39 minutes flight time, on 9 October the V59 was destroyed in a forced landing while being ferried to Jumo in Dessau (see crash photos). The experienced test pilot Dipl.Ing. Harry Schilling of Jumo took off from Langenhagen at 1136 hours. Four minutes after takeoff Schilling noticed a heavy smoke trail behind the aircraft and decided to put the aircraft down in a freshly-plowed field 10 km east of Langenhagen. In the ensuing crash-landing Harry Schilling was killed and the V59 was completely destroyed. It was discovered that a fractured oil line to the propeller regulator of the Jumo 213 F had caused this tragic accident.

Opposite
These photographs depict one of the Fw 190 D-11 prototypes (V55 or V56) during roll-out at the Adelheide prototype works. In the background is the Fw 190 V30/U1, GH+KT, the second prototype of the Ta 152 H high-altitude fighter.

Jumo test pilot Harry Schiller lost his life in the crash of the Fw 190 V59. (Sander)

The Fw 190 V59 was completely destroyed in an attempted force landing. (Sander)

Fw 190 V60

Werknummer 350 157

Code: TG+MI

First flight on 10 October 1944. On 21 October test pilot Bernhard Märschel flew the aircraft from Adelheide to Langenhagen. On 29 October the V60 went to Junkers Motorenbau in Dessau to replace the V59, which had been lost in a crash. There it was fitted with the Jumo 213 F1, which had a strengthened transmission. So equipped, the V60 achieved a maximum speed of 716 km/h at critical height of 9000 m. In mid-March 1945 the V60 was in the midst of an engine conversion.

Fw 190 V61

Werknummer 350 158

Code: VI+QM

The V61 was the last of the D-11 series prototypes. It entered testing on 14 October 1944 and the same day was flown from Adelheide to Langenhagen with test pilot Märschel at the controls. Focke-Wulf's famous chief test pilot, Hans Sander, flew the V61 at Langenhagen on 9 November before it was transferred to the *E-Stelle Rechlin* for flight trials on 19 November 1944.

The fates of all these prototypes remains a mystery. It has been suggested in several publications that the Fw 190 V58 was used operationally by the *Würgerstaffel* with the tactical code "Red 4". This is extremely unlikely, however, as Junkers did not begin engine trials with the aircraft until 27 March 1945. As well, according to a Focke-Wulf list of prototypes dated 18 Oct. 1944, it had two MG 131 machine-guns (like the D-9). More probable is the use of a production D-11 by the *Verbandführerschule der G.d.J.* (Unit Leaders School of the Commanding General Fighters), whose aircraft are known to have worn higher than usual aircraft numbers. An example of this is offered in Experten Decals No. 3, which includes side views and photographs of D-11 "Red 4", whose original tactical markings were "Chevron 58". It is known that the Fw 190 V55 was at Reinsehlen airfield (near Soltau) on 6 April 1945. It may have been blown up by German troops, together with the Fw 190 V18/U2, WNr. 0 040, CF+OY, the well-known Ta 152 H prototype, before the British occupied the airfield. The airfield in Reinsehlen would have been a treasure trove for any Fw 190/Ta 152 enthusiast on 6 April 1945, for Hans Sander noted the following experimental aircraft parked there:

Fw 190 V18/U2, code CF+OY, Werknummer 0 040, Ta 152 H prototype

Fw 190 V32/U2, code GH+KV, Werknummer 0 057, Ta 152 H-1 prototype

Ta 152 H-0, code CW+CD, Werknummer 150 004, Ta 152 H-0 pre-production aircraft

Fw 190 V55, code GV+CV, Werknummer 170 923, prototype Fw 190 D-11

Fw 190 V73, code TX+PQ, Werknummer 733 705, Fw 190 A-8 with Panzerblitz racks

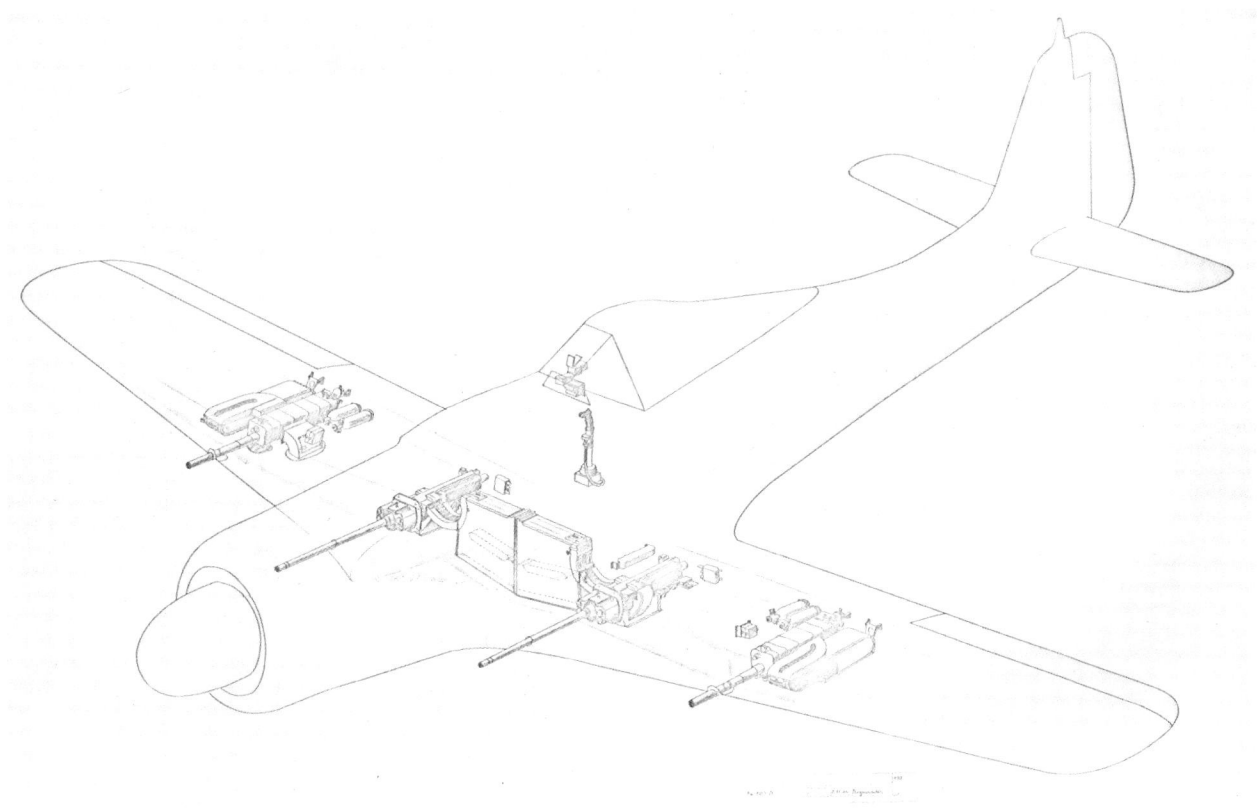

The armament of the Fw 190 D-11, consisting of two 20-mm cannon in the wing roots and two 30-mm weapons in the outer wings.

8.3 Report on Testing

The Fw 190 V55 to V61 prototypes logged a total of 53.2 flying hours by 27 December 1944. Testing was seriously delayed by the large number of engine failures experienced with the Jumo 213 F. The absence of cockpit pressurization made itself felt during high-altitude flights. Pilots experienced painful cramping in their limbs at heights above 11 000 meters, however these disappeared again on descent below 10 000 meters.

Based on the experienced gained by 27 December 1944, the Jumo 213 F was not considered ready for general service. In addition to engine failures described previously, some sort of engine problem was encountered on virtually every flight. In most cases the cause was not known, which meant that several pieces of equipment usually had to be replaced to eliminate the problem. The most serious technical problem was the so-called "supercharger surging", which was described in a previous chapter.

Below: At the end of the war several Fw 190 D-11s were captured virtually intact in Bad Wörrishofen. Here *Werknummer* 220 009 (White Double Chevron) is seen at the edge of a wood. Some Fw 190 D-11s had been flown out prior to the end of the war, as on 24 April, when Franz Bernhard, a former member of JGr. 10, ferried one such aircraft from Bad Wörrishofen to Schongau.

Bottom: Fw 190 D-11 "Chevron 61" at Bad Wörrishofen. Complete power plant units are visible in the background.

The wreck of "Chevron 61" at Bad Wörrishofen.

8.4 Further Development and Fw 190 D-11 Performance Enhancement

The Fw 190 V56 was used in various performance-enhancing experiments. In one, all gaps in the engine cowling were sealed with rubber. This measure, which was tested successfully using the Fw 190 D-9 *Werknummer* 210 002, TR+SB, resulted in a 17 km/h increase in maximum speed. This development resulted in a request for an engine cowling which was attached to the airframe instead of the engine. A roller chain was installed between the engine cowling and the fixed nose ring to secure the forward mounting. It was planned to introduce the airframe-mounted cowling with the introduction of the Jumo 213 EB engine for the Fw 190 D-11/D-12 and D-13 series. Junkers was to prepare the Jumo 213 EB for the new cowling from the outset. There were also plans to add the airframe-mounted cowling to the Ta 512 C and Ta 152 H to improve performance. By March 1945 a decision still had not been made on a Fw 190 D testbed, however the airframe-mounted cowling was tested with satisfactory results using a Ta 152 H, WNr. 150 004, the Ta 152 C V6, WNr. 110 006, and the Ta 152 C V7, WNr. 110 007.

Focke-Wulf was forced to alter its plans for the Fw 190 D-11 as a result of changes in planning by Jumo. Junkers proposed the following schedule for engine deliveries:

1.) Jumo 213 F engines with the low-pressure MW 50 system were to be delivered until approximately 1 March 1945. Emergency power was locked out in third gear and ventilation lines had to be installed to overcome supercharger surging.

2.) Deliveries of Jumo 213 F1 engines to begin approximately 1 March 1945. Emergency power again available in all gears and ventilation valve installed to eliminate supercharger surging.

A little girl sits peacefully in the cockpit of "Chevron 57". This aircraft, *Werknummer* 220 011, was also found at Bad Wörrishofen in nearly intact condition. Such high aircraft numbers were used by the Unit Leaders School of the Commanding General Fighters.

[3] R4M = Air-to-air rocket successfully used by the Me 262 A-1a jet fighter.

3.) These engines to be replaced by the Jumo 213 F1 engine with high-pressure MW 50 system beginning approximately 24 April 1945.

4.) The Jumo 213 EB with intercooler and Jumo annular radiator to be introduced approximately 1 June 1945.

The Fw 190 D-11 equipped with the Jumo 213 F1 and high-pressure MW 50 system was assigned the designation Fw 190 D-11/R20, while the Fw 190 D-11/R11 (bad weather fighter with *Rüstsatz 11*) was redesignated as the Fw 190 D-11/R21. In fact Focke-Wulf installed a high-pressure MW 50 system in the Fw 190 V56 and the aircraft was ready to fly on 7 March 1945. No test results are known to exist.

It was planned to retrofit the Fw 190 D-11 with racks for R4M[3] and *Panzerblitz* rockets, however the chaotic situation during the final months of the war prevented this from happening.

8.5 List of Fw 190 D-11 Prototypes

This table provides an overview of all prototypes which were built or converted for the Fw 190 D-11 series.

Prototype	Werk-Nr.	Code	First Flight	Purpose
Fw 190 V55	170 923	GV+CV	06/06/44	FW test-bed
Fw 190 V56	170 924	GV+CW	14/08/44	FW test-bed
Fw 190 V57	170 926	GV+CY	19/08/44	FW performance aircraft
Fw 190 V58	170 933	GV+DF	29/08/44	To Tarnewitz test-center on 01/09/44
Fw 190 V59	350 156	TG+MH	13/09/44	Jumo test-bed, lost on ferry flight on 09/10/44
Fw 190 V60	350 157	TG+MI	10/10/44	To Jumo, Dessau on 13/11/44
Fw 190 V61	350 158	VI+QM	14/10/44	To *E-Stelle Rechlin* on 19/11/44

CHAPTER NINE

The Fw 190 D-12/D-13 - The Fastest Doras Come too Late

The Fw 190 D-11 prototypes had already provided valuable information concerning the installation of the Jumo 213 F in the Fw 190 airframe. The next variants of the Fw 190 D were to possess a more powerful armament in keeping with RLM requirements. The result was the Fw 190 D-12 and D-13. These were the last two versions of the Fw 190 with the Jumo 213 engine and brought the type to its peak of performance.

9.1 New Requirements

Not until May 1944 did the *Luftwaffe* High Command issue a requirement for Focke-Wulf to install the Jumo 213 F engine with two-stage supercharger in the standard D-9 airframe. In May 1944 efforts to ready the Fw 190 D-9 for production were in full swing, and Focke-Wulf subsequently began planning a series of prototypes for the new D-11 series. The RLM viewed the installation of the new engine as low risk, for the

The restored Fw 190 D-13 in the Champlin Fighter Museum in the USA. (Sander)

performance of the Jumo 213 F at lower altitudes was identical to that of the Jumo 213 A with single-stage supercharger as installed in the Fw 190 D-9. By the autumn of 1944 Focke-Wulf had six prototypes of the new under variant test, but then the OKH suddenly changed its mind about the D-11.

Unlike the Jumo 213 A, the Jumo 213 F was designed to accommodate a centrally-mounted *Motorkanone* (20 or 30 mm). This led to the last two Jumo-engined variants, the Fw 190 D-12 and D-13. The production D-12 was to have been equipped with a 30-mm MK 108 *Motorkanone* and the D-13 with a 20-mm MG 151/20. Although Focke-Wulf had always intended for an engine-mounted cannon to from part of the D-series' armament, it was not until the adoption of the Jumo 213 F engine that this became possible. The originally-planned heavy armament of two additional fuselage weapons and cannon in the outer wings had to be abandoned out of weight considerations.

Copy of the Fw 190 D-12 Development Report dated 3 January 1945:

Subject: Fw 190 D-12 with Jumo 213 F

Task: <u>I. As part of the requested effort to improve performance, the Jumo 213 F engine is to be installed in the production Fw 190 D in place of the Jumo 213 A.</u>

To the extent possible, the installation of the 213 F engine is to based on that of the 213 A engine (9-8213 E) developed by Focke-Wulf; MW 50 injection is planned in place of the supercharger air cooler.

<u>II. Because of problems being encountered with overloading of tires (700 x 175), the planned strengthening of the Fw 190 D's central armament has now been established as:</u>

Production Fw 190 D-12
        Fuselage: 1 MK 151 engine-mounted cannon
        Wing roots: 2 MG 151

        Production Fw 190 D-13
        Fuselage: 1 MK 108 engine-mounted cannon
        Wing roots: 2 MG 151

These variants are to make up 50% of the entire program.

Note: Fuselage-mounted MG 131s deleted along with outer wing cannon.

III. It is planned to further increase the range of the D-12 series through the addition of unprotected fuel tanks.

1) Construction Drawings
(a) Preliminary engine drawings to Opel   by 8 Jun. 44
        Completion of design by Opel   July 1944

(b) Airframe Drawings by 30 Jun. 44
Addendum per Task II by 30 Aug. 44
Addendum per Task III by Nov. 44

2) Prototypes for I: 7 engine test-beds are being built by the Fw prototype works.

The aircraft are conversions of A-8s, <u>however installation of the engine cannon and associated airframe modifications are not being carried out.</u>

The <u>outer wing and fuselage armament</u> is to be removed.

The 115-l auxiliary tank is to be installed in all aircraft together with the MW 50 system.

1. V55, WNr. 170 923 ready to fly 6 Aug. 44
2. V56, WNr. 170 924 ready to fly 14 Aug. 44
3. V57, WNr. 170 926 ready to fly 19 Aug. 44
4. V58, WNr. 170 933 ready to fly 29 Aug. 44 (Tarnewitz)
5. V59, WNr. 350 156 ready to fly 13 Sept. 44 (crashed 9 Oct. 44)

<u>Committee 10 13 337</u>

6. V60, WNr. 350 157 ready to fly 10 Oct. – 13 Nov. Jumo
7. V61, WNr. 350 158 ready to fly 14 Oct. – 18 Nov. Rechlin

<u>Committee 10 13 338</u>

3) <u>Prototypes for II:</u> To be converted to the ultimate weapons standard are:

D-12 3 aircraft
D-13 2 aircraft converted from A-8s

<u>For D-12</u> 8. V62, WNr. 732 053 ready to fly Jan. 45 +
   9. V64, WNr. 730 254 ready to fly Jan. 45 +
   10. V63, WNr. 350 166 ready to fly 16 Oct – 11 Nov. Tarnewitz

<u>For D-13</u> 11. V65, WNr. 350 165 ready to fly 20 Oct. – 19 Nov. Tarnewitz
   12. V71, WNr. 350 167 ready to fly 15 Nov. – 9 Dec. Tarnewitz/Rechlin

(+ Completion delayed by shortages of engines and personnel, currently in final assembly.)

4) Series D-12/R11   Fieseler   Jan. 45
                      Arado   Feb. 45

    D-13/R11   Roland Arbg. Jan. 45

5) Delivery Standard:
    Power plant   Jumo 213 F (9-8213 H-1)
    Radios   FuG 16 ZY, 25, 125
    PKS 12 autopilot
    Heated windscreen
    MW 50 system installed in all aircraft
    From factory with ETC 504 under fuselage and 300-liter tank

    Revi EZ 42 see Dev. Report XV f 1,2 of 19 Oct. 44

6) Operating and servicing manuals are to be ready for the start of production.

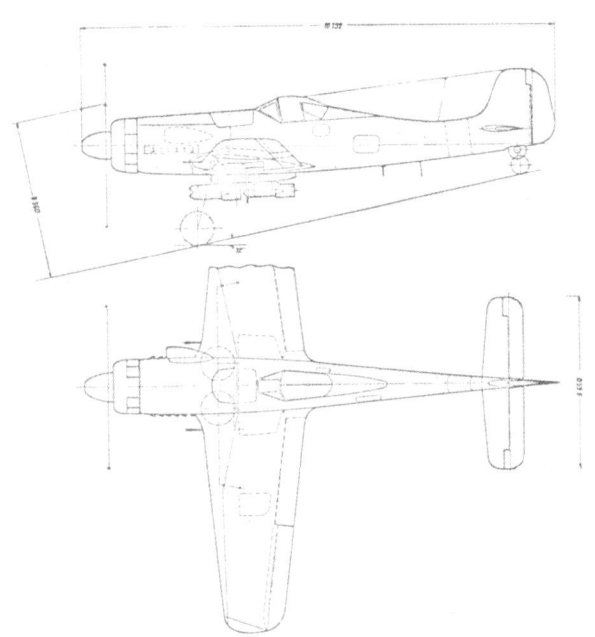

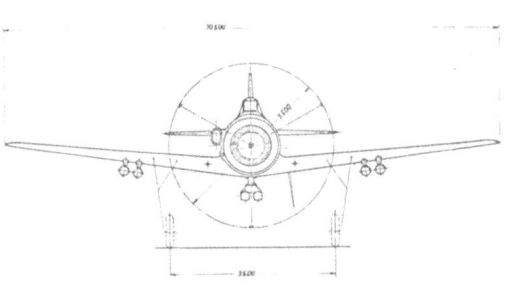

Schlachtflugzeug Fw 190 D-13 (Übersicht)
mit TSA 2 D-Anlage
Triebwerk: Jumo 213 E B

Focke-Wulf drawing of the Fw 190 D-13 CS fighter powered by the new Jumo 213 EB engine.

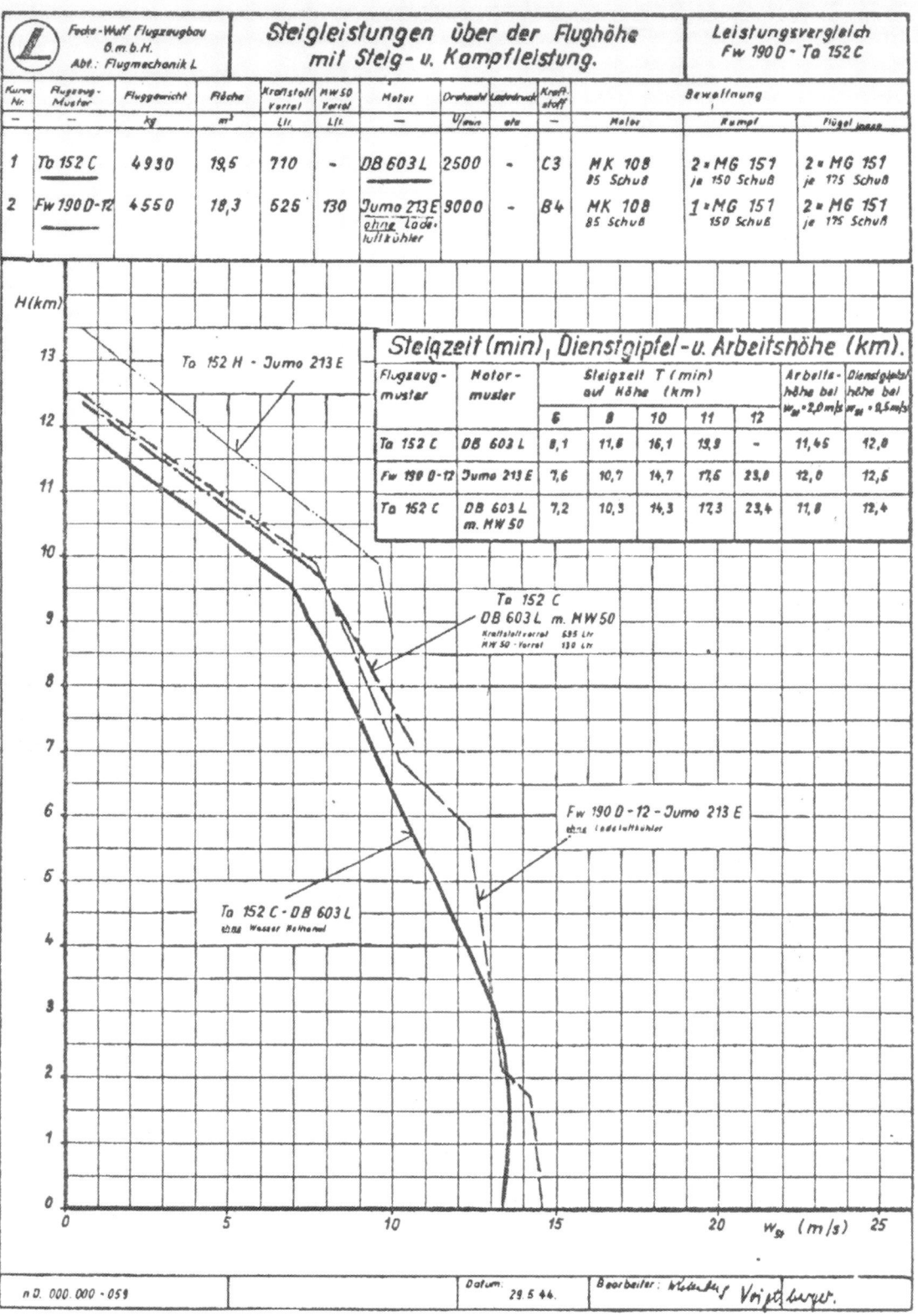

Graphic comparison of the rates of climb of the Fw 190 D-12 and the Ta 152 C.

Focke-Wulf Flugzeugbau G.m.b.H.
Abt.: Flugmechanik L

Horizontalgeschwindigkeit über der Flughöhe mit Steig- u. Kampfleistung.

Leistungsvergleich
Fw 190 D - Ta 152 C

Kurve Nr.	Flugzeug-Muster	Fluggewicht	Fläche	Kraftstoff Vorrat	MW 50 Vorrat	Motor	Drehzahl	Ladedruck	Kraftstoff	Bewaffnung Motor	Bewaffnung Rumpf	Bewaffnung Flügel innen
—	—	kg	m²	Ltr.	Ltr.	—	U/min	ata	—			
1	Ta 152 C	4930	19,5	710	-	DB 603 L	2500	-	C3	MK 108 85 Schuß	2 × MG 151 je 150 Schuß	2 × MG 151 je 175 Schuß
2	Fw 190 D-12	4550	18,3	525	130	Jumo 213 E ohne Ladeluftkühler	3000	-	B4	MK 108 85 Schuß	1 × MG 151 150 Schuß	2 × MG 151 je 175 Schuß

n.J. 000. 000 - 059 | Datum: 28.5.44. | Bearbeiter: Kolemberg Voigtsberger.

Vorteil: Nachdem der Leistungsgewinn durch Wasser-Methanol-Zusatz von der Firma Daimler-Benz auch für Steig- u. Kampfleistung als gesichert bezeichnet wird, ergeben sich für die Ta 152 über dem gesamten Höhenbereich bessere Flugleistungen gegenüber der Fw 190 D.

Bei der Fw 190 D mit 213 E ist ein Leistungsgewinn durch Wasser-Methanol nicht erzielbar, weil hier der Zusatz als ausschliesslicher Ersatz für die Ladeluftkühlung gebraucht wird.

Focke-Wulf Flugzeugbau G.m.b.H.

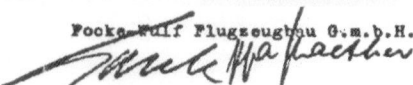

Graphic comparison of the maximum speeds of the Fw 190 D-12 and the Ta 152 C.

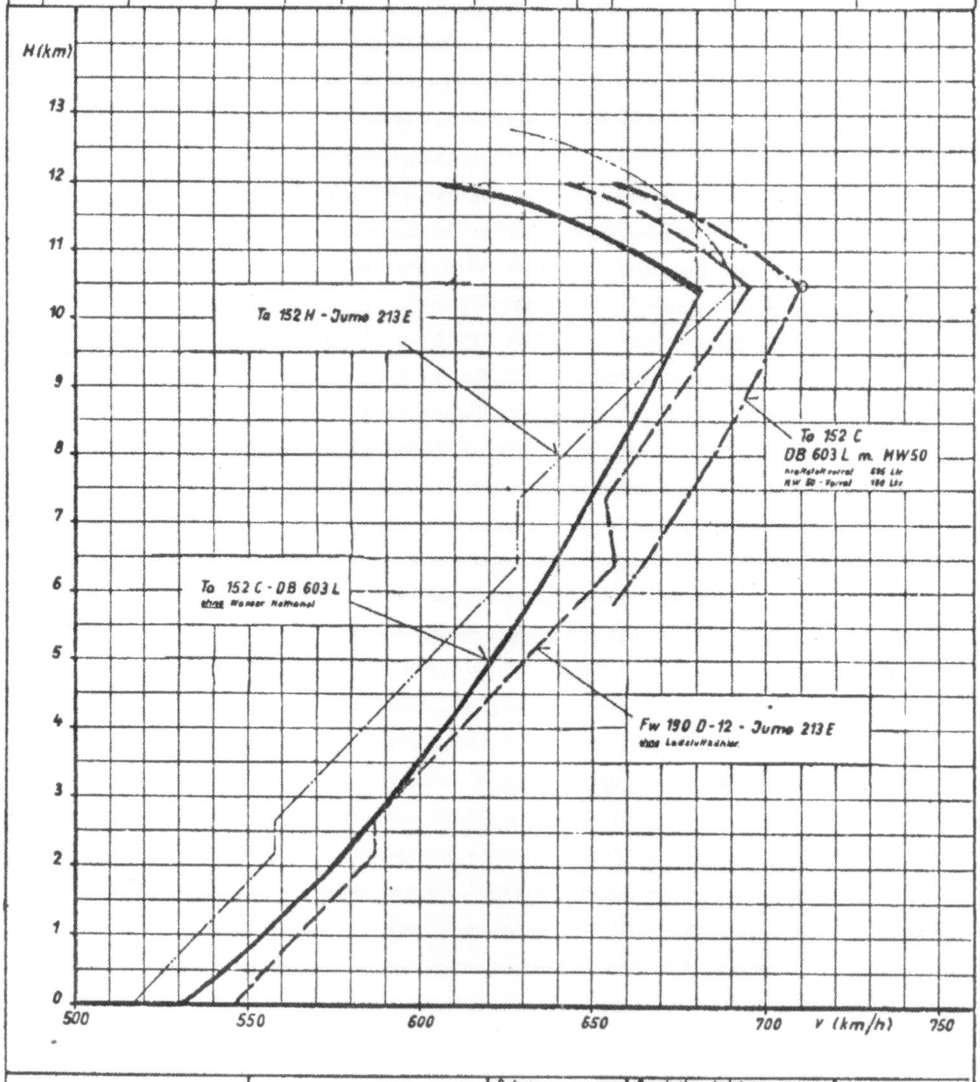

9.2 Prototypes for the new Variants

Focke-Wulf produced a total of five new prototypes for the Fw 190 D-12 and D-13. To assist in readying the Jumo 213 F for service use, Focke-Wulf included the prototypes of the cancelled Fw 190 D-11 in subsequent testing. Like the new D-12/D-13 prototypes, the seven D-11 prototypes had been converted from Fw 190 A-8 production aircraft. These seven prototypes lacked provision for the engine-mounted cannon and the associated airframe modifications, and the outer wing and fuselage-mounted weapons were removed. As well, in all cases the MW 50 system and 115-liter methanol-water tank had to be installed.

The focus of testing for the five new prototypes was the installation and operation of the centrally-mounted 20-mm or 30-mm cannon. The new *Motorkanone* had to made ready for service use. Two of the prototypes were therefore sent directly to the experimental weapons station in Tarnewitz. By that time, November 1944, there were growing problems at the prototype works in Adelheide. A shortage of personnel seriously hampered the construction of at least two prototypes by Focke-Wulf and there were further delays in testing. The two prototypes sent to Tarnewitz, the V63 and V65, were delivered with the old motor mounts, and the forward armored tubes for the *Motorkanone* were missing altogether. The *E-Stelle* subsequently had to request that all the missing parts be sent by courier.

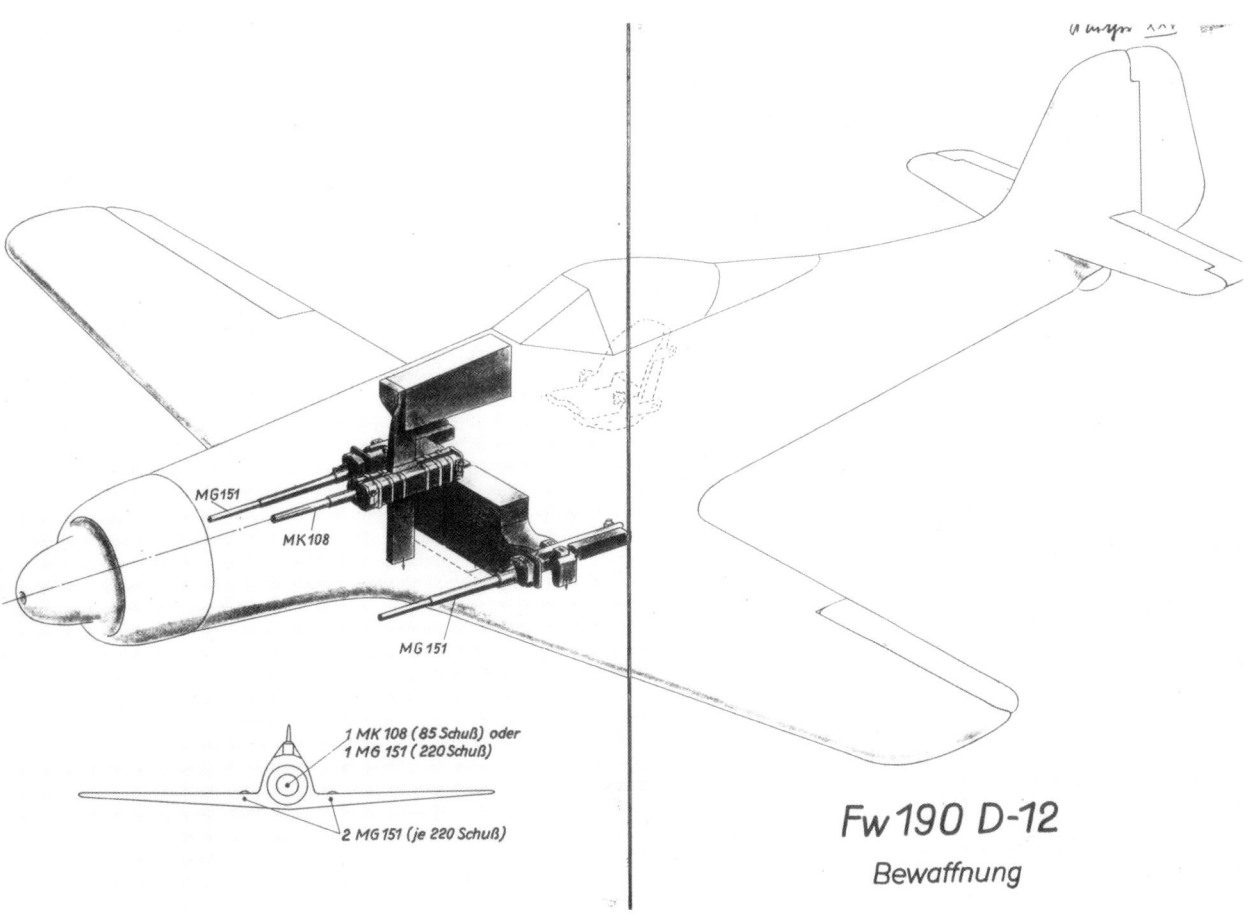

Armament of the Fw 190 D-12.

At the end of 1944 the engine which was to power the Fw 190 D-12/D-13 series, the Jumo 213 F with MW 50 injection, was still not ready for service. Like the earlier D-11 series, testing was handicapped by an engine still under development.

1.) Deliveries of Jumo 213 F engines with the low-pressure MW system (BNE system) were to continue until approximately 1 March 1945. For these engines use of emergency power in third gear was blocked and ventilation lines had to be installed to eliminate supercharger surging.

2.) Deliveries began on or about 1 March 1945 of Jumo 213 F1 engines cleared for use of emergency power and ventilation valve fitted to eliminate supercharger surging.

3.) From about 25 Apr. 1945 these engines were to be replaced in production by the Jumo 213 F1 engine with high-pressure MW system.

The Jumo 213 F's most serious problem, however, was its supercharger gearing, which was too weak. As a result, the first 200 Jumo 213 E/F engines to be delivered encountered problems in the high range (see Chapter 9.4 Problems with the Jumo 213 F).

9.3 The New Prototypes

The following summary provides a brief examination of the prototypes for the Fw 190 D-12 and D-13 planned and actually built by Focke-Wulf. All information is taken from official documents.

Fw 190 V62
Experimental Fw 190 D-12
Werknummer 732 053
Manufacturer's code SQ+DQ
First flown by test pilot Bernhard Märschel at Adelheide on 20 January 1945 (2 flights). On 24 February the V62 was transferred to the Junkers Motorenbau in Dessau where it was fitted with the latest Jumo 213 F-1 engine with strengthened supercharger gearing. The aircraft was to be used to test the new engine and the hydraulic MW 50 system. A shortage of personnel seriously hampered Junkers' efforts, nevertheless work was almost complete at the end of March 1945. Speed measurements were planned using takeoff, combat and emergency power at various altitudes up to 10000 meters.

The Fw 190 V65 was captured by the Allies intact at Travemünde at the end of the war.

Fw 190 V63

Experimental Fw 190 D-12
Werknummer 350 166
Manufacturer's code CS+IB

Aircraft ready to fly at Adelheide on 16 October 1944. First test flight by Bernhard Märschel on 20 October. After three more test flights at Adelheide, on 1 November 1944 Märschel flew the V63 to Langenhagen. There, on 1 November, it was test-flown by chief pilot Hans Sander before being transferred to the Weapons Test Center at Tarnewitz. The first official mention of the V63 in Tarnewitz appears in Weekly Report 46/44 dated 18 November. At that time the V63's armament consisted of one engine-mounted MK 108, one fuselage-mounted MG 151 and one MG 151 in each wing root. The engine's thrust line was minus 52 min., as a result of which the downward adjustment range of the weapons in the wing roots was incompatible with that of the engine-mounted cannon. Consequently the engine had to be realigned.

Fw 190 V64

Experimental Fw 190 D-12
Werknummer 730 254
Manufacturer's code SD+VM (probably)

Scheduled to begin testing in January 1945. Like the V62, final assembly of the V64 was seriously hampered by the shortage of personnel in the prototype shop. Virtually nothing is known about this aircraft. No mention of it appears in the log books of Hans Sander or Bernhard Märschel. The aircraft was transferred to Salzwedel on 14 February 1945. An entry in the log book of Rechlin test pilot Baist on 23 March 1945 makes reference to a Fw 190 D-12 with the manufacturer's code SD+VM. In all likelihood this was the Fw 190 V64.

The Fw 190 V65, prototype for the Fw 190 D-13, discovered at the end of the war.

Fw 190 V65
Experimental Fw 190 D-13
Werknummer 350 165
Manufacturer's code CS+IA
Ready to fly on 20 October 1944. Bernhard Märschel made the first flight in the aircraft at Adelheide on 13 November, followed by test flights on 16 and 17 November. On 19 November the V65 was transferred to the *E-Stelle Tarnewitz*, like the V63 nine days earlier. The *E-Stelle* complained that the Fw 190 V65 also lacked the positive engine position (+ 1 deg.) required to enable the cannon in the wing roots to be adjusted properly. When weapons trials began at the beginning of December, the engine-mounted cannon displayed a tendency to jam. The weapons mounted in the wing roots performed satisfactorily. Later reports also made reference to the problem of aligning the wing root weapons.

Unlike all the other prototypes, the fate of the Fw 190 V65 is known: it was captured in Travemünde at the end of the war.

Fw 190 V71
Experimental Fw 190 D-13
Werknummer 350 167
Manufacturer's Code CS+IC
Ready to fly on 15 November 1944. Test pilot Märschel flew the V71 twice at Adelheide on 17 November. On 10 December the Fw 190 V71 was transferred to the *E-Stelle Rechlin* for testing.

In the last known development report for the Fw 190 D-12/D13 series dated 3 January 1945, Focke-Wulf was not able to give any concrete information as to when the Fw 190 V62 and V64 would be ready to fly.

Table of Fw 190 D-12/D-13 Prototypes

Prototype	Series	WNr.	Code	Ready to Fly	First Flight	Remarks
Fw 190 V62	D-12	732 053	SQ+DQ	20/01/45	20/01/45	Transferred to Jumo in Dessau on 24/02/454 for engine trials.
Fw 190 V63	D-12	350 166	CS+IB	16/10/44	19/10/44	Transferred to the E-Stelle Tarnewitz for weapons trials on 10/11/44.
Fw 190 V64	D-12	730 254	SD+VM	01/45		Not yet under test on 27/12/44. Transferred to Salzwedel on 14/2/45.
Fw 190 V65	D-13	350 165	CS+IA	20/10/44	13/11/44	To the E-Stelle Tarnewitz on 19/11/44. Captured in Travemünde.
Fw 190 V71	D-13	350 167	CS+IC	15/11/44	17/11/44	To the E-Stelle Rechlin on 10/12/44 for flight tests.

Both prototypes were still in the final assembly stage in January 1945. The delays in the completion of the two prototypes were caused by the non-availability of engines and the acute shortage of personnel. At that late stage of the war even skilled workers were being called away for military service.

The first mention of the Fw 190 V62 in a log book was by Bernhard Märschel on 20 January 1945 at Adelheide. Märschel, Hans Sander and *Obfw.* Friedrich Schnier were Focke-Wulf's last three test pilots. Unfortunately. Friedrich Schnier's log book has been lost, consequently it is impossible to provide a complete description of the last Focke-Wulf prototypes.

With the exception of the Fw 190 V65, which was captured in Travemünde, the fates of the Fw 190 D-12/D-13 series prototypes are not known.

9.4 Problems with Jumo 213 F

The Fw 190 D-9 and its Jumo 213 A engine represented a significant advance in German fighter performance. The Fw 190 D-12 and D-13, which were powered by the Jumo 213 F engine, offered a further increase in performance. With its two-stage, three-speed supercharger, the Jumo 213 F developed 2,100 h.p. for takeoff using MW 50 boost (special emergency power) and 1,750 h.p. at 6000 meters. The supercharger gearing

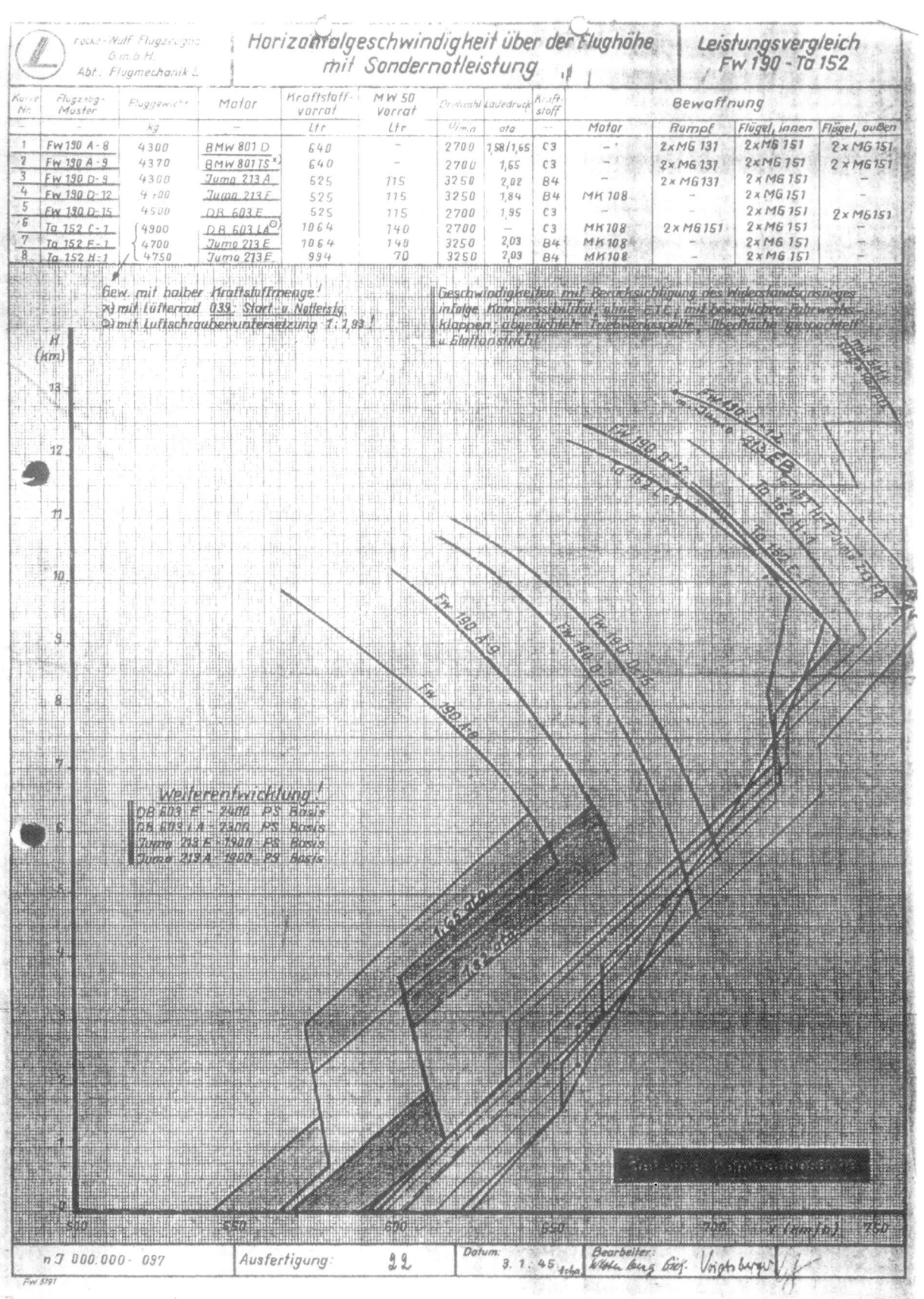

proved too weak in the first 200 engines, consequently special emergency power had to blocked for third gear. This meant that special emergency power was only available to 6000 meters, above which performance was similar to the Jumo 213 A. This situation did not change until the introduction of the Jumo 213 F-1, which had more robust gearing and could be operated with no restrictions. Of the original 200 engines, 100 were supposed to have been converted to F-1 standard by the Junkers technical field service.

There was another problem. As the radiator of the Fw 190 D-12/D-13 was designed too small, in high-speed flight the cooling gills had to be opened slightly (15% of streamlined position). According to Jumo, this resulted in a speed loss of 20 km/h at altitude. This limitation would not be eliminated until introduction of the Jumo 213 EB, which had supercharger air cooling and which could fit into the airframe of the Fw 190 D-12 with only minor modifications. The Jumo 213 EB was also expected to produce an additional 200 h.p., which according to the manufacturer would result in a further speed increase of 20 km/h. Introduction of the Jumo 213 EB in the Fw 190 D-12 series and the new Ta 152 H was expected to take place in June 1945. The resulting version of the D-12, designated the Fw 190 D-12/R25, would have been in the same speed class (in excess of 750 km/h) as the latest Allied fighter aircraft, such as the P-47 M Thunderbolt and the Supermarine Spitfire F. 21. Focke-Wulf estimated that the D-12 would be capable of 770 km/h at a height of 9500 meters. Estimated maximum speed at low level was 613 km/h. The D-12 would thus have been the fastest piston-engined fighter produced in Germany, surpassing even the Ta 152 H.

The conversion to the Jumo 213 EB engine would have been accompanied by adoption of a 130-liter MW 50 tank in the fuselage. It was also planned to modify the D-series to accommodate four bag-type fuel tanks in the wings. Six bag tanks, as carried by the Ta 152 H, was not possible for reasons of cost and tire load. After the adoption of bag tanks, the MW 50 fluid would have been housed in the inner left bag tank. With the extra fuel capacity the Fw 190 D-9/R25 would have had a maximum range of 1705 km. All of these changes were in plans for the future, however, which were brought to an abrupt end by the rapidly approaching end of the war.

9.5 Production

The new Fw 190 D-12 and D-13 variants were supposed to enter production in January 1945. Production start-up was scheduled as follows:

Fw 190 D-12/R11 by Fieseler in January and Arado in February 1945
Fw 190 D-13/R11 by the Roland Consortium in January 1945

Opposite
This performance sheet dated 3 January 1945 illustrates the tremendous performance of the Fw 190 D-12 with the Jumo 213 EB engine. The speed curve for the Fw 190 D-12 does not even fit onto the page any more.

This target for the start of production could not be met, even though it had been announced in the Focke-Wulf development report of 3 January 1945. The dismal military situation resulted in production of both variants being delayed until March 1945. The RLM blamed Focke-Wulf for the delay, citing its failure to deliver construction drawings to the companies which were to build the types under license. Production of the Jumo 213 F was also delayed. While in January 20 engines had been delivered, in February it was only three.

On 9 January 1945 there was a meeting with Daimler Benz at Fieseler in Kassel. Daimler Benz wanted to determine if thirty Fw 190 D-12 airframes were available for conversion to Fw 190 D-14 standard. It was told that the first Fw 190 D-12 would not be completed until late January-early February at the earliest. Fieseler was unable to offer any further dates for the other 29 Fw 190 D-12s. It must be assumed that the situation worsened as Germany's fortunes declined. It is therefore likely that only a handful of aircraft were completed by war's end. One such machine, Fw 190 D-13 *Werknummer* 836 017, was captured at the end of the war. The Fw 190 D-13 first appears in the aircraft distribution plans of the *Gen.Qu. 6 Abt.* in March 1945. According to this, just two Fw 190 D-13s were delivered to the units that month. There is no reference in the report to any Fw 190 D-12.

When the war ended the Allies discovered ample evidence that the Fw 190 D-12/D-13 series was on the verge of entering production. At Weser Flugzeugbau, for instance, the Allies discovered 30 complete Fw 190 D-12 fuselages. The two factories producing the D-12 and D-13 were designed for an output of 200 completed fuselages per month. 7,000 workers were employed in the two factories.

Soll-Zahlen nach LP 227

Baureihe	Verw. Zweck	Motor	Firma	1945							
				1	2	3	4	5	6	7	8
Fw 190 D-11	J	8213 H-1	FW	40	140	230	50	--	--	--	
Fw 190 D-12/R11	J	8213 H-1	GFW	30	70	140	220	210	...	...	
			ArW	--	50	100	160	240	...	...	
Fw 190 D-13/R11	J	8213 H-1	WFG	30	70	180	200	200	...	...	

FW - Focke-Wulf   GFW - Fieseler Werke   ArW - Arado Werke   WFG - Arbeitsgemeinschaft

The Fw 190 D-12/D-13 - The Fastest Doras Come too Late

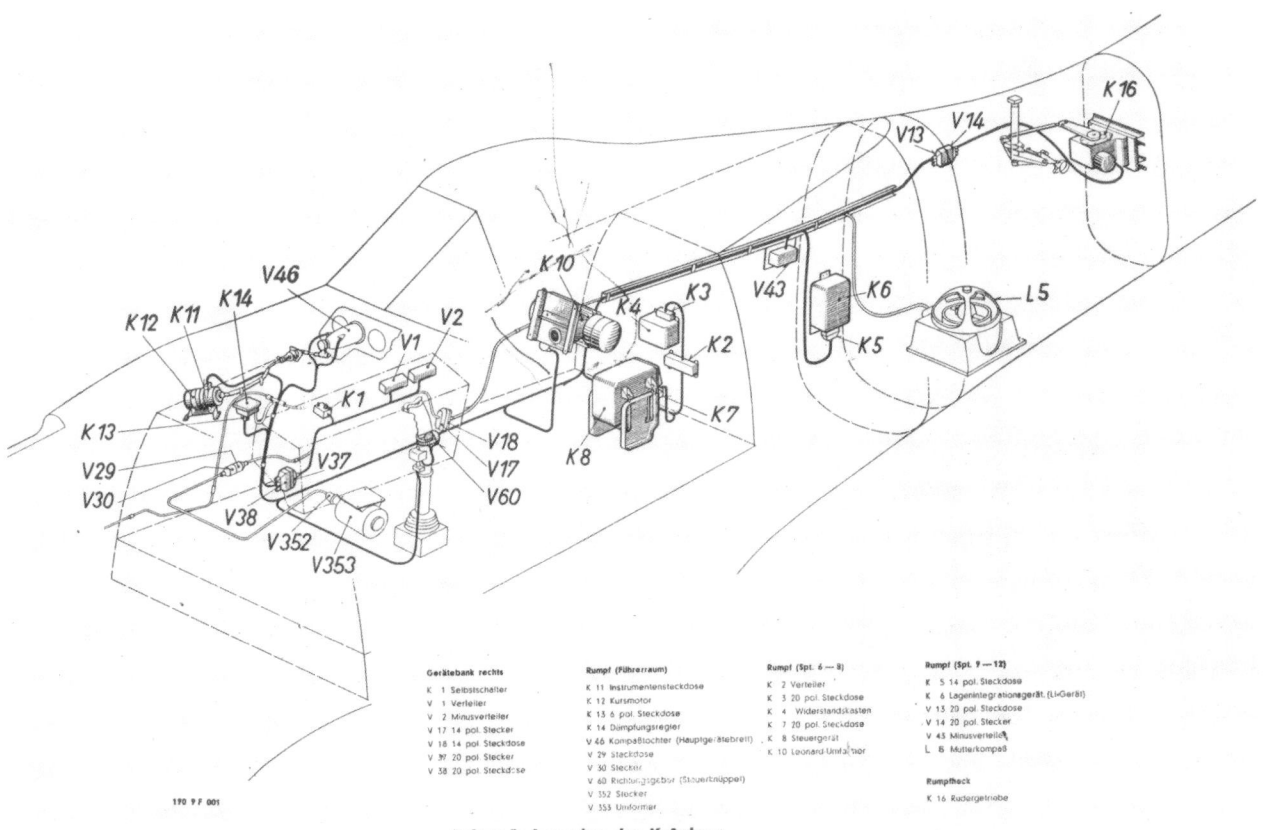

Anlage 1: Lageplan der K-Anlage

According to the Central Aircraft Committee's Delivery Plan 227 dated 11 January 1945, planned production figures for the Focke-Wulf Fw 190 D-11 to Fw 190 D-13/R11 were as follows:

As well, the series was to be fitted with *Rüstsatz R11* from the beginning. This bad-weather equipment set consisted of the PKS 12 autopilot, backup turn-and-bank indicator, heated windscreen and FuG 125 radio. The Patin autopilot was a single-axis type, controlling the rudder only and thus easing the pilot's workload in instrument conditions, as when climbing or descending through cloud. The so-called "Turn Control" was the only control for the pilot. This device had a double-pole toggle switch for engaging and disengaging the system, and a double-pole, five-position switch with a central position and two positions to the left and right for initiating an automatic turn at a selected rate (1 or 2 degrees per second). The elevators and ailerons were operated manually.

The PKS 12 autopilot was discovered during restoration of the sole surviving Fw 190 D-13, *Werknummer* 836 017, which is on display today in the Champlin Fighter Museum.

This illustration depicts the complete autopilot system. The turn control describe in the text (V60) is located on the stick grip. The mechanism which controlled the rudder (K 16) was discovered during the restoration of "Yellow 10". This confirmed without a doubt that the aircraft was a Fw 190 D-13/R11.

9.6 Comparison Flight between the Fw 190 D-13 and the Hawker Tempest

The performance of the Fw 190 D-13 was demonstrated in a mock combat with a Hawker Tempest of the RAF which took place shortly after the end

"Yellow 10" of JG 26 (below) was captured toward the end of the war. *Major* Lange (above) flew this aircraft in a mock combat against a Hawker Tempest of the RAF on 25 June 1945.

of the war. The performance of the Tempest was close to that of the Spitfire. Powered by a Napier Sabre II engine rated at 2,180 h.p., the Tempest had a maximum speed of 697 km/h at 5400 meters. How this mock combat came about is best described by the German pilot who flew the Fw 190 D-13. Dr. Heinz Lange was then a *Major* in the *Luftwaffe* and had commanded the fighter wing JG 51 at the end of the war. His recollections of these events are repeated here:

The date was 28 April 1945. I had only recently assumed command of the Jagdgeschwader "Mölders" and had flown back to East Prussia, where the I. and III. Gruppe and the Stabsstaffel were located. There all my efforts to get these elements of the Geschwader back were in vain: the I. Gruppe was disbanded, elements were incorporated into the III. Gruppe, while all remaining personnel were supposed to go to the army.

I nevertheless managed to get a large part of the membership of the Geschwader back to Swinemünde. From there, on 28 April we proceeded to Schmolow in Pomerania, where we rejoined the IV. Gruppe, our air signals company and the elements of the Stabsstaffel which had remained there. At that airfield we took on strength several Fw 190 D-9s. This type was the best the Luftwaffe had to offer, apart from the Me 262.

The D-9 was somewhat longer because of its Jumo 213 engine and the annular radiator in front of it. From the front the aircraft appeared to have a radial engine. It was somewhat inferior to other versions of the Fw 190 in a turn, but it had an outstanding rate of climb. It also had an excellent turn of speed in level flight. There was no opportunity to test-fly the aircraft, for we had to move again the next day, to Nebenlübke.

Over Neubrandenburg we encountered four Soviet La 7s. In the ensuing engagement Oberfeldwebel Rauch, formerly of the Stabsstaffel, who had recently been awarded the Knight's Cross, shot down one of the enemy aircraft for the unit's last victory.

With this victory, IV. Gruppe had shot down 115 enemy aircraft against just five losses in the final three weeks of the war, or since the start of the Battle of Berlin. On 30 April we moved to Redlin near Parchim. On 1 May we flew a mission over Schwerin and Berlin. Oberfeldwebel Marquardt and Oberfeldwebel Buss were lost in this engagement – this time our opponents were Spitfires. Heinz Marquardt survived the war and later became an Oberstleutnant in the Bundeswehr. We never heard any more of Oberfeldwebel Buss.

On 2 May we were transferred to Flensburg. This was my last flight in the Fw 190 D-9 during the war, but not my last flight in this wonderful machine. We were interned by the English. Then, on 25 June 1945, almost two months after the surrender, our colleagues of the Royal Air Force proposed a fly-off between our Dora 9 and one of the Hawker Tempests stationed in Flensburg. The Tempest was just about the best English piston-engined fighter, but having been stationed in the east we had never encountered the type.

The ammunition was removed from my aircraft – of course – and the tanks were filled with just enough fuel for a half-hour flight. And then up we went. I was assigned an area near Husum and a maximum altitude of 3000 meters. A dogfight was held in this area, I in the Dora 9 and a Canadian pilot in the Royal Air Force Tempest. We flew as in wartime, and after some time I succeeded in outclimbing the Tempest and engaged it in a turning fight from above.

Of course our pilots and ground crews, some of whom were able to observe the spectacle from the ground, were enthusiastic about the outcome. After landing we had an exchange of technical thoughts with the British. Prior to this they hadn't spoken to us much, as there was a ban on fraternization.

This bought my career as a fighter pilot to an end. Even though I and my comrades of JG 51 Mölders only flew the Fw 190 D-9 a few times and therefore are unable to offer a more detailed assessment of its qualities, I will never forget that we found the machine fantastic and tried to find suitable words of praise like those which Adolf Galland used after flying the Me 262 for the first time: "It was if an angel was pushing".

Designation	Fw 190 D-13	Hawker Tempest Mk V[9]
Purpose	*Fighter, fighter-bomber*	*Fighter, fighter-bomber*
Empty weight	3,490 kg	4,082 kg
Takeoff weight	4,440 kg	5,216 kg
Wingspan	10.50 m	12.50 m
Length	10.20 m	10.27 m
Height	3.36 m	4.90 m
Wing area	18.30 m²	28.05 m²
Wing loading	242 kg/m²	179 kg/m²
Power plant	Junkers Jumo 213 F-1	Napier Sabre IIA, B or C
Takeoff power	2,050 HP	2,180 HP
Fuel	B4/87 Octane	100 Octane
Fuel capacity	525 l + 140 l MW 50	1,146 l (252 gal. total)
Range	745 km	1,191 km
Range with auxiliary tanks	1,250 km[10]	2,462 km
Speed at low level	572 km/h 608 km/h with MW50	605 km/h
Maximum speed	738 km/h	695 km/h
at maximum boost altitude	11.5 km	5.24 km
Rate of climb at ground level	22 m/s	22.25 m/s
Time to climb to 3000 m	3.6 min	2.8 min (3,050 m)
Time to climb to 6000 m	7.6 min[11]	6.55 min (6,100 m)
Time to climb to 8000 m	10.7 min	14.0 min (9,150 m)
Time to climb to 10000 m	14.7 min	23.15 min (10,360 m)
Service ceiling	12.8 km	11.125 km
Armament	2 x MG 151/20, 1 x 30mm Mk108	4 x 20mm Hispano MkII cannon
Bomb load	max. 500 kg	2 x 454 kg

[9] The Tempest performance data come from Boscombe Down tests of JN 731 in March 1944.
[10] With 300-l fuel tank under fuselage.
[11] At combat power.

Opposite
Top: Hawker Tempest fighter of the RAF.

Bottom: Before it was shipped to the USA, the Fw 190 D-13 "Yellow 10" was given the transfer number USA 14. It was later assigned the code FE-118.

In fact, later research determined that the aircraft flown by *Major* Lange in the simulated combat against the Tempest had been the Fw 190 D-13 "Yellow 10", *Werknummer* 836 017. It was also found that another German pilot had been permitted to fly "Yellow 10" after the war. Oblt. Günther Josten, who later rose to the rank of *Oberst* in the *Bundeswehr*, flew the Fw 190 D-13 on the same day. In his diary he wrote: "I never would have thought it possible. Today I was allowed to test fly a Focke-Wulf Fw 190 D-13 for the Americans. Wonderful! Something pleasant to do for a change. I enjoyed it immensely."

Author's Note: It is an established fact that there was little to choose between the Fw 190 D-13 and the Fw 190 D-9 at a height of 3000 meters, the approximate altitude at which the mock combat took place. With the

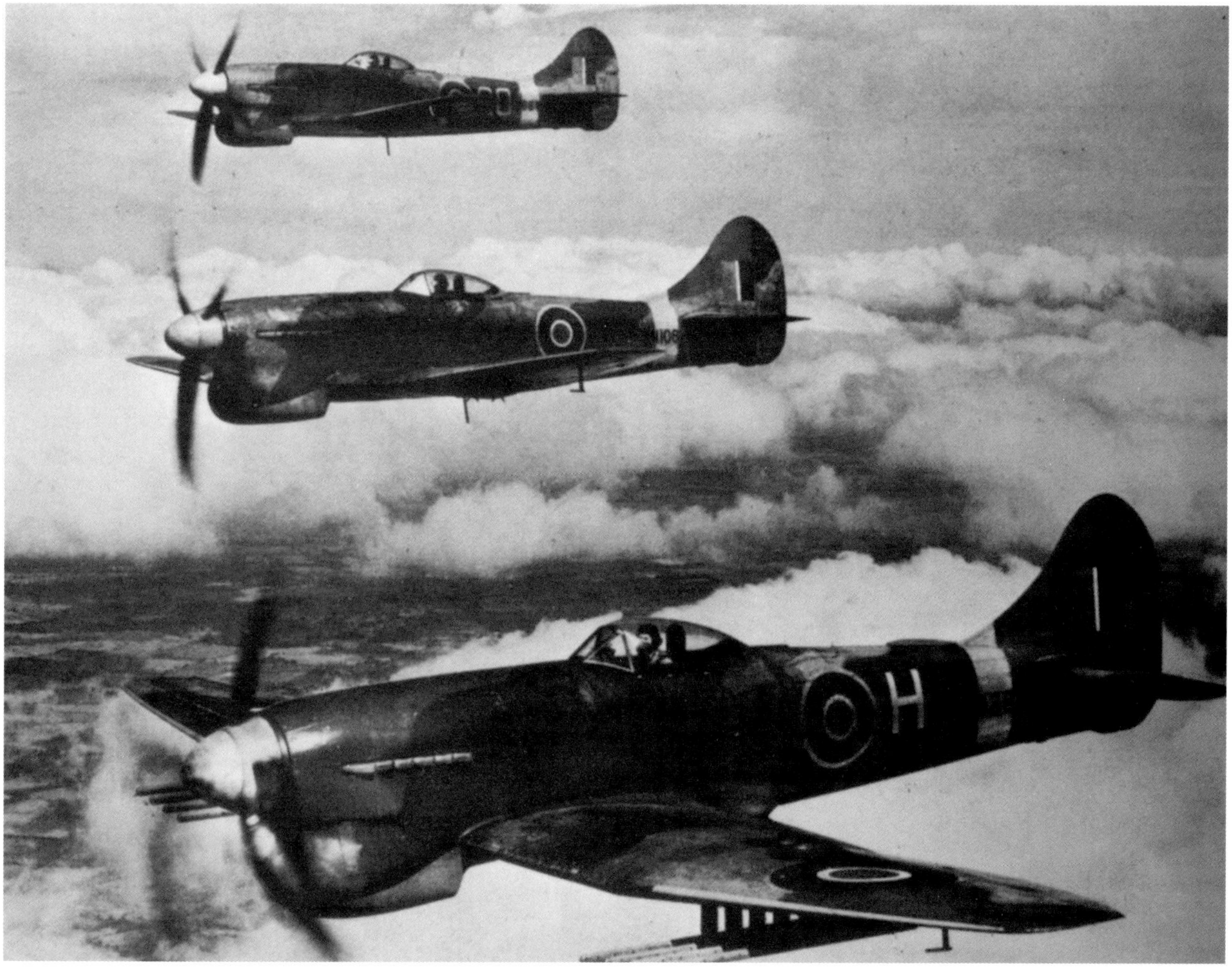

The Fw 190 D-12/D-13 - The Fastest Doras Come too Late

161

supercharger in low gear, the ratings of the two engines were almost identical. The D-13's more efficient propeller may have given it a speed advantage of 15 km/h compared to the standard D-9 (as determined by the *E-Stelle Rechlin*). It is also surprising that the German aircraft was able to prevail in the simulated combat without MW 50 injection for its Jumo 213 F engine.

The performance comparison between the Tempest and the D-13 shows that the Fw 190 D-13 was somewhat slower than the British fighter at low level. Only through the use of MW 50 injection was the D-13 able to match the Tempest. As altitude increased, however, the D-13's speed advantage became more pronounced, due to the superior high-altitude characteristics of the Jumo 213 F engine.

The Fw 190 D-13 was spared the fate that awaited most German aircraft at the end of the war. Instead of being scrapped it was transported to the USA for testing aboard the British aircraft carrier HMS Reaper. Many of the captured aircraft were later forgotten. They were either stored or languished in corners of American airfields. It is believed that the Focke-Wulf was donated to the Technical University in Atlanta, Georgia.

Almost twenty years later, in 1966, the D-13 was purchased by Lloyd Freeman. Then, in 1970, Dave Kyte bought the aircraft. He began the fist effort to restore the D-13 in Santa Barbara, however illness forced him to abandon his plans and the aircraft was sold to Doug Champlin. Champlin sent the D-13 back to Germany for restoration. After two and a half years of painstaking effort by the small Seebauer Company owned by Art and Christa Williams, the Fw 190 D-13 was completely restored. No less an authority than Kurt Tank served as an advisor on the project. Many parts were missing, such as control surfaces, propeller and most of the instruments. The advantage of restoring the aircraft in Germany and replicating parts there was the use of the metric system.

"Yellow 10", seen here wearing the American star and the transfer number USA 14.

The Fw 190 D-12/D-13 - The Fastest Doras Come too Late

Above: Yellow 10 today in the Champlin Fighter Museum. (Wildmoser)

Left and below: The Fw 190 D-13 in 1966. The wings have been removed and the fuselage rests on jacks on the floor of a hangar.

After approximately 5600 hours work, on 26 March 1976 the D-13 was returned to America. It was repainted as "Yellow 10" and bore the "Ace of Spades" emblem of JG 53. Experts believe that Major Franz Götz initially flew this machine as *Kommodore* of JG 26, after which it was transferred to JG 51 (Götz retained the "Ace of Spades" emblem in memory of his earlier service with JG 53). Once painted, the aircraft was put on display in the Champlin Fighter Museum in Mesa, Arizona. "Yellow 10" is still there today. At present it is undergoing further restoration work. It has been discovered that the wings are something less than an exact fit. It turns out that the wings were mixed up during the time the machine was in storage.

Pages 165-166
An attempt was made to restore the D-13 in 1971. Here the aircraft has been partly disassembled at Santa Barbara airport.

Two more photographs depicting *Werknummer* 836017 in poor condition. In contrast to the fuselage, the Jumo 213 F engine appears to be in excellent condition. (Weber)

These two close-up photographs of the Fw 190 D-13 during restoration provide an excellent view of the Jumo 213 F. As may be seen, not a millimeter was wasted in installing the engine in the production airframe.

Two close-ups of the Jumo 213 F.

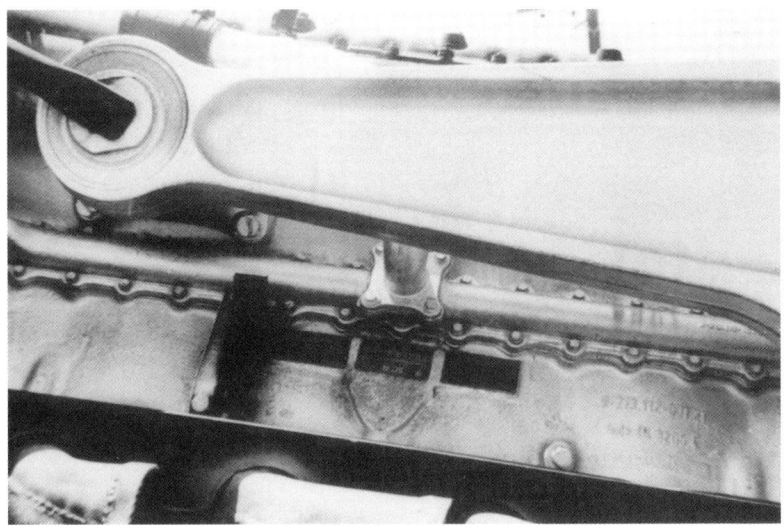

These three photographs depict the Jumo 213 F from above, the incomplete tail assembly and the port engine bearer with the attached engine block with manufacturer's plate.

Planned Equipment Sets (Rüstsätze) for the Fw 190 D-12 and D-13

Fw 190 D-12

R1   Original designation for the Fw 190 D-13 with engine-mounted MG 151/20
R5   Four protected fuel tanks in the wings with MW 50 high-pressure system in fuselage
R11 Bad-weather equipment consisting of PKS 12, FuG 125, heated windscreen and backup turn-and-bank indicator
R14 Torpedo aircraft with Schloss 504 for carriage of LT 1 B torpedo
R20 MW 50 high-pressure system installed
R21 MW 50 high-pressure system with PKS 12 autopilot, FuG 125, heated windscreen and backup turn-and-bank indicator
R25 With Jumo 213 EB (only in Fw 190 D-12 with MK 108). MW 50 high-pressure system in wing, 140-l auxiliary fuel tank in fuselage

Fw 190 D-13

R5   Four protected fuel tanks in the wings with MW 50 high-pressure system in fuselage
R11 Bad-weather equipment consisting of PKS 12, FuG 125, heated windscreen and backup turn-and-bank indicator
R21 MW 50 high-pressure system with PKS 12 autopilot, FuG 125, heated windscreen and backup turn-and-bank indicator

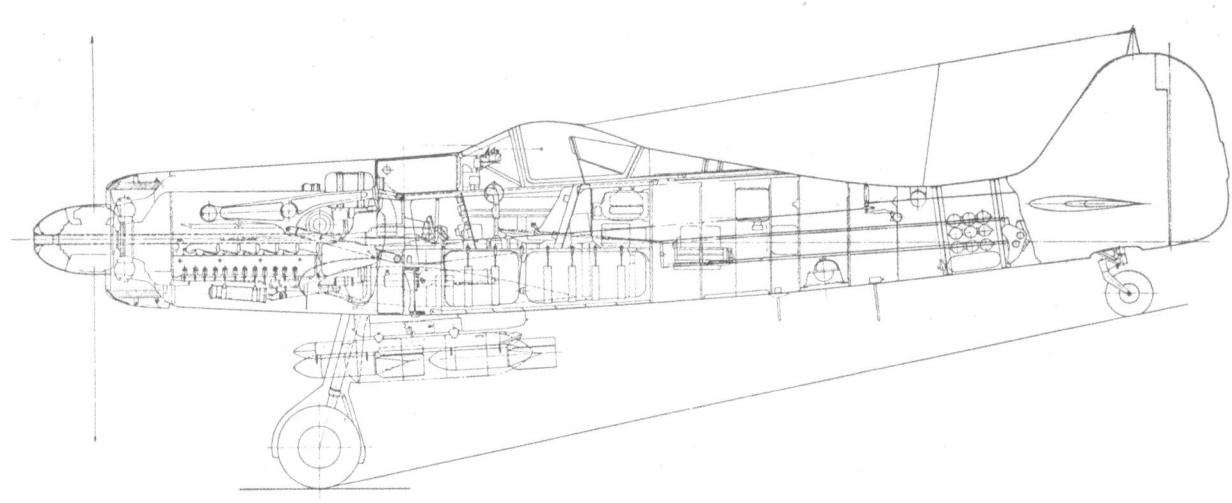

Schlachtflugzeug Fw 190 D-13 (Längsschnitt)
mit TSA 2 D-Anlage
Triebwerk: Jumo 213 E B

Planned close-support variant of the Fw 190 D-13 powered by the Jumo 213 EB. (Focke-Wulf)

9.7 The Focke-Wulf Fw 190 D-12/R14

On 30 December 1944 Focke-Wulf concluded an intensive study to determine the suitability of various versions of the Fw 190 and Ta 152 for the role of torpedo-carrier. The sub-types that were included in the study were the Fw 190 F-8, F-9, D-9, D-12 and the Ta 152 C-1.

The study concluded that under the existing conditions the Fw 190 D-9 was most suitable. As a result, it was decided to install a torpedo rack designed by MWN of Neubrandenburg on a Fw 190 D-9 for trials. As production of the Fw 190 D-9 was supposed to end in May 1945, the Fw 190 D-12 was proposed as a replacement. The Jumo 213 F high-altitude engine was poorly suited for this role, therefore it was proposed that the proven Jumo 213 A, which was still in production, be installed in the torpedo-carrier instead. The planned installation of four additional fuel tanks with a combined capacity of 310 liters would have increased the torpedo-carrier's radius of action considerably. The wing tank system could also have been replaced by the *Doppelreiter* system.

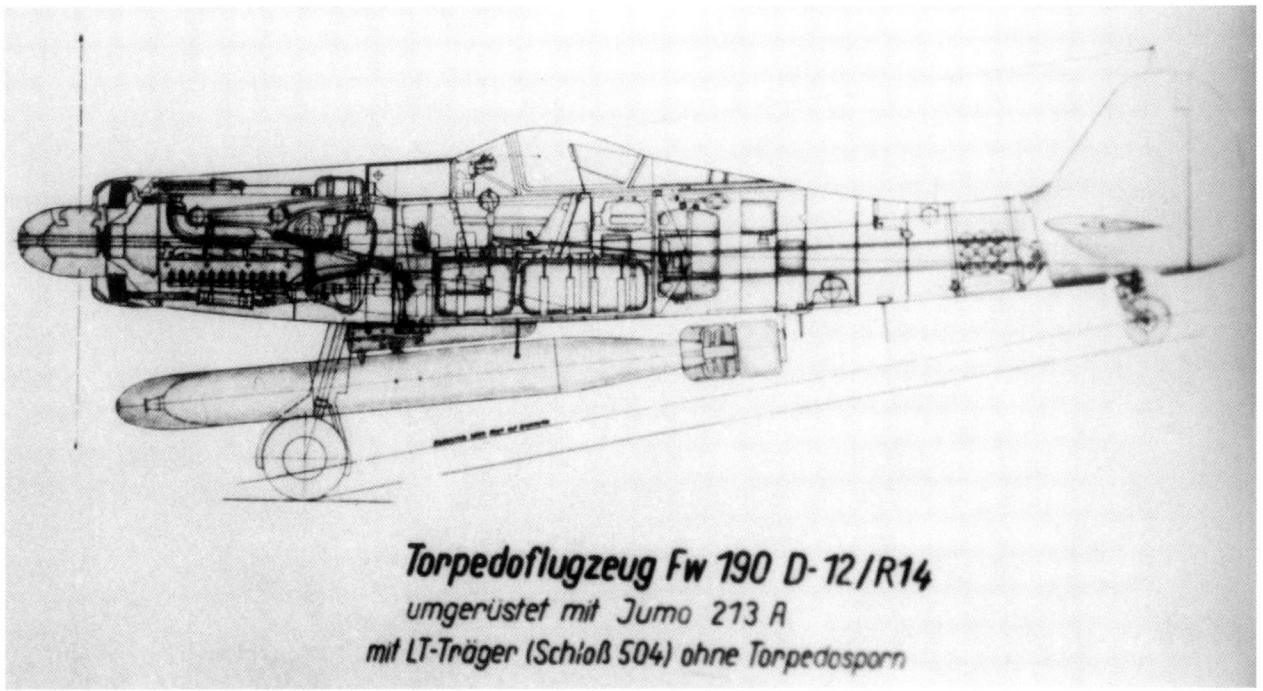

Focke-Wulf drawing of the Fw 190 D-12/R14, which was to have been powered by the Jumo 213 A engine.

Focke-Wulf produced a torpedo-carrying fighter in 1943 in the form of the Fw 190 A-5/U14. The basic concept was carried over to the torpedo-armed version of the Fw 190 D.

Focke-Wulf Fw 190 D-12/R14 Specification		
Power plant:	Junkers Jumo 213 A	
Armament:	2 MG 151/20 (250 rounds per gun)	
Payload:	LT 1 B short (780 kg) or LT 1 B long (850 kg) torpedo	
Equipment:	FuG 16 ZY, FuG 25a, FuG 101a in the wing, emergency compass, backup turn-and-bank indicator, PKS 12 autopilot	
	Fw 190 D-12/R14	**Fw 190 D-12/R14 with wing tanks**
Weight with short torpedo:	4990 kg	5210 kg
Weight with long torpedo:	5060 kg	5280 kg
Fuel: (310 l in wing tanks)	664 l B4	974 l B4
Speed to and from target at 3000 m[1]	560 km/h / 605 km/h	557 km/h / 616 km/h
Range at 3000 m[2]	900 km	1365 km

[1] At combat power (3,000 rpm)
[2] At economical cruise (2,100 rpm)

The fuel system consisted of two normal fuel tanks with a combined capacity of 524 liters plus a 140-liter long-range tank in the rear fuselage. The planned four-tank system in the wings increased capacity by 310 liters.

Right and opposite: Although the first torpedo-carrying version of the Fw 190 failed to achieve production status in 1943, Focke-Wulf was working intensively on a new torpedo-carrier. Focke-Wulf conducted a comparative study of the Fw 190 F, Fw 190 D and Ta 152 C/R14 to determine which was best-suited to the role of torpedo aircraft.

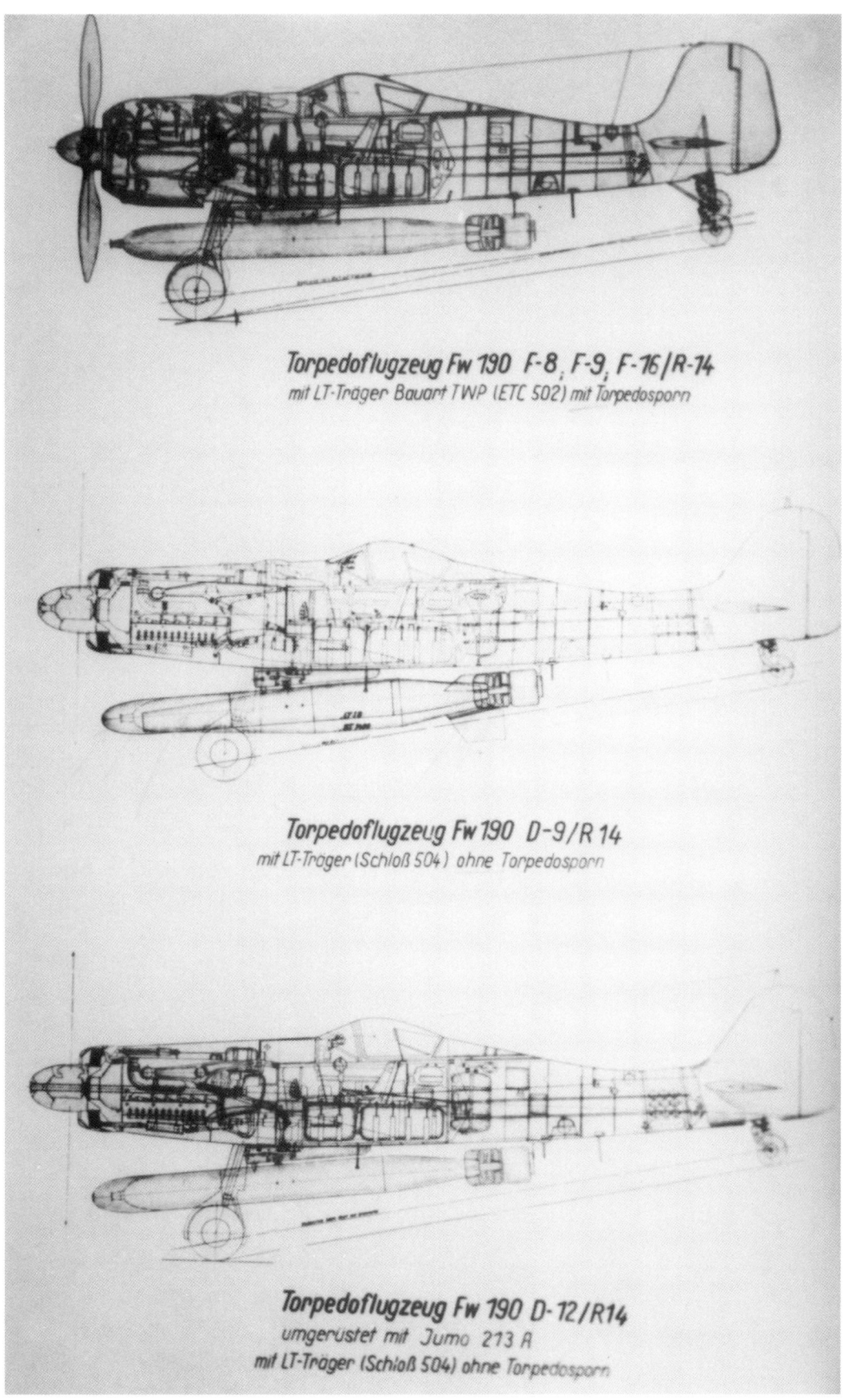

CHAPTER TEN

Rebirth of an Old Idea - The Fw 190 and Daimler-Benz Engines

The first Focke-Wulf Fw 190 D-9 fighters were received by German fighter units in the late autumn of 1944. Almost immediately the aircraft was given the fitting nickname of "*Langnase*" (Long-Nose) by its pilots. Unlike the *Dora*, however, the first of the long-nosed Focke-Wulfs had been powered by a Daimler Benz in-line engine. The Fw 190 V13 had first flown in the spring of 1942, powered by a pre-production version of the DB 603 A engine. Focke-Wulf made plans to produce a version of its fighter powered by the DB 603 A, to be designated the Fw 190 C, however the RLM refused to approve the installation of the DB 603 in the Fw 190. After the initial trials of the DB 603 in the Fw 190 in the spring of 1942, Daimler Benz continued to develop the engine. By 1944 the DB 603 G version was in full production. It was rated at 1,900 h.p. with a maximum boost altitude of 8300 m. Designed for use with methanol-water and nitrous-oxide injection, the DB 603 G entered service in April 1944 in the Messerschmitt Me 410 B-1 heavy fighter and the Heinkel He 219 A-5 *Uhu* night fighter. The next significant improvement was to be provided by the DB 603 L, which was rated at 1,820 h.p. for takeoff and 1,400 h.p. at emergency power at a height of 10000 meters. The DB 603 L was also suitable for MW 50 and GM 1 injection. Unlike the DB 603 L, the DB 603 LA had no intercooler, and the methanol-water mixture was used for supercharger air cooling. According to Focke-Wulf documents, the Fw 190 D-14, like the earlier Fw 190 D-11 powered by the Jumo 213 F, lacked the space for an intercooler, and the company therefore proposed the installation of the DB 603 LA.

With production of the Fw 190 D-9 already in full swing, the RLM began having doubts about Junkers Motorenbau's ability to produce sufficient numbers of the Jumo 213. In addition to the Jumo 213 A for the Fw 190, the Jumo 213 F for the Fw 190 D-12 and the Jumo 213 E for the Ta 152 E and Ta 152 H major production variants, Jumo was now also expected to deliver the Jumo 004 turbojet engines for the Me 262. To

Like the Fw 190 V76, the Ta 152 V6 was powered by the DB 603 E engine.

ensure that fighter production was not hampered by a shortage of Jumo engines, the RLM issued instructions for a version of the Fw 190 D powered by the DB 603 engine.

10.1 The Fw 190 D-14 and D-15

In late autumn 1944 Focke-Wulf received a development contract to install the Daimler-Benz DB 603 E/A engine (DB 603 E with DB 603 A gearing) in the production Fw 190 D-12 airframe. This new variant, which was designated the Fw 190 D-14, was largely similar to the Fw 190 D-12, except that the latter's Jumo 213 F engine was to be replaced by the DB 603 F and later the DB 603 LA. Focke-Wulf was ordered to convert a Fw 190 D-12 to D-14 standard to serve as prototype for the new series. The situation was deteriorating rapidly, however, and production of the Fw 190 D-12, which was supposed to begin in January, was delayed until March. On 1 February, following a conference at the Air Armaments Staff on 26 January, the requirement for the Fw 190 D-14 was dropped, in order to avoid further delays in beginning production of the Fw 190 D-12. By this time as well, priority had been given to the DB 603 LA for installation in the Ta 152 C, which was to replace the Focke-Wulf Fw 190. Another probable factor in the demise of the Fw 190 D-14 was delays in development of the DB 603 LA because of further technical changes.

The DB 603 E was planned for the Fw 190 D-14 and D-15 production variants. It was rated at 1,800 h.p. at low level. Use of MW 50 injection increased output to 2,400 h.p. (Daimler-Chrysler)

Daimler Benz originally wanted to produce thirty Fw 190 D-14 prototypes itself, all conversions of existing aircraft. The engine maker requested that fifteen Fw 190 D-11s be delivered to it in January 1945 and fifteen Fw 190 D-12s in February. On 9 January representatives of Daimler Benz visited Fieseler in Kassel. Daimler Benz now hoped that Fieseler could provide thirty Fw 190 D-12 airframes for conversion by the end of February 1945, however the company's representatives learned that the first D-12 airframe would not be completed until the end of January at the earliest. As well, Fieseler was unable to say when additional Fw 190 D-12s would become available.

On 31 January 1945 the D-14 program was halted by the air armaments staff. Both Focke-Wulf and Daimler Benz opposed the decision, as both expected great things from the Fw 190 D-14. Cancellation of the D-14 halted planning for prototype conversion and subsequent production of the type by Arado.

The production Fw 190 D-14 was to have been built to the following standard:

DB 603 EA power plant

Armament: MK 108 Motorkanone, two MG 151/20 cannon in wing roots

Revised panel in front of windscreen, Daimler Benz design

Radio equipment: FuG 16 ZY, FuG 125

The Fw 190 D-15 was the last of the planned Fw 190 D sub-variants. The airframe of the D-15 was based on that of the Fw 190 A-8/F-8, construction of which was similar to the Fw 190 D-9. The aircraft was to be powered by a DB 603 E engine with MW 50 boost. Installation of the Daimler Benz engine meant that the fuselage-mounted armament had to be deleted, however this loss of firepower was to be compensated for by the installation of two MK 108 cannon in the outer wings. Radio equipment consisted of a Fug 16 ZY and FuG 25. Procurement of a bad-weather version of the D-15 with the R15 equipment set was uncertain at that time, however every aircraft was to leave the factory with the ETC 501 rack and 300-l external fuel tank. Plans called for Fw 190 A-8/F-8 airframes to be converted to Fw 190 D-15 standard by Focke-Wulf, NDW and Lutherwerk beginning in April-May 1945. In any case, the first production aircraft was to go to Langenhagen for performance trials. The Fw 190 D-15 was only planned as an interim series, to avoid disrupting preparations for building the D-12 in quantity. In a development report dated 13 March 1945, Focke-Wulf wrote:

> *The armaments staff has now requested a conversion of the Fw 190 A-8 with the DB 603 E instead of the D-14 series (D-12 with DB 603) previously planned. The reason is to avoid delaying the start of D-12 production. The new series has been designated the D-15.*

The military situation prevented this converted version of the Fw 190 from coming to fruition. The Fw 190 D-15/R11, the bad-weather version, suffered a similar fate.

The DB 603 production at Daimler Benz in late 1944.

To gather information on the new type as quickly as possible, Daimler Benz wanted to produce thirty prototypes of the Fw 190 D-15 series by way of the conversion process. This was in fact begun, in March 1945. The first fifteen Fw 190 D-9s for conversion to the DB 603 E were delivered to Daimler Benz in Echterdingen from 11 to 17 March 1945. According to the manufacturer, the DB 603 E was capable of producing 1,800 h.p. for takeoff, which was increased to 2,400 h.p. with MW 50 boost. The following D-9s were delivered to Echterdingen for conversion:

11 March	*Werknummer* 601 071
12 March	*Werknummer* 601 098, 601 093, 601 096, 601 075, 601 089, 601 102
13 March	*Werknummer* 601 063, 601 079, 601 289, 601 104, 601 286
14 March	*Werknummer* 601 099
16 March	*Werknummer* 601 068
17 March	*Werknummer* 601 080

Only one of these D-9s is believed to have been converted to Fw 190 D-15 standard and test-flown.

Copy of Development Report on the Fw 190 D-15 Dated 13 March 1945

Task: The armaments staff has now requested a conversion of the Fw 190 A-8 series with the DB 603 E instead of the previously planned D-14 series (D-12 with DB 603 E) in order to avoid interrupting production of the D-12.

This variant has been designated Fw 190 D-15.

Extent of Modifications:

a) Fuselage   Reinforcement of the fuselage and Frame 1
Changes in internal equipment, ventilation, etc.
New panel in front of windscreen (DB)
New oil tank in Frame 1
500-mm fuselage extension with enlarged fin and rudder.

b) Wing   Changes and strengthening as D-9

c) Engine   New control linkages etc.

d) Armament   2 x MG 131 in fuselage deleted
2 x MG 151 in wing roots
2 x MK 108 in outer wings

e) Special Material   115-l tank behind Frame 8, no fuel pump, fuel transferred by compressed air from supercharger. Change to fuel operation on ground by switching one line. Tank must be cleaned first.

f) External Weapons   ETC 501 (conversion to ETC 504 cancelled)

g) Equipment   No changes (RPM indicator, firewall plugs, etc.)

Construction Drawings:
Construction drawings ready to be picked up in Eilsen SB III on 13/3 at 1800 hours.

without panel in front (to be delivered by DB)
without autopilot (D-15/R11)
these can be delivered later by ....

Prototype Construction:
The first converted aircraft will serve as prototype and is to be delivered to Langenhagen for testing.

Fw 190 D-15 WNr. ....ready to fly.........

4.) Series: D-15   FW beginning April (A-8 conversions)
                          NDW beginning April
                          Lutherwerke beginning May (Factory X)
                          (status of D-15/R11 to be determined)

Delivery Standard:
      Power plant   DB 603 E (9-8603 C2/TE) to be delivered by Daimler Benz
                              Airframe company must procure generators

      Radios   FuG 16 ZY and FuG 25

      Special Materials System   MW 50 system installed

      Armament   2 x MG 151 in wing roots
                              2 x MK 108 in outer wings

      Gunsight   Revi 16 b or EZ 42
      (as available)

      ETC 501   installed on every aircraft with 300-liter drop tank

      Autopilot   PKS 12 and FuG 125 as required

6.) Notes: a) The engines must be controlled between SA F4 and TZ2.

                      b) The panel in front of the windscreen 9-8603.929-000 is to be built according to plans supplied by DB. Clarification between SA F4 and TZ2 required.

                      c) DB intends to eventually deliver the DB 603 LA for the D-15 (Engine 9-8603 C2/TLA), installation of which is possible in the existing airframe. Airframe changes include a revised oil tank, changes to the special materials system and possible fuselage reinforcements (related to reduced load factor).

d) As DB will not be able to deliver the airframe-mounted engine cowling on time, the airframe manufacturer will have to install joint cover panels similar to those of the D-11, 12 and 13.

e) Procurement of the oil tank by SA F4.

7.) DB requests that an engine acceptance instructor be sent for the purpose of checking a fully-equipped engine, specifically the engine mounts.

8.) Handbooks: and servicing manuals to be prepared by start of production.

10.2 The Fw 190 V76 and V77 Prototypes

In October 1944 Daimler Benz received its first two Fw 190 D-9s from the Focke-Wulf factory in Sorau. *Werknummer* 210 040, TS+DN, was handed over in Echterdingen on 8 October 1944 and *Werknummer* 210 043, TS+DQ, on 10 October. While *Werknummer* 210 040 was immediately disassembled and the fuselage sent to Backnang for conversion, 210 043 remained at Echterdingen, Daimler Benz's test center, for performance tests with the Jumo 213 A. In charge of flight testing at Echterdingen (Daimler Benz Plant 60 V) was *Flugkapitän* Ellenrieder. Focke-Wulf designated the aircraft the Fw 190 V76 (WNr. 210 040) and V77 (W.Nr 210 043). Earlier research by Daimler Benz had shown that

Opposite
This Daimler Benz graph illustrates the better speed and rate of climb of the Fw 190 D powered by the DB 603 engine.

What has often been described as a mock-up was in fact the conversion of one of the two Fw 190 Ds with the DB 603 engine.

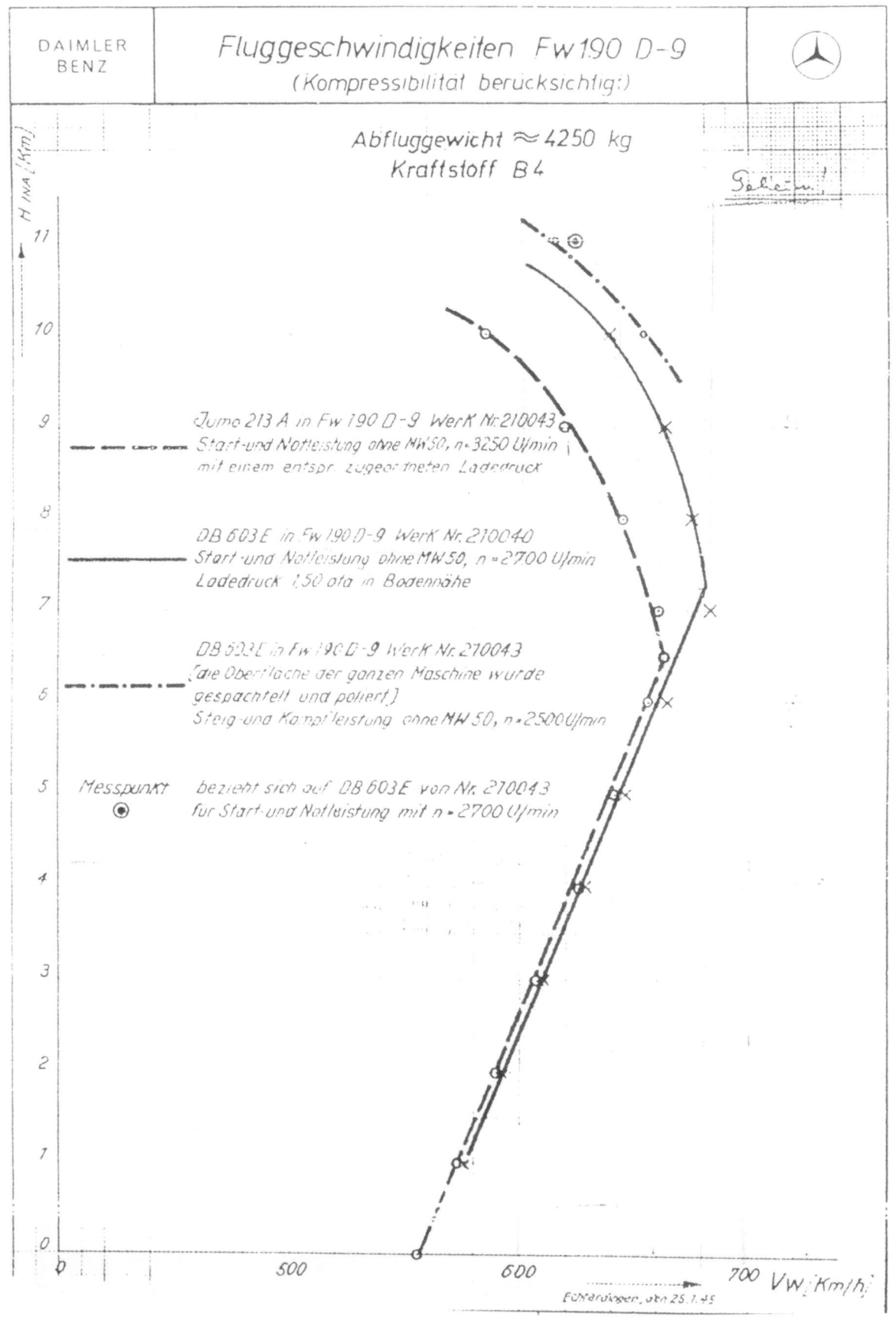

Parts of Fw 190s can still be found at Echterdingen today, such as this supercharger air intake for the DB 603 engine of the Fw 190 D-15.

the DB 603 E motor, though somewhat larger than the Jumo 213, would fit in the airframe of the Fw 190 D-9. Despite the absence of construction drawings from Focke-Wulf, 210 040 was returned to Echterdingen one month later, on 15 November 1944. The re-engined V76 took to the air for the first time on 20 November. As the accompanying illustration shows, the V76's maximum speed was 680 km/h at 7500 meters compared to 660 km/h at 6500 meters by the Jumo-powered V77. The performance disparity increased with altitude, and at 10000 km the V76 was 52 km/h faster. This was clear proof that the DB 603 performed better with the DB 603 E engine than with the Jumo 213 A.

When the performance measuring flights had been completed (4 hours and 45 minutes), the V77 also went to Backnang for conversion. The V77 returned to Echterdingen shortly before the end of the year. It made its first flight powered by the DB 603 E on 10 January 1945. All seams were filled and the aircraft was waxed and polished. Thus finished, the V77 proved 20 km/h faster than the V76 at all altitudes. Testing was not over yet, however. The V77 was subsequently fitted with a DB 603 EC engine with MW 50 injection and, thus equipped, began flying again in mid-February 1945. Before the war ended the V76 was fitted with the new and more powerful DB 603 LA. The engine was delivered from Backnang to Echterdingen at the beginning of March 1945.

Both prototypes were used for preliminary testing for the new Fw 190 D-14 and Fw 190 D-15 series. Flugkapitän Ellenrieder flew TS+DN for the last time on 14 March 1945 and TS+DQ on 9 March 1945. The ultimate fate of the two prototypes is unknown.

10.3 The Two Fw 190 D-14 Prototypes

Focke-Wulf Fw 190 V76

Werknummer:	210 040
Power plant:	DB 603 E, engine no. 644; later DB 603 LA
Manufacturer's code:	TS+DN
Delivered to Daimler Benz:	8 Oct. 1944
First flight with DB 603 E:	20 Nov. 1944

Focke-Wulf Fw 190 V77

Werknummer:	210 043
Power plant:	DB 603 E, later DB 603 EC with MW 50
Manufacturer's code:	TS+DQ
Delivered to Daimler Benz:	10 Oct. 1944
First flight with DB 603:	10 Jan. 1945

10.4 Results of Testing

Both converted aircraft showed excellent results from the outset. Daimler Benz compiled a report on the Fw 190 D-9/DB 603 E test program on 27 January 1945. In it, Daimler Benz concluded that the results achieved at Echterdingen with the Jumo-powered Fw 190 D-9 were almost identical to the speeds measured by the *E-Stelle Rechlin*. B4 fuel was used for all performance-measurement flights and takeoff weight in all cases was 4250 kg. Powered by a Jumo 213 A, the V77 was largely similar to the D-9. It achieved 662 km/h at the maximum boost altitude of 6500 meters. The V76 powered by the DB 603 reached 666 km/h at the same height. The maximum speed of the Fw 190 D-9 fell off above the Jumo 213 A's maximum boost altitude and from there the performance gap widened. At the DB 603 E's maximum boost altitude of 7400 meters the V76 achieved a maximum speed of 678 km/h, 22 km/h better than the D-9 with its Jumo 213 A. At 10000 meters the speed difference was 52 km/h. Following conversion to the DB 603, the V77's external surfaces were waxed and polished, which increased speed by an additional 20 km/h. Of course, the same would have applied to the Fw 190 D-9. In its initial form, the V77 was powered by a Jumo 213 A whose takeoff rating had been increased to 1,900 h.p. The DB 603 E was nevertheless superior across the entire performance spectrum.

Knowing what we know today, one has to ask why this step in the development of the Fw 190 was taken so late. The better performance spectrum and maximum boost altitude of the DB 603 E compared to the Jumo 213 A were convincing arguments for a variant of the Fw 190 D powered by the DB 603. As well, according to Focke-Wulf documents, the DB 603 was a more reliable power plant than the Jumo engine. Given the adverse conditions under which German fighters were operating at that time, this is a not insignificant factor. The fact is, that this step could have been taken a year earlier with good results. Was the Ta 152 C, which was promoted by the RLM, a better solution? Despite the absence of construction drawings from Focke-Wulf, conversion of the V76 by Daimler Benz took much less time (about one month) than construction of the Ta 152 C. The converted Fw 190 V76 first flew on 20 November 1944, before the new-build Ta 152 CV 6 (12 Dec. 44).

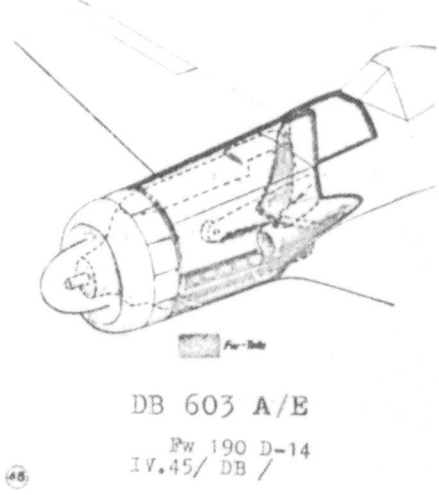

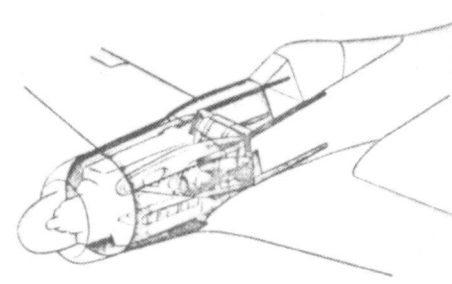

These drawings depict the extent of the changes in the Fw 190 D-14 and D-15 series.

10.5 The Big Mistake

Thus ends the interesting story of the first Fw 190 D-series aircraft with the DB 603 in-line engine. In spite of promising beginnings, production was never begun, and the few converted Fw 190 Ds had no opportunity to demonstrate their potential in action.

Curiously, the DB 603 was repeatedly rejected as a power plant for the Fw 190 D because officialdom believed that it was too heavy compared to the Jumo 213 A. In response to this assertion, Daimler Benz compared the weights of the Jumo 213 A removed from the Fw 190 D-9, WNr. 210

040, and its own 9-8603 C1 (DB 603 E) engine. With cowling and propeller the DB 603 weighed 1644.75 kg. The Junkers engine weighed 1642 kg. The weight difference was thus only 2.75 kg in favor of the Jumo 213. In making its performance estimates, however, Focke-Wulf factored in a weight difference of 128 kg in favor of the Jumo 213 A. This fateful error was not discovered until November 1944. As well, no consideration was given to the DB 603's advantages from a production standpoint, for example its use of sheet steel instead of the light metal used in the Jumo 213 and the better armoring of the DB 603's annular radiator. The question of engine weights lead to a heated exchange of correspondence between Daimler Benz, the RLM and Focke-Wulf.

It remains to be said that the Fw 190 D-14 and D-15 were developed much too late (large-scale production of the DB 603 E had begun at the beginning of 1944), that Daimler Benz expended much time and effort on this program, and that the development of this promising engine-airframe combination had to be halted before it had really begun.

Fw 190 D (Jumo 213)
Jäger, Jabo

Fw 190 A-Flügel mit neuem Übergang Rumpf-Flügel
Rumpfverstärkung (Triebwerk)
Rumpftonne, C-Heck
Keine Flügelaußen-Waffen,-Lasten
(nur D-11 MK 108)

Stand vom 1.1.45.
Blatt 3

Ausführung	Serie	Fertiger	1943	1944	1945	Muster
2 MG 131 Rumpf oben; 2 MG 151 Flügelwurzel; ETC 504 (Rumpf); keine Flügelaußenwaffen	D-9 (Jumo 213A)	Fw / Arbgm / GFW				V53 / V54
MW (Methanol-Wasser) Nachrüstung und Einl auf in lfd. Serie					MW Einschleusen in lfd. Serie nach Erprob.	
Schlechtwettereinsatz; PKS 12; FuG 125; Heizscheiben	D9/R11 (Jumo 213A)	Fw				V72 (FuG 125)
Zwischenserie D9 - D12/13; MG 151 und MK 108; Einbau MG 151 an stelle MK 108 möglich.	D-11 (Jumo 213F)	Fw				V55 / V56
MK 108 zentral; 2 MG 151 Fl.-Wurzel; PKS 12; FuG 125, 25; Heizscheiben; MW Anlage	D-12/R11 (Jumo 213F)	Arado / GFW				V72 (FuG 125) / V62 / V64
1 MK 151 in Motorlafette; 2 MG 151 Flügelwurzel; PKS 12; FuG 125, 25; Heizscheiben	D-13/R11 (Jumo 213F)	Arbgm				V77 / V72 (FuG 125)
Kraftstoffbehälter im Flügel; Sonst wie D-12, 13/R11	D12/R5 (Jumo 213F)	Arado / GFW				
	D13/R5 (Jumo 213F)	Arbgm				
Einführung des Revi EZ 42 (Adler-Anlage) nach Deckung des Bedarfes für Ta 152.						

Einmotorige Jäger: Leistungsdaten

Flugzeugmuster	Fw 190 A-8	Fw 190 A-9	Fw 190 D-9	Fw 190 D-12	Ta 152 H-0	Ta 152 C-0	Ta 152 E-0	Fw 190 (D-9)	Fw 190 [D-9]	Ta 152 (C-0)
Motormuster	BMW 801 D	BMW 801 F	Jumo 213 A	Jumo 213 F	Jumo 213 E	DB 603 L	Jumo 213 E	DB 603 A	DB 603 E	DB 603 E
Bewaffnung: Motor	—	—	—	1×MK 108	1×MK 108	1×MK 108	1×MK 108	—	—	1×MK 108
Rumpf	2×MG 131	2×MG 131	2×MG 131	—	—	2×MG 151	—	2×MG 131	2×MG 131	2×MG 151
Flügel innen	2×MG 151	2×MG 151	2×MG 151	2×MG 151	2×MG 151	2×MG 151	2×MG 151	2×MG 151	2×MG 151	2×MG 151
Flügel außen	2×MG 151	2×MG 151	—	—	—	—	—	—	—	—
Abfluggewicht (kg)	4 300	4 370	4 300	4 420	4 760	4 830	4 675	4 400	4 400	4 770
Höchstgeschwindigkeit mit Notleistung am Boden (km/h)	548 (578)	560	576 (612)	572 (608)	540 (580)	(576)	547 (581)	556 (607)	563 (607)	543 (590)
" (km/h)	644 (652)	666	685 (702)	738 (738)	720 (742)	(753)	712 (744)	672 (691)	687 (706)	667 (684)
in Volldruckhöhe (km)	6,3 (5,5)	6,4	6,6 (5,7)	11,6 (11,6)	10,7 (9,5)	(10,5)	10,7 9,5	7,0 (5,1)	8,3 (6,9)	8,2 (6,8)
Höchstgeschwindigkeit mit Kampfleistung (km/h)	614	638	675	710	704	(710)	695	660	675	654
in Volldruckhöhe (km)	5,8	6,1	6,6	10,9	10,5	(10,5)	10,5	6,9	8,3	8,2
Steigleistungen m. Kampfleistung										
Dienstgipfelhöhe w_{st}=0,5m/s (km)	9,95 (10,6)	10,8	11,1 (11,6)	12,8 (13,4)	13,5 (13,7)(13,9)	(13,0)	12,4 (12,9)	11,0 (11,4)	11,6 (12,0)	11,1 (11,5)
Arbeitshöhe w_{st}=2,0m/s (km)	9,25 (9,9)	10,1	10,4 (11,0)	12,3 (13,0)	12,9(14,4)(13,3)	(12,5)	11,9 (12,4)	10,4 (10,8)	11,0 (11,4)	10,5 (10,9)
Steiggeschwindigkeit (m/sec)	9,6 (14,0)	11,7	12,7 (18,5)	9,0 (8,2)	9,7 (14,5)	(10,9)	7,6 (13,0)	12,1 (19,6)	10,7 (16,5)	9,1 (14,6)
in Volldruckhöhe (km)	5,5 (4,9)	5,75	5,8 (4,8)	10,3 (11,2)	9,9 (8,8)	(9,5)	9,9 (8,8)	6,0 (4,0)	7,5 (5,9)	7,5 (5,9)
Steigzeit auf 10 km (min)		19,6	16,8 (12,5)	13,1 (10,9)	13,6 (10,1)	(10,9)	15,6 (10,9)	17,1 (12,9)	15,0 (11,2)	18,4 (13,6)
Rollstrecke auf Beton (m)	430	390	365	355	295	380	375	420	385	420
Startstrecke bis 20 m (m)	715	600	570	575	495	605	595	630	600	635
Steiggeschwind. b. Abheben (m/s) (Flg. im Startzustand)	9,7	11,5	11,3	12,9	12,0	12,9	12,8	10,6	11,1	10,7
Leistungsverluste bei geänderter Bewaffnung:			2MG151+1MK108		× mit GM1		3×MK 103	2MG151+2MK108	2MG151+2MK108	
Δ V_{max} in V.Dr.H. (km/h)			10		Staatsgeheimnis!		10	10	10	
Δ w_{st} (m/sec)			0,45		Geheimhaltungspflicht beachten		0,70	0,45	0,45	
Δ H Dienstgipfelhöhe (m)			150				300	150	150	

Geschwindigkeiten ohne Berücksichtigung des Widerstandsanstieges aus Kompressibilität, ohne ETC unter dem Rumpf, mit bewegl. Fahrwerks-Klappen, Oberfläche gespachtelt u. Glattanstrich.

Leistungen gelten nur für Luftrad 035 bei 035 ist zusätzlich Leistungsverlust im BL-Ast vorhanden

Eingeklammerte Werte gelten für Sondernotleistung (Start-u Notleistung mit MW50) Bei Fw 190 A 8 für Notleistung und erhöhtem Ladedruck!

1. 10. 1944   Vogtsberger.

Einmotorige Jäger: Rechnerische Flugstrecke und Flugdauer.

Flugzeug-Muster	Abflug-Gewicht (Kg)	Bewaffnung:		Gesamt-Kraftstoff-Vorrat (L)	Kraftstoffunterbringung				MW50 Vorrat (l)	Schmierstoff-Vorrat (l)	Vorh. Radlast (kg)	Drehzahl U/min Flughöhe	Gesamt-Flugdauer (h) x)		Flugstrecke (Km) xx)		Mittlere Fluggeschwindigkeit Km/h o)	
					Rumpf-behälter	Rumpf-Zus.Beh.	Flügel-behälter	Abw.Beh. u.d.R.					0 Km	7 Km	0 Km	7 Km	0 Km	7 Km
Fw 190 A-8	4 390	Rumpf	2×MG 131 je 450 Schuß	640	525	115	—	—	—	55	1820	2300¹⁾	1,20	1,48	610	775	510	580
BMW 801D	4 720	Flügel I.	2×MG 151 je 250 Schuß	940	525	115	—	300	—	60	1960	2000²⁾	2,10	2,18	910	1035	435	435
		Flügel a.	2×MG 151 je 150 Schuß									2300	1,80	2,15	900	1120	500	574
												2000	3,15	3,31	1310	1500	425	485
Fw 190 A-9	4 420	Rumpf	2×MG 131 je 450 Schuß	640	525	115	—	—	—	55	1835	2400	1,02	1,28	520	705	510	615
BMW 801F	4 750	Flügel I.	2×MG 151 je 250 Schuß	940	525	115	—	300	—	60	1975	2000	2,14	2,00	910	965	424	506
		Flügel a.	2×MG 151 je 150 Schuß									2400	1,59	1,91	780	1060	500	620
												2000	3,34	3,08	1350	1440	474	496
Fw 190 D-9	4 270	Rumpf	2×MG 131 je 450 Schuß	525	525	MW50 Füllung	—	—	115 i.Ru.Z.B.	60	1805	3000	0,69	0,97	385	505	557	665
Jumo 213 A	4 560	Flügel I.	2×MG 151 je 250 Schuß	825	525	MW50 Füllung	—	300	115 i.Ru.Z.B.	60	1930	2100	1,63	1,74	680	755	418	468
												3000	1,18	1,46	645	835	552	660
												2100	2,88	2,94	1170	1255	412	461
Fw 190 D-12	4 440	Motorkan.1×MK 108 80 Schuß		525	525	MW50 Füllung	—	—	140 i.Ru.Z.B.	60	1880	3000	0,66	0,90	365	475	554	677
Jumo 213 F-1	4 730	Flügel I.	2×MG 151 je 250 Schuß	825	525	MW50 Füllung	—	300	140 i.Ru.Z.B.	60	2000	2100	1,64	1,65	690	745	421	487
												3000	1,13	1,37	610	765	549	671
												2100	2,70	2,79	1155	1250	415	482
Fw 190 D-12/R5	4 750	Motorkan.1×MK 108 80 Schuß		890	525	70	295	—	70 i.Fl.	60	2010	3000	1,38	1,60	760	920	549	662
Jumo 213 EB	5 050	Flügel I.	2×MG 151 je 250 Schuß	1190	525	70	295	300	70 i.Fl.	60	2135	2100	2,9	2,91	1220	1300	427	467
												3000	1,97	2,14	1025	1235	543	655
												2100	4,0	4,01	1635	1705	415	467
Fw 190 D-15	4 530	Flügel I.	2×MG 151 je 250 Schuß	525	525	—	—	—	115 i.Ru.Z.B.	60	1920	2300	0,82	1,06	420	565	574	632
DB 603 EB	4 820	Flügel a.	2×MK 108 je 50 Schuß	825	525	—	—	300	115 i.Ru.Z.B.	60	2050	1900	1,10	1,39	485	710	440	570
												2300	1,43	1,64	715	895	509	624
												1900	1,92	2,22	815	1130	430	557
Ta 152 C-1/R11	5 115	Motorkan.×MK 108 85 Schuß		914	594	—	320	—	150 i.Fl.	60÷70	2220	2300	1,62	1,80	815	990	511	609
DB 603 LA	5 385	Rumpf 2×MG 151 je 150 Schuß		1214	594	—	320	300	150 i.Fl.	60÷70	2335	2000	—	3,00	—	1375	—	463
		Flügel I.	2×MG 151 je 175 Schuß									2300	2,27	2,37	1105	1295	505	602
												2000	—	4,01	—	1795	—	476
Ta 152 H-1/R11	5 250	Motorkan.1×MK 108 85 Schuß		914	574	GM1-Füllung	400	—	70 i.Fl.	60÷70	2260	3000	1,67	1,61	678	895	534	652
Jumo 213 E-1	5 510	Flügel I.	2×MG 151 je 175 Schuß	1214	574	GM1-Füllung	400	300	70 i.Fl.	60÷70	2375	2100	3,26	3,16	1335	1570	410	505
												3000	1,74	2,00	920	1145	530	647
												2100	4,27	4,19	1735	2070	406	500

Verbräuche entsprech. den Angaben der Motorfirmen + 12,5 % Sicherheitszuschlag.
- o) Mittlere Geschwindigkeiten = arith. Mittel aus An- und Rückflug.
- x.) Flugdauer einschließlich Zeit für Steigen und Gleiten aus Flughöhe.
- xx.) Rechn. Flugstrecke ohne taktische Abzüge, einschl. Steig- u. Gleitflugstrecke! Abzüge für Warmlaufen, Rollen, Start, Steigen, Gleiten, Durchstarten und Restmenge sind berücksichtigt!
- u.d.R. = Abwurfbehälter unter dem Rumpf.
- i.Fl. = Ungeschützte Zusatzbehälter im Flügel.
- Ru.Zus.Beh. = Rumpfzusatzbehälter
- 1) Entspricht höchstzulässiger Dauerleistung.
- 2) Entspricht wirtschaftlicher Reiseleistung.

Staatsgeheimnis! Geheimhaltungspflicht beachten.

Vogtsberger. 15. III. 1945.

Chef TLR		FLUGZEUG-BAUREIHEN-BLATT Fw 190					Chef TLR Fl.Nr.8554/44 gKdos(B-2) 550 Ausfertigungen 1.8.44	
Baureihe	Triebwerk	Bewaffnung – Beladung	Abwurf-Anlage	Kraftstoff	FT-Gerät	Sonstiges		Bemerkung
Fw 190 D-9 (J)	Jumo 213 A	2 MG 131/je 475 Sch / MG 151/20/175 Sch / MG 151/20/175 Sch	ETC 501	2 Rumpfbehälter zus. 520 l, 115 l Beh. wahlweise Methanol oder Reichweite.	FuG 16Z FuG 25a	D-9 erhält Bewaffnungsverstärkung, Außenflügel 2 MK 108 bezw. 2 MG 151, MG 131 fallen weg. Umstellung erfolgt innerhalb der Serie.		
Fw 190 D-9/ R-11 (J)	"	wie A-8/R-11	"	" zusätzlich 1 x 300 l abwerfbar	" FuG 125	Schlechtwetterjagd, Jägerkurssteuerung		
Fw 190 D-11 (J)	Jumo 213 E	2 MG 131/je 475 Sch / MG 151/20/175 Sch / MG 151/20/175 Sch	"	"	FuG 16Z FuG 25a	Nur Einzelflugzeuge für Triebwerkserprobung.		
Fw 190 D-12 (J)	"	MK 108/55 Sch / MG 151/20/220 Sch / MG 151/20/220 Sch	"	2 Rumpfbehälter 520 l 115 l Methanol	"	Methanol zur Leistungssteigerung bzw. in Höhe für Ladeluftkühlung		
Fw 190 D-12 R-11 (J)	"	"	"	"	" FuG 125	Schlechtwetterjagd, Jägerkurssteuerung		
Fw 190 D-13 (J)	"	MG 151/20/250 Sch / MG 151/20/220 Sch / MG 151/20/220 Sch	"	"	FuG 16Z FuG 25a			
Fw 190 F-3/ R-1 (S)	BMW 801 D	2 MG 17/je 1000 Sch / MG 151/20/220 Sch / MG 151/20/220 Sch	2x ETC 50 unter jeder Fläche ETC 501 unter d.R.	2 Rumpfbehälter 520 l	"			
Fw 190 F-8/ R-1 (S)	"	ETC 50(71) / 2 MG 131/je 475 Sch / MG 151/20/220 Sch / MG 151/20/220 Sch	"	" 115 l im Rumpf	"			

CHAPTER ELEVEN

The End

At the end of April 1945 the last German fighter units gradually began to disintegrate. Supplies of materials and fuel came to complete stop. With no fuel, some German aircraft were blown up to prevent them falling into the hands of the enemy. Many aircraft survived the end of the war, however, and machines of all types litter the former *Luftwaffe* airfields. Many of these were Focke-Wulf machines.

The victorious Allies were extremely interested in flyable German aircraft. As well as the Me 262 and He 162 jet fighters, the most sought after included the Fw 190 D-9 and D-13. The Americans shipped four such aircraft to the United States aboard the aircraft carrier HMS Reaper. The following aircraft were loaded aboard the carrier in France:

1. Fw 190 D-13
    USA 14   later FE 118/T2-118   WNr. 836 017

2. Fw 190 D-9
    USA 12 or 15 later FE 119/T2-119   WNr. 210 016

3. Fw 190 D-9
    USA 12 or 15 later FE 120/T2-120   WNr. 601 392

4. Fw 190 D-9
    USA 13   later FE 121/T2-121   WNr. 401 392

1. FE 118: This D-13, Yellow 10 of I./JG 26, was captured by the English in Flensburg. It was initially assigned the code USA 14. Together with other captured aircraft it was shipped to the USA aboard the carrier HMS Reaper. Its first appearance in the records at Freeman Field was on 17 May 1946. The aircraft subsequently went to the Georgia Institute of Technology in Atlanta.

This badly damaged Fw 190 D-9 was found by American troops near Halle an der Saale. It probably belonged to II./JG 6.

The wreck of *Werknummer* 600 434, a Fw 190 D-9.

Wrecked Fw 190 D-9, WNr. 210 256, Frankfurt-Rebstock, spring 1946.

2. FE 119: This D-9 was captured as White 14 of the 5. Staffel of II. Gruppe/JG 26, also at Flensburg. It was initially assigned the code USA 12 or 15. It is first recorded at Freeman Field on 1 August 1945. On 13 September 1945 the D-9 was flown from Newark to Freeman Field by Lt. William V. Haynes. During a demonstration at low level FE 119 crashed and Lt. Haynes was killed.

3. FE 120: This D-9 was also captured by the RAF at Flensburg and is believed to have served with JG 26. First mention of the aircraft in the USA is at Wright Field on 1 August 1946. It is known to have flown a test program there. The aircraft was subsequently placed in storage and was later transferred to Silver Hill. In 1975 the machine was moved to the USAF Museum at Wright-Patterson AFB. There it is on display as Chevron 1 of IV.(Sturm)/JG 3 Udet.

4. FE 121: This D-19 was captured as Black 5 of JG 26 at Flensburg. It was initially assigned the code USA 13 by the English and later the American code FE 121. It was in flyable condition at Freeman Field between May and August 1946. The subsequent fate of the D-9 is uncertain, but it does not appear to have survived.

Below: During the Red Army's rapid advance into East Prussia, Soviet troops captured brand-new Fw 190 D-9s at Marienburg, site of a large Focke-Wulf factory. The aircraft were marked with red stars and then flown against the Germans.

Bottom: At war's end: Fw 190s with propellers removed. In the foreground is a Fw 190 D-9.

Above: White 14 in Flensburg.

Right: Despite its poor quality, this photograph confirms the correctness of the "1" code of the 4. *Gruppe*.

Below and opposite top: These photographs show the complete restoration of Fw 190 D-9, *Werknummer* 601 088 (FE 120) in the 1970s for the USAF Museum in Wright Patterson. The original finish has been stripped to the bare metal.

Werknummer 601 088 as it looks today, in the markings of IV.(Sturm)/JG 3 Udet at Wright Patterson, Ohio.

Two photographs depicting the captured Fw 190 D-9, FE 121, *Werknummer* 401 392. Above it is seen still in German markings, while below it has American codes and overpainted swastika.

Pages 195-196: The following series of photographs shows FE 121, a captured Fw 190 D-9, from several perspectives. The paint scheme is pure fantasy and has nothing to do with the aircraft's original camouflage finish. The photographs were taken in the USA while the aircraft was under test.

Bibliography

Fw 190 C-1/C-2 / Fw 190 D-1/D-2

Daimler Benz memo on the installation of the DB 603 in the Fw 190 dated 6 Feb. 1940.

Daimler Benz letter Fw 190 with DB 603 of 14 Feb. 1940

Focke-Wulf letter concerning the installation of the DB 603 of 12 Feb. 1940

Focke-Wulf List of Variants of 18 Nov. 1942

Focke-Wulf summary of prototypes and Fw 190 B-G series of 4 Dec. 1942 with revisions on 16 March 1943 and 29 May 1943.

Focke-Wulf report concerning Fw 190 V17 to V23 with Jumo 213 of 22 Apr. 1942

Focke-Wulf memo Fw 190 V19 to V23 of 21 May 1942

Focke-Wulf report Fw 190 with Jumo 213 over Fw 190 C test-bed now with Jumo 213 of 30 Jan. 1943

Focke-Wulf report concerning BMW 8035 in Fw 190 of 6 Apr. 1943

Focke-Wulf evaluation of various power plants in the Fw 190 fighter aircraft (Fw 190 V19) of 6 Aug. 1943

Junkers report on the Fw 190 V20 with Jumo 213 C of 29 Nov. 1943

Junkers memo on Jumo 213 in Fw 190 or Ta 152 of 18 May 1944

Flight Reports

Flight report Fw 190 V13/0 036/SK+JS, 4th and 5th flights on 14 Mar. 1942

Flight report Fw 190 V13/0 036/SK+JS, 6th flight on 17 Mar. 1942

Flight report Fw 190 V13/0 036/SK+JS, 7th and 8th flights on 9 Apr. 1942

Flight report Fw 190 V13/0 036/SK+JS, 9th-12th flights on 18 Apr. 1942

Flight report Fw 190 V13/0 036/SK+JS, 35th flight on 30 Jul. 1942

Flight report Fw 190 V15/0 037/CF+OV, 1st-4th flights on 9 May 1942

Flight report Fw 190 V15/0 037/CF+OV, 13th-14th flights on 23 June 1942

Flight report No. 6 Fw 190 V15/0 037/CF+OV, 42nd flight on 8 Dec. 1942

Flight report No. 7 Fw 190 V15/0 037/CF+OV, 43rd (18 Dec. 1942) to 58th (29 Jan. 1943) flights

Flight report No. 5 Fw 190 V17/0 039/CF+OX, 9th (11 Jan. 1943) to 20th (29 Mar. 1943) flights

Flight report No. 1 Fw 190 V20/0 042/TI+IG, 1st (23 Nov. 1943) to 34th (28 Mar. 1944) flights

Flight report No. 3 Fw 190 V20/0 042/TI+IG, 52nd (1 Jun. 1944) to 69th (25 Jun. 1944) flights

Flight report No. 1 Fw 190 V21/0 043/TI+CH, 1st (13 Mar. 1944) to 27th (26 Apr. 1944) flights

Ta 153 A-1

Calculations Ta 153 Ra-1 fuselage, wing, power plant of August 1943

Focke-Wulf performance comparison Ta 153 – Me 209 of 6 Aug. 1943

Messerschmitt weight comparison Ta 153 (Fw 190 D) – Me 209 of 30 Jul. 1943

Fw 190 D-9

Development report Fw 190 D-9 with Jumo 213 A, Page XV b2, b3 of 31 May 1944

Development report Fw 190 D-9 with Jumo 213 A, Page XV b2, b3 of 20 Jun. 1944

Fw 190 D-9 Aircraft Handbook Part 0 General Information — Nov. 1944 issue

Fw 190 D-9 Aircraft Handbook Part 8C Special Weapons Systems – D. (Luft) T.2190 D-9, January 1945 issue

Fw 190 D-9 Aircraft Handbook Part 8 E Camera Equipment – D. (Luft) T.2190 D-9, January 1945 issue

Fw 190 A-8, A-9 Aircraft Handbook Part 9 A General Equipment – D. (Luft) T.2190 A-8, January 1945 issue

Supplement No. 1 Patin PKS 12 Fighter Autopilot, also applicable to Fw 190 D-9, January 1945 issue

Focke-Wulf designations Fw 190 and Ta 152 of 4 Aug. 1944

Focke-Wulf Program for Type Testing of 18 Aug. 1944

Junkers Monthly Reports *TAM – Gruppe Luftwaffe* from Sept. 1944 to March 1944

Focke-Wulf Performance Summary Fw 190 D/Ta 152 of 1 Oct. 1944

List of Major Component Subcontractors for the Fw 190 and Ta 152 of 25 Oct. 1944

Junkers – Fw 190 D-9 with Jumo 213 A in Front-Line Service, Experiences to Date, 1 Nov. 1944

Comparison of Fw 190 F, D and Ta 152 C/R14 Torpedo Aircraft of 30 Dec. 1944

Jumo 213 Engine Failures with Focke-Wulf, 25 Jan. 1945
Design Meeting on Changes for Installation of R4M, Panzerblitz and Wing Bomb Carriers of 14 Mar. 1945
Focke-Wulf Type Summary of 3 Jan. 1945 and 21 Mar. 1945

Flight Reports
Fw 190 V53, WNr. 170 003, Report No. 2 of 19 Oct. 1944, 66th Flight (21 Jul. 1944) to 99th Flight (26 Sept. 1944)
Fw 190 D-9, WNr. 210 002, Report No. 1 of Oct. 1944, 1st Flight (15 Sept. 1944) to 15th Flight (2 Oct. 1944)
Jumo Crash Report Fw 190 D-9, WNr. 210 048, with MW 50 system, 21 Oct. 1944

Fw 190 D-11
Development Report Fw 190 D Page XV e 10 of 28 Nov. 1944 – Fw 190 D-11 with addenda
Focke-Wulf Report Jumo 213 F Engine Failures as of 25 Jan. 1945
Testing Report Fw 190 D-11, D-12, D-13 with Jumo 213 F Engine of 27 Dec. 1945
Summary of Reports on Testing of Fw 190 D-11, D-12, D-13 with Jumo 213 F of 20 Mar. 1945
Focke-Wulf Type Summaries of 3 Jan. 1945 and 21 Mar. 1945
Report on Engine Changes Fw 190 D-11, D-12, D-13 of 9 Mar. 1945
Development Report – Airframe-Mounted Engine Cowling for Fw 190 D-11/D-12/D-13

OMW Acceptance Record Fw 190 D-12, TG+MI, *Werknummer* 350 157 of 30 Oct. 1944
Focke-Wulf Memo Concerning Crash of the V59, *Werknummer* 350 156, of 10 Oct. 1944

Flight Reports
Flight Report No. 1 Fw 190 V56 of 27 Sept. 1944
Flight Report No. 2 Fw 190 V56 of 13 Feb. 1945
Focke-Wulf Correspondence Concerning MW 50 System in the V56 of 29 Sept. 1944

Fw 190 D-12/D-13
Focke-Wulf Testing Report Fw 190 D-11, D-12, D-13 with Jumo 213 F Engine of 27 Dec. 1945
Focke-Wulf Summary of Reports on Testing of Fw 190 D-11, D-12, D-13 with Jumo 213 F of 20 Mar. 1945
Focke-Wulf Type Summaries of 3 Jan. 1945 and 21 Mar. 1945
Focke-Wulf Report on Engine Changes Fw 190 D-11, D-12, D-13 of 9 Mar. 1945
Focke-Wulf Development Report – Airframe-Mounted Engine Cowling for Fw 190 D-11/D-12/D-13

Focke-Wulf Comparison of Fw 190 F, D and Ta 152 C/R14 Torpedo Aircraft of 30 Dec. 1944

Junkers Weekly Reports to the OMW Air Division of 5-18 Mar. 1945 and 19-23 Mar. 1945

Junkers Monthly Report to the OMW Air Division of March 1945

Fw 190 D-14/D-15

Development Report Fw 190 D Page XV g 1, 2 "Fw 190 D-14 with DB 603 AE" of 29 Nov. 1944

Development Report Fw 190 D Page XV g 1, 2 "Fw 190 D-14 with DB 603 AE" of 1 Feb. 1945

Development Report Fw 190 D Page XV m 1-3 "Fw 190 D-15 with DB 603 E" of 13 Mar. 1945

Daimler Benz Report to the OKL on Testing of the Fw 190 D-9 with 9-8603 C1 Engine, 27 Jan. 1945

Focke-Wulf Type Survey Lists of 5 Jan. 1945 and 21 Mar. 1945

Performance Comparison Fw 190 D/Ta 152 with Jumo 213/DB 603, 1 Oct. 1944

Letter from Daimler Benz to RLM Concerning Weights of Jumo 213 A and DB 603 E Engines, 15 Nov. 1944

Daimler Benz Report on the Status of the Installation of DB 603 E in the Airframe of the Fw 190 D, 2 Feb. 1945

Daimler Benz Weekly Report No. 34/44 Werk 60 V, (Experimental Department Echterdingen), 28 Nov. 1944

Literature

Luftfahrt International – *Triebwek Daimler Benz 9-8603 B 1*
FLUGZEUG 3/87 – *Vergleichsfliegen zwischen Fw 190 D-9 and Tempest*
FLUGZEUG 6/94 – *Unternehmung Bodenplatte*
War Prizes – Phil Butler

For their kind assistance and support, I would like to sincerely thank Peter Achs, Heinrich Beauvais, Frank Berger, Thomas Besemer, Richard Chapman, Dipl.Ing. Peter W. Cohausz, Hans-Joachim Ebert of the DASA, Richard Faltermair, Udo Hafner of the Luftfahrtarchiv Hafner, Herr Heintzer and Dr. Niemann of the Daimler-Chrysler AG Historical Archive, Frau Burgmaier and Frau Piroth of the Dornier-Fairchild Company Archive, *Oberst* (Rtd.) Wilhelm Goebel of the Gemeinschaft der Jagdflieger, Dr. Jur. Heinz Lange, Gerd Lanio, Dipl. Grafiker Ulrich Leverenz, *Oberstleutnant* (Rtd.) Karl-Heinz Ossenkop, Peter Petrick, Stephen Ransom, Christoph Regel, Frau Ursula Schaefer of the Deutschen Technikmuseum Berlin, Günther Sengfelder, Axel Urbanke, Eberhard Weber, Hans Günther Wildmoser of the Flugwerk GmbH and the EADS Bremen.

Finally, with great respect, I would like to express my appreciation to the late Herr Dipl.Ing. Hans Sander, chief test pilot and chief engineer of the "Type Testing" Department of Focke-Wulf, for the important information he provided and his insightful comments.

Color Aircraft Profiles

Color Aircraft Profiles

Fw 190 V17 test bed aircraft for Jumo 213 engine installation, WNr. 0039

Fw 190 D prototype "V 53" DU+JC, WNr. 170 003, with four MG 151/20 wing cannon

Fw 190 D-9, Ofw. Werner Hohenberg, I./JG 2, "Black <II" WNr. 210 194, January 1, 1945

Fw 190 D-9, Oblt. Oscar Romm, Staf.Führer. IV./JG 3, "Black <<" WNr. unknown, February 1945

Fw 190 D-9, pilot unknown, of 11./JG 26, "White 9" WNr. 500 342, November 1944

Fw 190 D-9, Uffz. Rank, possibly 5./JG 26 or JGr.10, "White 1" WNr. unknown, April 1945, with R4M-Bordracketen under wing

Fw 190 D-9 of Lt. Heinz Marquardt, 13./JG 51, "White 11" WNr. 213 097, April 1945

Fw 190 D-9 of Oblt. Hans Dortenmann, III./JG 54, "Rote 1" WNr. 210 003, November 1944

Fw 190 D-9 of Hptm. Klaus Faber, JV 44, "Red 13" WNr. 400 240, April 1945

Fw 190 D-11 prototype V56, WNr.170924, flown by Prof. Kurt Tank, October 21, 1944

Fw 190 D-11, Stab. pilot unknown, VFS G.d.F., "<57" WNr. 220011, April 1945

Fw 190 D-13, Maj. Franz Lange, G.Kom., JG 51, "Yellow 10" WNr. 836017, April 1945

Also from the Publisher

Focke-Wulf Ta 152
The Story of the Luftwaffe's Late-War, High-Altitude Fighter

Dietmar Harmann

One of the best fighter aircraft of the Second World War – a masterpiece produced by chief designer Kurt Tank. With a large number of photographs – some previously unpublished – and drawings, this book details the development history of the Ta 152. It also illustrates the hopelessness of Germany's efforts late in the war to deploy advanced aircraft in large numbers.

Size: 8 1/2" x 11" • over 165 b/w photographs and line drawings • 144 pp.
ISBN: 0-7643-0860-2 • hard cover • $35.00